Advance praise for
What Is Sexual Harassment?

"It's no secret that people's definitions of sexual harassment differ wildly and that those definitions can have a huge impact on everyday lives. But just how do those definitions get made and fixed into place, and why do they differ? In this complex, much-needed study of sexual harassment as concept and legal practice in the United States and France, Abigail Saguy unlocks that puzzle with extraordinary grace. Rooted in rigorous comparative research, *What Is Sexual Harassment?* answers its own question with no-nonsense lucidity and cutting intelligence."

—Joshua Gamson, author of *Freaks Talk Back:*
Tabloid Talk Shows and Sexual Nonconformity

"This is a remarkable book, both in terms of methodology and theory. This work will be an indispensable tool for anyone concerned with defining the concept of sexual harassment. The comparative approach demonstrates its heuristic importance, as Saguy shows a remarkable mastery of different social and legal cultures."

—Françoise Gaspard, author of *A Small City in France*

What Is Sexual Harassment?

What Is Sexual Harassment?

From Capitol Hill to the Sorbonne

Abigail C. Saguy

UNIVERSITY OF CALIFORNIA PRESS

Berkeley   Los Angeles   London

University of California Press
Berkeley and Los Angeles, California

University of California Press, Ltd.
London, England

© 2003 by the Regents of the University of California

Library of Congress Cataloging-in-Publication Data

Saguy, Abigail Cope, 1970–
    What is sexual harassment? : from Capitol Hill to the
Sorbonne / Abigail C. Saguy.
        p. cm.
    Includes bibliographical references and index.
    ISBN 0-520-23740-4 (cloth : acid-free paper)—
ISBN 0-520-23741-2 (paper : acid-free paper)
    1. Sexual harassment—Law and legislation—United
States.   2. Sexual harassment—Law and legislation—
France.   3. Sexual harassment—United States.   4. Sexual
harassment—France.   I. Title.
KF3467 .S24 2003
344.7301'4133—dc21   2002153268

Manufactured in the United States of America
12 11 10 09 08 07 06 05 04 03
10 9 8 7 6 5 4 3 2 1

The paper used in this publication is both acid-free and
totally chlorine-free (TCF). It meets the minimum requirements of ANSI/NISO Z39.48-1992 (R 1997) (*Permanence of
Paper*) ♾

To my parents

CONTENTS

FIGURES

TABLES

ACKNOWLEDGMENTS

This book has been several years in the making and has benefited from the generous support of many people and institutions. As an undergraduate student at Wesleyan University, I began researching the French women's movement under the guidance of Charles Lemert and with support from a Davenport Grant. At the Ecole Normale Supérieure (ENS) and the Ecole des Hautes Etudes en Sciences Sociales (EHESS), where I completed a DEA (French MA) in Social Science, I expanded the study to a cross-national comparison of the French and American women's movements, under the supervision of Serge Moscovici.

The research for this book proper began in the context of my doctoral dissertation, conducted jointly at Princeton University and at the EHESS. I received much-needed support from the Department of Sociology at Princeton University and the following Princeton University–based research grants: the program in French Studies, the Center of International Studies, the Compton Fund, the Council on Regional Studies, and the Center of Domestic and Comparative Policy Studies. The National Science Foundation, the French government (*subvention de cotutelle*), the Council for European Studies, and the Princeton Society of Fellows of the Woodrow Wilson Foundation also provided generous funding. After completion of the dissertation, a two-year research grant from the Robert Wood Johnson Foundation's Program in Health Policy at Yale University gave me funding and time free from departmental and teaching responsibilities, which allowed me to revise and update this book in a much more timely fashion than would have been otherwise possible.

I am greatly indebted to my interviewees for the time they generously spent talking to me and, in many instances, for helping set up other interviews. The members of the Association Européenne Contre les Violences Faites aux Femmes au Travail (AVFT, European Association Against Violence Toward Women at Work) deserve special thanks. In addition to allowing me use of their extensive legal, media, and academic archives, AVFT members spent countless hours answering questions about French law and politics, facilitating contacts for interviews, and providing valuable feedback. I am especially in debt to Catherine LeMagueresse, Marie-Victoire Louis, and Gisèle Amoussou for their precious insights and friendship. Marie Huret and *L'Express* magazine saved me several days of archival work by providing access to the newsmagazine's electronic archives.

I am eternally grateful for the time, energy, patience, encouragement, and friendship that my dissertation advisor, Michèle Lamont, has given me over the years. I also feel incredibly fortunate to have received sustained and careful comments, as well as warm encouragement, from Viviana Zelizer and Paul DiMaggio. Many other current and former members of Princeton's Sociology Department took the time to read and comment on this project over the years. I am especially grateful for the feedback I received from Frank Dobbin, Erin Kelly, and Sara Curran. I owe Bruce Western thanks for his patient advice with media coding and statistics.

I also received useful feedback from colleagues and friends outside of Princeton's Sociology Department. In the first two years of this project, Miriam Ruchman and Holly Sukel read and commented on several drafts of my work, listened and commented on presentations, suggested useful reading, and provided much needed emotional support. Over the years, Jerrob Duffy shared his knowledge of American law. Erik Bleich, Mia Cahill, Cynthia Epstein, Judith Ezekiel, Eric Fassin, Marion Fourcade-Gourinchas, Michal Frenkel, Catharine MacKinnon, Serge Moscovici, Geneviève Paicheler, Vicki Schultz, Joan Scott, Susan Silbey, John Skrentny, Laurent Thévenot, and Kathrina Zippel each provided important comments on my written work.

Several local workshops, study groups and conferences provided opportunities to present my ongoing work and receive feedback, including Princeton's Sociology Department's Joinder on Organizations, Institutions, and Economic Sociology (JOIE) and Dissertation Support Group (DSG). Members of Princeton Society of Fellows of the Woodrow Wilson Foundation, especially Stan Katz and Dirk Hartog, offered helpful critique and guidance during the two years I spent as a Woodrow Wilson fellow. I presented parts of this project to the Princeton-Rutgers Conference on the Sociology of Culture, in the Department of Sociology of New York University, and Princeton University's "Graduate Women's Studies Colloquium." During the 1998–1999 academic year, I found a supportive and enriching intellectual community in the Sociology of Law Study Group at Columbia University.

Over the years, I have also presented pieces of this project at several national and regional professional conferences and workshops, including the American Sociological Association, the Eastern Sociological Association, the Law and Society Association, the Council of European Studies, and the Communitarian Council. I am grateful to Reva Siegel and Catharine MacKinnon for inviting me to present my work in a stimulating conference they organized on sexual harassment law in February 1998 and to conference participants for their input. Finally, I received useful comments and questions following invited presentations at UCLA's Sociology Department, the University of Massachusetts at Amherst's Sociology Department, the University of Minnesota's Sociology Department, and the Robert Wood Johnson Foundation Health Policy Program at Yale University.

In the past year that I have spent revising this book, the Robert Wood

Johnson Foundation scholars and faculty at Yale have provided collegial support, intellectual stimulation and helpful critique. A special thanks goes to Kim DaCosta, Evan Lieberman, Kimberly Morgan, and Erik Oliver. I have also benefited from the feedback of Jim Jasper, Rod Benson, Robin Stryker, and Michael McCann.

For assistance in the transcription of in-depth interviews, I was lucky to find excellent help from Naim Antaki, Joanne Augustin, Jennifer Boittin, Michelle Coyne, Dana Deaton, Juliette Dellecker, Anne Fonteneau, Yvette Ho, and Holly Sukel. While at Yale, Rachel Berger and Erin Lyons provided excellent library assistance and, in the case of Rachel, media coding. At the University of California Press, Naomi Schneider, Kate Warne, Annie Decker, and Sierra Filucci provided support and guidance. Elizabeth Berg copyedited the final manuscript. Rene Almeling and Ellen Wight assisted in proofreading the edited manuscript and galleys, respectively.

To carry out this research, I made several trips to France. My mother and father-in-law, Irit and Dov Slomka, and sometimes my sister and brother in-law, Méïtal and Daniel Amzallag, not only put a roof over my head and delicious food on my plate for weeks at a time, but they encouraged me in my fieldwork and listened to my ideas. My friend Isabelle Pessiot used both her practical and academic knowledge of French society to facilitate my fieldwork in a variety of ways. When I needed a quiet place not far from home to write, Charlotte Elkin and Tamara Kroll graciously lent me their apartment as a daytime "office."

Over the past ten years, Dotan Saguy has transcribed many an interview, solved countless computer crises, edited my French, listened and critiqued several presentations, and helped me navigate PowerPoint, Excel, and Access, often coming up with creative ways to analyze or present my data. As my husband and now the father to my daughter, Dotan's love and devotion are a source of pure joy, comfort, and inner strength. My daughter Claire was conceived and born during the final year of revisions. Her imminent arrival motivated me to make fast progress on the manuscript, and her presence has already enriched and sweetened my life more than I could have imagined possible.

Finally, I probably would never have embarked on this research, or the earlier research projects that led up to this one, without the love, support, and encouragement of my parents, Rita and Charles Smith. My mother was always on the lookout for relevant press articles and was a wonderful person with whom to discuss emerging findings and the writing process. A sociologist himself, my father also served as a sound-board for ideas and as an excellent editor. I dedicate this book to them.

The Making of a Concept

During the two years that Teresa Harris worked as a manager at Forklift Systems, an equipment rental company, Charles Hardy, the company's president, often insulted her and made her the target of unwanted sexual innuendos. Charles asked Teresa on several occasions, in the presence of other employees, "You're a woman, what do you know?" or said things such as "We need a man as the rental manager"; at least once, he told her she was "a dumb-ass woman." Again in front of others, he suggested that the two of them "go to the Holiday Inn to negotiate Teresa's raise." Charles occasionally asked Teresa and other female employees to get coins from his front pants pocket. He threw objects on the ground in front of Teresa and other women, and asked them to pick the objects up. He made sexual innuendos about Teresa's and other women's clothing.

When Teresa complained to Charles about his conduct, the latter expressed surprise that Teresa was offended, claimed he was only joking, and apologized. Based on his promises that he would stop his behavior, Teresa stayed on the job. But then the behavior began anew: While Teresa was arranging a deal with one of the company's customers, Charles asked her, again in front of other employees, "What did you do, promise the guy some sex Saturday night?" Shortly after this incident, Teresa collected her paycheck and quit.[1]

Is this sexual harassment? Actually, it depends on when and where the behavior took place. Before 1993, when the U.S. Supreme Court ruled in favor of Teresa Harris in *Harris v. Forklift Systems*[2] reversing the Court of Appeals for the Sixth Circuit, Charles Hardy's behavior was arguably not severe or pervasive enough to constitute sexual harassment under American law. Less than twenty years before that, the term "sexual harassment" did not exist in the United States or in American law. Today, the meaning of sexual harassment in the United States is still in a state of flux. However, the behavior that Teresa Harris suffered at the hands of Charles Hardy falls squarely within one of two legally recognized forms of sexual harassment: hostile environment, in which a boss or colleague creates an abusive or hostile environment by making unwanted sexual comments, demands for sex, sexual jokes, or sexist insults that are "sufficiently severe or pervasive as to alter the conditions of a victim's employment and to create an abusive working environment."[3] If Charles Hardy had told Teresa Harris that unless she gave in to his sexual advances he would fire or demote her or take away some of her job benefits, she would have been subject to the second kind of sexual harassment: quid pro quo sexual harassment.[4]

Though the concept of sexual harassment has spread across the globe, it still means different things in different places.[5] For instance, during the time the research for this book was conducted, French law only recognized the quid pro quo version of sexual harassment, so that the kind of behavior suffered by Teresa Harris would not be sexual harassment under French law.[6] Unlike American law, which defined sexual harassment as a form of group-based discrimination, French law framed it as a form of interpersonal violence. This legal framing was preserved in subsequent legal reform, suggesting that predictions about cultural and political convergence across the globe[7] are incomplete.

These national legal differences stem from the fact that although feminists demanded sexual harassment laws in both countries, they encountered distinct political, legal, and cultural constraints and resources. Particularly important were understandings of group-based discrimination and discrimination law in the United States and the salience of hierarchical boundaries, interpersonal violence, and anti-American sentiment in France. As is shown in subsequent chapters, these legal differences have had a far-reaching impact on wider social understandings of sexual harassment in the two countries. Rather than simply reproducing national legal definitions of sexual harassment, however, American and French corporations and the press responded to national sexual harassment law based on their own institutional practices and traditions, as well as external constraints and resources. Likewise, national legal definitions of sexual harassment greatly informed the way in which individuals conceptualized sexual harassment. However, individuals also innovated upon legal definitions to varying degrees, based on the extent of their training in the law combined with the degree to which legal definitions coincided with broader, taken-for-granted social assumptions about right and wrong.

THE IMPORTANCE OF NAMING SEXUAL HARASSMENT

The past three decades have seen an influx of women into the paid labor market[8] and growing legitimacy of the *idea* that women are equal, rather than subservient, to men. The greater acceptance of the concept that women are men's equals has made sexual harassment laws possible, and the existence of such laws has, in turn, further legitimized and enforced gender equality. Coined in 1975 by American feminists,[9] the concept of "sexual harassment" assumed a worldview in which women were not always flattered by sexual attention but could instead be extremely aggravated by it. By labeling as "sexual harassment" the way many men treat their female coworkers as sex objects, feminist activists and, later, the courts suggested that sexual or sexist aggression should not be an unavoidable part of women's employment. In so doing, they challenged cultural assumptions about gender (the social implications of being a man or a woman), sexuality, and the workplace.[10] Moreover, this new label potentially transformed the way women who are ogled, propositioned, or groped at work experience and respond to such behavior, as well as their level of outrage or self-blame. Likewise, naming sexual harassment transformed how the men who ogle, proposition, or grope them regard their own behavior and the sense of entitlement or guilt they feel. The belief that such behavior is wrong arguably serves to prevent some men from committing such acts at all.

The formulation of sexual harassment as a concept and a body of law *at all*, as well as the particular way it is conceptualized, thus has important implications for gender equality, for expectations and behaviors linked to sexuality, and for what sorts of social interactions are considered appropriate or desirable in the workplace in particular and in other public and private spheres more generally. Yet, we know very little about how and why this term has been transformed so quickly from an esoteric phrase to a taken-for-granted concept. The bulk of American research on sexual harassment assumes a priori that there exists a particular definition of sexual harassment, one usually based on current legal doctrine. In so doing, these studies take current legal definitions for granted rather than examining how they are historically and nationally contextual. They lose sight of the fact that earlier in United States history "sexual harassment" meant something different or nothing at all. They do not examine the meaning sexual harassment has outside of the courtroom or for different individuals. Moreover, they do not capture how, given different institutional or ideological conditions such as those found abroad, we may have ended up with a very different understanding of what "sexual harassment" entails and why it is wrong.

THE INADEQUACY OF ESSENTIALIST
NATIONAL CHARACTER EXPLANATIONS

That sexual harassment is conceptualized differently in the United States and France makes intuitive sense to many people. Americans having lived in France share anecdotes about France's more "laissez-faire" sexual environment, where physical touching and sexual banter is still a common and even valued feature of French workplaces. Others talk more critically about how in France the climate is more sexist and oppressive for women, and sexual coercion and humiliation remain commonplace, to the detriment of female workers. Few French are surprised to hear that sexual harassment is taken more seriously in the United States. For many, this information coincides with their impressions of American workplaces as repressive and intolerant of sexual innuendo. For others, the United States is "ahead of" France in matters of gender equity. For many, the United States is a country of contradictions, a place where workplaces are both more women-friendly and also dangerously invasive of people's personal lives.

However, when people venture to explain such national differences, they usually appeal to essentialist accounts of national character, which explain national variation as the product of exaggerated and ahistorical "cultural" differences. The mass media in both countries affirm that Americans are uptight and puritanical compared to the French, who are more at ease with matters sexual. For instance, a *New York Times* article on sexual harassment policy in France[11] reports:

> When one thinks of France, certain images spring to mind. The accordion. Foie gras. Ah, yes, the French lover, whose seductive skills have long seemed as much a birthright as a good Bordeaux. Eroticism has helped define the country. The disclosure by the former president, François Mitterrand, of a decades-long relationship with a mistress created barely a ripple — and when it did, it was an approving one.

This article and others like it gloss over the fact that surveys show that most French *dis*approve of marital infidelity.[12] Indeed, they say nothing about how this disapproval kept Mitterrand's extramarital affair a dirty secret during his lifetime. More importantly, however, reports such as this one treat cultural differences as widely agreed upon and unchanging.

In fact, culture, whether this term is used to denote norms, values, beliefs, expressive symbols, or any number of the "totality of man's products,"[13] is multivalent and highly contested.[14]

The issue of sexual harassment is fascinating from a sociological point of view precisely because it represents a crack in previous configurations of gender and sexuality, a place where cultural change is taking place. The popular French view that Americans are obsessed with sexual harassment because they are "puritans" fails to account for how ideas about what are appropriate and inappropriate ways for men to treat their female coworkers or subordinates have changed tremendously in the past several decades. As an American woman in her seventies told me recently: "When I was working, my boss used to chase me around his desk. It happened when we were alone in the office and I hated to go into his office to ask him something because of that, but other than that, he wasn't a bad guy." This woman's comments reveal the extent to which cultural expectations about work, gender, sexuality, and hierarchical authority have changed in the United States during her lifetime. The formulation of sexual harassment as a social problem is part of this process. As such, it needs explaining, and the ahistorical supposition that Americans are puritanical and the French are sexually permissive will not do.

Indeed, the "permissive" French have had laws against sexual harassment since the early 1990s and the "puritanical" Americans have prohibited sexual harassment not because it is a form of deviant sexuality but because it compromises women's employment opportunities. According to American jurisprudence, employers can be held liable for sexual harassment occurring among employees and be made to pay compensatory and punitive damages under Title VII of the Civil Rights Act of 1964, which makes it illegal to discriminate on the basis of race, color, religion, sex, or national origin.

In contrast, under French law, a male supervisor who fires a female subordinate because she refuses to have an affair with him has committed a penal misdemeanor, for which he alone (and not his employer) is held responsible. His action is not condemned as an instance of sex discrimination.[15] Rather, this man has committed a misdemeanor akin to the crime of rape by using his authority as supervisor to try to coerce a woman into having sexual relations with him, much as a rapist uses physical force to compel his victim into having sexual relations. Indeed the connection between sexual harassment and rape is made in the French penal code, which classifies sexual harassment with rape, sexual battery, and exhibitionism in the section on sexual violence, rather than with group-based discrimination. While rape is a *crime*, however, the other three, including sexual harassment, are *délits* (misdemeanors), which are tried in a different court and carry much lighter penalties. Although the sexual harassment penal statute allows for a maximum penalty of one year behind bars or a fine roughly equivalent to $14,000, actual sentences typically involve only suspended jail sentences of two months, a couple of thousand dollars in fines, and small compensatory damages paid to the plaintiff (usually less than the equivalent of $3,000).

These distinct legal approaches have important material consequences, including the kind of relief a victim of sexual harassment can receive, the likelihood that employers will take preventive or remedial measures against sexual harassment, as well as the kinds of punishment sexual harassers can expect. Moreover, these legal distinctions affect the ways in which people understand the harm done when they or others sexually harass or are harassed and how seriously they take such behavior. More generally, these legal approaches shape a variety of taken-for-granted understandings of political rights, acceptable and unacceptable behavior, and social responsibility, to list a few prominent examples.

While legal institutions have shaped both American and French conceptions of sexual harassment, sexual harassment is not solely a legal issue in either country. American employers have created their own rules and regulations that define sexual harassment differently from American law. Within such companies, some behavior, like sexist jokes or comments that fall short of the legal test of severity or pervasiveness, is considered sexual harassment in the company. Moreover, rather than condemn the behavior as sex discrimination, many American human resource departments condemn sexual innuendo of any kind because it is considered to detract from the bottom line and standards of professionalism. Likewise, the American mass media, which also play a role in defining sexual harassment, often lose sight of the discrimination component when they report on high-profile sexual harassment cases as sexual and often political scandals.

That sexual harassment is a form of interpersonal violence, rather than a form of sex discrimination, is the dominant view in French law and corporations. Some French feminist activists, however, have promoted an analysis of sexual harassment as a form of sex discrimination. These activists have also argued that the French Parliament should prohibit the kind of behavior that American courts classify as hostile environment sexual harassment, an argument with which many French people agree.[16] Finally, the French media reports focus on *American* sexual harassment scandals as revealing American excesses of litigiousness, feminism, and puritanism.

The view that current American conceptions of sexual harassment are the product of a natural evolution toward a more gender-equal society overlooks how these particular understandings of sexual harassment are situational. Indeed, the contrast with France shows how a different institutional, political, historical, and cultural context can foster an extremely different conception of sexual harassment. The way sexual harassment is understood and addressed has important consequences for gender equality, sexuality, and the workplace, yet we know very little about why and how this problem has been conceptualized differently in different countries. This book seeks to answer this question, using as case studies the United States and France, major industrialized democracies with strong commitments to civil rights but which have adopted different definitions of sexual harassment. Not only important in its own right, this question is also useful for shedding light on the more general question of how social meaning is created, reproduced, and challenged.

GENERAL ARGUMENT OF THE BOOK

I argue that, in both the United States and France, the career of "sexual harassment," as social concept, body of law, and object of company rules, has been shaped by concerted efforts on the part of local social actors, like feminists, to change taken-for-granted assumptions about gender, sexuality, and the workplace. I thus embrace the concept of "social agency," or the idea that social actors have "free will" or autonomy to change their social environment. However, I further argue that the key social actors involved in struggles over legal and nonlegal definitions of sexual harassment were constrained and enabled by *social structure, relations among institutions and countries,* and *cultural and political traditions* specific to their national and institutional context.

"Social structure" is a sociological concept that refers to stable patterns of social behavior or rules that limit what sorts of conduct are possible or likely in a given social context. Social structures are often conceptualized as contained within particular institutions, such as the courts or the legislature. However, interconnections among different institutions, which vary cross-nationally, have had important implications for the conceptualization of sexual harassment and other social problems, as have interactions between the United States and France, an aspect too often neglected by cross-national research. By "cultural and political traditions," I am referring to collective customs, beliefs, and reasoning that govern everyday interactions or, more specifically, political behavior. My distinction between social structure, relations among institutions and countries, and cultural and political traditions is a heuristic device, a useful starting point for unpacking complex social behavior. In reality, as the empirical data will show, the lines among these concepts are often blurred. For instance, institutions are often considered the building blocks of social structure. However, they can also be analyzed as practical norms in routine activity.

Legal systems function as social structure by dictating who can make or change laws (such as lawmakers, judges, lobbyists, dictators, and so on) and through which processes (such as legislative debates, court precedent, decree, and so on). A common-law system, like that of the United States, for instance, allows courts discretion in building case law through jurisprudence to an extent that is unparalleled in a civil law system, like that of France. In the case of sexual harassment, the common-law system provided American feminists a valuable entryway into the lawmaking process that their French counterparts did not enjoy. This structural opportunity also entailed inherent constraints. For instance, to win their case, American feminists and lawyers have had to make a *legal* case in U.S. courtrooms that sexual harassment violates an existing statute. For strategic and intellectual reasons, they chose to build sexual harassment jurisprudence on Title VII. This, in turn, has compelled them to stress certain aspects of the harm of sexual harassment, such as group-based discrimination and employment consequences, and downplay others, such as sexual violence and behavior outside of the workplace. Preexisting laws, such as Title VII in the United States, were thus also part of the social structure that influenced the ways in which sexual harassment could or could not be legally defined.

French feminists faced different structural opportunities and constraints. Because of French legal structure, the avenue for legal reform lay not in the courts but in Parliament, especially in 1991 when a *window of opportunity* emerged in the form of penal code reform. Here state feminists (feminists employed by the state, in roles such as minister or secretary of women's rights, or as independent lawmakers) were obliged to engage in political compromise to get sufficient support for their bill, a standard practice of the parliamentary process. In French parliamentary debates, state feminists thus narrowed the scope of the sexual harassment bill to target only quid pro quo forms of sexual harassment and framed[17] the problem as an abuse of hierarchical power rather than gender discrimination in order to convince their (male) socialist colleagues to vote for their bill. French feminists were less able to build on discrimination law, as it was narrowly defined, poorly enforced, and lacked legitimacy in France. Rather, the French sexual harassment penal statute was ultimately inscribed in the preexisting section on sexual violence, a placement that had consequences for how the wrong of sexual harassment would be conceptualized and addressed.

Other institutions are governed by their own sets of rules and routines. The American mass media, often controlled by business and dependent on advertisement revenues, are under great pressure to produce news that sells, making sexual harassment scandals particularly compelling. Due largely to the more narrow scope and recent passage of sexual harassment law in France as well as greater legal constraints on the media, there were no home-grown French sexual harassment scandals before 2002.[18] However, the French press, which also faces intense competition, has found that American scandals make for titillating stories with a moral: beware of "American excesses." Corporations tend to be driven by profit-maximization, assuming that the government does not heavily subsidize them. In the case of the United States, this has led corporations to address sexual harassment largely as a practice that can hurt the bottom line, not only through costly lawsuits but also by affecting reputation and employee productivity.

The courts, corporations, and mass media have further interacted in ways that have increased attention to sexual harassment in the United States. By holding employers liable for sexual harassment occurring in their workplace, American sexual harassment law has accorded employers with "ownership"[19] of this social problem to a far greater extent than has French law, which holds only individual harassers, and not employers, legally responsible for their behavior. In the United States, corporate responses to the law can have a feedback effect on the courts.[20] For instance, American corporations initially enacted sexual harassment policies and training programs in the hopes that they could be used to shield themselves from liability. Over the years, the U.S. courts have officially recognized these policies as important elements of an affirmative defense against employer liability.[21]

By reporting on the most expensive sexual harassment lawsuits, the mass media inflate the perceived risks of legal action for employers, thereby increasing the odds that companies will take preventive action.[22] According to several commentators, media reporting on Anita Hill's accusations against Clarence Thomas and her treatment during the Senate hearings facilitated President Bush's signing of the Civil Rights Act of 1991, which greatly strengthened sexual harassment law, in particular by allowing plaintiffs to sue for punitive damages.[23]

In addition to their structural aspects, laws also function as *cultural symbols* that legitimize *cultural and political traditions.*[24] For instance, the existence of affirmative action and Title VII makes Americans likely to think that group-based discrimination, such as racism or sexism, is an important source of inequality, or at least to see race and gender as salient social categories.[25] Even if they believe group-based discrimination is exaggerated or that antidiscrimination law goes too far, Americans will, on the whole, be more familiar with the concept than their French counterparts, who have neither a political history of civil rights equivalent to the American movement nor strong employment discrimination laws.[26] This means that Americans are more likely to conceptualize a range of behavior, including sexual harassment, as forms of gender discrimination. The French, on the other hand, are more likely to conceptualize inequality in terms of class divisions and hierarchy, since ideas about class struggle and abuse of power are embedded in French social history and are perpetuated by state institutions like the French Communist and Socialist parties. Similarly, America's developed antidiscrimination jurisprudence institutionalizes and legitimizes expectations that (labor) markets should be fair, a more important and central belief in the United States, where there is a low degree of "decommodification" and a high degree of liberalism, than in France, where there is greater suspicion of the market.[27]

Based on peoples' perceptions of dominant cultural and political traditions, individuals also have different expectations about what their peers are willing to believe or do. For instance, even though the French state-feminist supporters of the 1991 sexual harassment bills were personally sympathetic to the argument that sexual harassment is a form of gender discrimination and violence against women, they framed the behavior as a form of hierarchical abuse because they thought this argument would resonate more with their male Socialist colleagues. Sometimes there is a considerable gap between what members of a community personally believe and what beliefs they ascribe to their peers, so that groups of people may act contrary to their own wishes because they falsely believe they are conforming to the larger group.[28]

These cultural differences have been accentuated by "boundary work"[29] on the part of French individuals. For instance, French lawmakers engaged in "boundary work" against the United States by drawing on the French media's representations of the "excesses" of American sexual harassment law to argue that French law should be more cautious in its approach to sexual harassment. According to the official French Senate report: "Recent press articles report that in [the United States] 'simply holding the door open for a woman can incite a severe reprimand,' and that most men admit to being very wary in interacting with women in the workplace."[30] The desire to avoid alleged American excesses was one of the reasons given by this senator, in his report, for limiting the scope of French sexual harassment laws. In his words: "It is certain that the excesses that are a product of exaggerated protective concern against sexual harassment in North America motivates the preference for a more restrictive but more realistic definition." Such negative perceptions of American responses to sexual harassment have also raised concern among French judges and the public at large about the danger of falling into "American excesses," a fear that has increased the stigma attached to sexual harassment victims and their advocates.[31]

This study follows in a tradition of work in cultural sociology, in which cultural attitudes and cultural content cannot be understood divorced from the organizational contexts in which they are produced.[32] While most studies focus on one institutional setting, this research triangulates among several, concentrating especially on the law, mass media, and corporations. It seeks to make sense of larger national patterns by examining how key national institutions have addressed sexual harassment, as well as the ways in which their respective approaches interact with each other.

I focus on four key groups of actors, including (1) feminist scholars, activists, and associations; (2) lawmakers, judges, and lawyers; (3) journalists and public figures; and (4) human resource managers and union activists. I examine how the actions of these social actors have been enabled and constrained by the three main institutional settings that have been primary sites for the conceptualization of sexual harassment: (1) the law; (2) the mass media; and (3) corporations.

METHODS AND DATA

This study draws on several sources of data, which were collected using multiple methods. First, I examined the major French and American sexual harassment legal texts, including statutes and jurisprudence. Second, using a detailed coding scheme and statistical analysis, I analyzed over six hundred randomly sampled articles about sexual harassment from the French and American press, published in 1975–2000. Third, I conducted almost sixty in-depth interviews with feminist activists, public figures (including Catharine MacKinnon, Phyllis Schlafly, Camille Paglia, Marie-Victoire Louis, Françoise Giroud, and Elisabeth Badinter), lawyers, human resource personnel, and union activists. Rather than a representative sample of French and Americans, the respondents are cultural entrepreneurs, who, through their jobs or volunteer activity, are likely to have a particular impact on the conceptualization of this social problem. I use the interviews with the activists to help reconstitute the legal and social movement history of sexual harassment. I also draw on the interviews with the activists, public figures, lawyers, human resource managers, and union representatives in my analysis of the actual meaning laws and press reports have for victims of sexual harassment and their advocates.

I further draw on the interviews with human resource personnel and union activists to examine the meaning of sexual harassment in the workplace of large multinational corporations. These respondents were employed in one of four work sites, including an American or French branch of an American multinational that I call "AmeriCorp," or an American or French branch of a French multinational that I call "Frenchco." In the case of the United States, I draw on secondary literature to put my findings from the American branches in a larger perspective. Because there is no comparable literature on French corporations, I conducted a series of short telephone interviews with representatives of twenty-three French branches of large multinational corporations. I draw on these to evaluate how French corporations respond to sexual harassment laws.[33]

BOOK OUTLINE

The next chapter, "Sexual Harassment Law on the Books: Opportunity Loss v. Violence," examines how and why American and French sexual harassment laws differ by body of law and definition of harm, scope, and remedy. In both countries, key social actors (feminists in both countries, lawyers and judges in the United States, lawmakers in France) mobilized for sexual harassment laws, but they encountered very different structural constraints and resources, institutions and institutional networks, and cultural and political traditions. These different national contexts, as well as global politics (namely negative French sentiment towards the United States) shaped the goals and strategies of social actors and, ultimately, the sexual harassment laws that ensued. In the United States, political traditions of antidiscrimination, a product of the 1960s civil rights movement, as well as antidiscrimination statutes and jurisprudence, made it particularly likely that American feminists would successfully conceptualize sexual harassment as a form of sex discrimination. In France, the legal system did not offer a ready-made mechanism like civil rights laws. On the other hand, two other kinds of resources were decisive: (1) the importance given to hierarchical boundaries, which are also institutionalized in French law; and (2) anti-American rhetoric, developed by the French media, on which certain influential lawmakers drew to argue that American sexual harassment law should not be taken as the model for France.

Chapter 2, "Sexual Harassment Law in Action: Legitimacy and Liability," examines the legal and corporate environment of sexual harassment.[34] This chapter shows how the differences that exist in sexual harassment laws have been compounded by the very different status sexual harassment has as a body of law and a social problem in each country. Briefly, the interviews demonstrate that the issue is taken much more seriously in the United States than in France. This chapter attributes this finding to national differences in cultural attitudes towards sexism and money, corporate cultures, legal differences (not limited to sexual harassment law), and the way in which national institutions, like courts, corporations, and mass media, interact or overlap. I further show how French social actors have reinforced these national differences by drawing symbolic boundaries against the United States.

Chapter 3, "Sexual Harassment in the Press: National Scandal, Pride, or Superiority?" examines how six of the main American and French presses have reported on sexual harassment. The American press has focused primarily on stories of sexual harassment as political scandal by covering accusations against high-profile political figures, like Supreme Court Justice Clarence Thomas or President Bill Clinton. Despite this focus, a substantial proportion of the American press has framed sexual harassment as an important social problem and a women's issue. The French press has reported less on sexual harassment than the American press, and when it has, it has focused on *American* rather than home-grown scandals. Analyses further show that when reporting on sexual harassment in the United States, as compared to reporting on France, French journalists are more likely to discredit plaintiffs and trivialize sexual harassment as a social problem, focusing instead on "American excesses" of feminism, puritanism, and litigiousness. As will become clear in the following chapters, the way the French media has presented sexual harassment as an "American problem" effectively discredits feminist activists, plaintiff lawyers, victims of sexual harassment, and others who are exposed to this problem in France. These patterns of reporting reflect both different "realities" in each country, such as the different scope of national sexual harassment laws and litigation, and media routines that favor simplification, individualism, symbolism, and "gotcha journalism."[35]

Chapter 4, "Discrimination, Violence, Professionalism, and the Bottom Line: How Interview Respondents Frame Sexual Harassment," analyzes how the interview respondents conceptualize sexual harassment. Three principal frames emerge: (1) a "discrimination frame," in which sexual harassment is condemned as a form of sex discrimination in employment, which was most common among the American respondents, especially the activists; (2) the "violence frame," in which sexual harassment is wrong because it is a form of interpersonal violence, which was more common among the French respondents; and (3) a "business frame," also common among the American respondents, especially human resource personnel, according to which sexual harassment is wrong because it is not "professional" and does not "add [economic] value" to companies. Chapter 4 thus complements Chapters 1 and 3 by demonstrating the extent to which individuals draw on public representations of sexual harassment produced by the legislature, courts, or mass media to make sense of this issue and the ways in which they innovate upon public definitions. This chapter reveals that strong national patterns exist but that individuals also demonstrate creativity as they improvise upon official definitions of sexual harassment.

The Conclusion, "Institutions, Framing, and Political Power," summarizes how the institutional patterns explored in Chapters 1–4 play out in the United States and France. I discuss the ways in which the law, corporations, and media interact, as well as how the interview respondents draw from different "cultural toolkits,"[36] depending on their national and institutional context. I conclude this chapter by discussing some of the lessons this study holds for sociology and by considering the political implications of debates regarding how sexual harassment should be defined.

As this book was going to press, French lawmakers revised French law to address sexual harassment among coworkers, and a scandal erupted around alleged incidents of sexual harassment in higher education. I address these events in the Epilogue, "Plus ça change, plus c'est la même chose." I argue that although these incidents seem to suggest that France is finally coming to resemble the United States in matters of sexual harassment, closer analysis reveals that important cross-national differences persist. For instance, although legal reform extended French sexual harassment laws to coworker harassment, it reinforced the French framing of sexual harassment as a form of interpersonal violence, rather than as an instance of group-based discrimination, and did little to reinforce employer liability. Media reporting on charges of sexual harassment in higher education revealed that for many French social commentators "universal" or gender-neutral questions of professors' power over students and class inequalities, and not sexism or sexual violence, remain the fundamental problems at stake. The events of 2002 also reveal that anti-American rhetoric remains an important political strategy for discrediting those who try to address the problem of sexual harassment in France.

ONE

Sexual Harassment Law
on the Books
Opportunity Loss v. Violence

After Forklift Systems' president Charles Hardy's sexist and sexually demeaning behavior drove Teresa Harris to quit her position as manager, she sued the company under Title VII of the Civil Rights Act of 1964 (CRA 1964), claiming that Hardy's conduct had created an abusive work environment for her because of her gender. The United States District Court for the Middle District of Tennessee found this to be "a close case," but held that Hardy's conduct did not create an abusive environment. The court found that some of Hardy's comments "offended [Harris], and would offend the reasonable woman," but that they were not "so severe as to be expected to seriously affect [Harris's] psychological well-being," nor had they "risen to the level of interfering with that person's work performance."[1] The United States Court of Appeals for the Sixth Circuit affirmed the District Court's decision.

In 1994, however, the Supreme Court reversed the Sixth Circuit decision, ruling that it had applied too high a standard by affirming that sexually harassing behavior must seriously affect the plaintiff's well-being. The "mere utterance of an epithet that engenders offensive feelings in the employee," behavior that the victim does not subjectively perceive to be abusive, or conduct that does not actually alter the conditions of the victim's employment do not constitute Title VII violations. However, this same ruling affirmed, "Title VII comes into play before the harassing conduct leads to a nervous breakdown."[2] In the unanimous decision, the Supreme Court argued that

> a discriminatorily abusive work environment, even one that does not seriously affect employees' psychological well-being, can and often will detract from employees' job performance, discourage employees from remaining on the job, or keep them from advancing in their careers. Moreover, even without regard to these tangible effects, the very fact that the discriminatory conduct was so severe or pervasive that it created a work environment abusive to employees because of their race, gender, religion, or national origin offends Title VII's broad rule of workplace equality.

While "psychological harm, like any other relevant factor, may be taken into account," according to the High Court, "no single factor is required."[3]

Four years after the Harris decision, the French Parliament considered a proposal for an amendment to its sexual harassment statute in the French penal code. The existing statute, which was passed in 1992 and had gone into effect in 1994, stated:

> The act of harassing another by using orders, threats, or constraint in the goal of obtaining sexual favors, by someone abusing the authority conferred by his position, is punished by [a maximum of] one year of imprisonment and [a maximum] fine of 100,000 F [$14,000].[4]

The new proposal would have added "pressure of any nature" to the "orders, threats, or constraints," to make the penal statute applicable to a wider range of conduct and to make it more consistent with the labor statute, which invokes "orders," "threats," "constraints" *and* "pressure of any nature."[5] Initially proposed in the National Assembly,[6] the bill was rejected twice by the more conservative Senate, where it was argued that the new term was too vague.[7] Ultimately, in a joint Senate–National Assembly meeting, Parliament added "serious pressure" to the penal statute as a compromise.[8]

These two instances of legal reform reveal many of the differences between American and French sexual harassment law (see Table 1). For instance, in the United States, the courts, rather than Congress, have created much of sexual harassment law. Second, the *Harris* decision reveals the extent to which sexual harassment is condemned in American law because it is an instance of employment discrimination, in which a person's *conditions of employment* are compromised because of that person's gender. It further reveals that, according to American law, sexual harassment need not involve an ultimatum that the employee engage in sex or risk losing her job; simply having to tolerate sexual demands and innuendo may alter an employee's conditions of employment if they are sufficiently severe or pervasive.[9] Finally, consistent with American sexual harassment law under Title VII, Teresa Harris sued the Forklift company for monetary damages, rather than pursuing Charles Hardy for either monetary damages or (through a state prosecutor) in a criminal court.

In France, Parliament, rather than the courts, has made sexual harassment law. The parliamentary debate further exposes the centrality in French law of *constraint*, which, made possible by "official *authority*," is used to force a person into engaging in sexual relations against her will.[10] Just as physical force is used to coerce a rape victim into having unwanted sexual relations, so here official authority is used to exert pressure to the same end. The French penal statute says nothing about gender discrimination or workplace consequences, revealing that it conceptualizes sexual harassment as a form of sexual violence, akin to but distinct from rape or sexual battery, rather than as a form of gender discrimination. Finally, under French penal law, it is the sexual harasser, not the employer, who is charged in criminal court, where he could be sent to jail and receive a fine, and who may also have to pay small compensatory damages to the victim.[11]

Table 1. *Sexual Harassment in U.S. and French Law*

	United States	France
Body of law	Employment law (civil); i.e., Title VII of CRA 1964	Penal law (criminal), labor law
Where law was chiefly created	Courts	Legislature
Groups most responsible for creating the laws	Feminist associations, lawyers/(feminist) legal scholars, judges	Feminist associations, elected officials, secretary of women's rights
Definition of wrong	1) Quid pro quo: exchange of employment benefits for sexual relations; (2) hostile environment: sexual or sexist behavior on the part of a boss or colleague that is sufficiently severe or pervasive to create a "hostile environment"	Abuse of authority to demand "sexual favors" from another (after legal reform in January 2002, abuse of authority is no longer necessary)
Larger values evoked	Equal employment opportunity	Physical safety and personal integrity
Main remedy	Monetary compensation paid to the harassed party by the employer (back pay, compensatory damages, punitive damages)	Penal: prison, fines, small compensatory damages; Labor: reinstatement, back pay

Sexual harassment is covered under employment law in the United States but in penal law in France. This is more than a technicality. Each body of law has had important implications for how sexual harassment has been legally defined and the remedy provided. In the United States, sexual harassment law has been created mostly as case law under Title VII of the CRA 1964, which states that, in businesses with fifteen or more employees, an employer may not "fail or refuse to hire or discharge any individual or otherwise discriminate against any individual with respect to his compensation, terms, conditions, or privileges of employment, because of such individual's race, color, religion, sex, or national origin."[12]

In order to address sexual harassment under Title VII, legal scholars, lawyers, and judges have had to argue that sexual harassment is a case of sex discrimination in employment. In so doing, they have stressed two dimensions of this problem: 1) the negative consequences it has on the targeted person's employment, and 2) that the behavior was motivated by or has the effect of sex discrimination. Why sexual harassment constitutes sex discrimination is ambiguous, but the dominant view is that sexual harassment violates formal equality principles, because members of one sex (usually women) are targeted for abusive behavior *because of their sex*.[13] By stressing employment repercussions and sex discrimination, the courts have, in effect, underplayed other dimensions, such as the target's psychological and physical well-being and gender-neutral causes of sexual harassment, like simple cruelty or poor impulse control.

Title VII applies strictly to the workplace, offering no protection from, say, a predatory doctor or landlord.[14] While other statutes have been used to prohibit sexual harassment in other places, the bulk of sexual harassment jurisprudence in the United States has focused on the workplace.[15] Also, while recognizing a greater range of *sexual* behavior as being in violation of Title VII, some legal scholars have argued that the courts have ruled that some egregious forms of nonsexual gender harassment (such as men telling female coworkers that women belong in the kitchen or sabotaging their equipment in manual jobs) are not covered under Title VII.[16]

In ruling that sexual harassment is a form of sex discrimination under Title VII, the courts have held employers responsible for sexual harassment among their employees. Concretely, this means that employees who have been sexually harassed can sue their employers for monetary compensation. The Equal Employment Opportunity Commission (EEOC) exists to enforce Title VII.[17]

In France, sexual harassment is covered under the penal code. The penal statute quoted above, which went into effect in 1994, qualified sexual harassment as sexual violence. Categorization is an important source of meaning. By situating sexual harassment with other forms of sexual violence, it is, in effect, defined as a form of sexual violence itself. What is and what is not sexual harassment is also given meaning relationally. Among the four kinds of sexual violence in this section — rape, sexual assault, exhibitionism, and sexual harassment — rape is the only *crime* (crime) among the four; the other three are *délits* (misdemeanors). Moreover, the maximum penalty for sexual harassment (and exhibitionism) — one year in prison and the equivalent of a $14,000 fine — is among the smallest of the group, revealing that sexual harassment is considered among the least serious.

According to French penal law, sexual harassment is also different from rape and sexual assault in that it does not involve physical contact. Rather, with sexual harassment, economic dependence and official authority alone are used to pressure a person into having sexual relations. If a boss not only tells his employee that she will have to sleep with him if she wants to keep her job, but also grabs her breast, he would be guilty not only of sexual harassment but also of sexual assault, according to French law. If he goes further and physically forces his employee into having sexual intercourse, legally speaking in France, he would be guilty of rape, in addition to assault and sexual harassment. Note that this is different in the United States, where, if Title VII is invoked, all forms of sexual violence at work are lumped together under the category "sexual harassment."[18]

French sexual harassment law is thus narrower in scope than American law, in that before January 2002 it recognized only those instances in which there was both abuse of hierarchical power and explicit demands for sexual activity.[19] However, unlike American jurisprudence under Title VII, the French penal statute extends beyond the workplace to other kinds of relations of power, such as that between a doctor and a patient, a teacher and a student, a state bureaucrat and a welfare recipient, or a landlord and a tenant. Rather than monetary damages from the employer, the French state can impose prison sentences and/or state fines on the harasser. The wronged party can also seek civil damages from the harasser during the penal trial, called "porter partie civile."[20]

Retaliation linked to sexual harassment, but not sexual harassment itself, is also covered in a statute in the French labor code, which went into effect in 1992, and states:

> No employee can be penalized nor dismissed for having submitted or refusing to submit to acts of harassment of an employer, his agent, or any person who, abusing the authority conferred by their position, gave orders, made threats, imposed constraints, or exercised pressure of any nature on this employee, in the goal of obtaining sexual favors for his own benefit or for the benefit of a third party.[21]

Employees who suffer employment retaliation linked to sexual harassment can claim reinstatement or (more likely) back pay under this labor statute, which also protects whistle-blowers from retaliation. The labor law further allows, but does not require, employers to discipline sexual harassers in the workplace.[22] Employers must include sexual harassment in the company's internal regulations and post them in the firm and places of recruitment.[23] Provisions of employer liability for sexual harassment, however, are extremely weak.[24] Because French labor law requires employers to provide justification for any dismissal, employers who are overzealous in penalizing employees for sexual harassment can be sued for wrongful discharge.[25]

AMERICAN LAW:
A PRODUCT OF ACTIVISM AND OPPORTUNITY

We have seen that the body of law in which sexual harassment is inscribed has important consequences for how this problem is conceptualized. This begs the question: Why did the United States end up addressing sexual harassment in employment law while France addressed this same problem through penal law? Was this a result of distinct strategies on the part of women's groups? Alternatively, was this a product of political or legal institutions? I show that it was a combination of the two, demonstrating how, in each country, feminists took advantage of the legal and political resources available to them and responded to the social constraints they faced. This led them to different bodies of law, which in turn shaped both the frame and remedy of sexual harassment in important and far-reaching ways.

In the United States, where much of law is created through jurisprudence, the courts offered American feminists access to the lawmaking process. After a few false starts, American feminists were able to successfully argue that sexual harassment was covered under Title VII of the CRA 1964, which prohibits employers from discriminating on the basis of race, color, religion, sex, or national origin. Feminists and others found that racial discrimination jurisprudence was particularly useful for expanding the scope of sexually harassing behavior prohibited under Title VII. However, certain characteristics of Title VII have limited the scope and effectiveness of American sexual harassment law. For instance, since Title VII applies only to the workplace, it is of little help in addressing sexual harassment outside of work. Because it only addresses discrimination, it is also poorly equipped to deal with any sadistic abuse of authority that is not discriminatory on the basis of sex, as the courts have defined it. Moreover, some have argued that, while recognizing a larger range of sexual forms of sex discrimination, the courts have increasingly overlooked nonsexual forms of gender discrimination.[26]

The earliest theorizing on sexual harassment in the United States emerged from women's own experiences. In a consciousness-raising group in 1974, Lin Farley discovered that each member had "already quit or been fired from a job at least once because we had been made too uncomfortable by the behavior of men."[27] Such discussions convinced Farley (and others) that this behavior needed a name; they decided that the term "sexual harassment" came "as close to symbolizing the problem as the language would permit."[28] Moving from personal experience to political action, members of this group joined with the NYC Human Rights Commission and the National Organization for Women (NOW) to help establish Working Women United (WWU), a resource center and activist organization for women who work outside of the home, focusing primarily on sexual harassment at work.[29] Other early women's movement organizations that dealt specifically with issues of sexual harassment included the Women Office Workers (WOW) in New York City, the Alliance Against Sexual Coercion in the Boston area, and 9to5 National Association of Working Women.[30]

In May 1975, WWU held the first "Speak Out Against Sexual Harassment" in Ithaca, New York and, as an anti-sexual harassment network grew within the existing women's movement, others followed.[31] Several surveys were conducted from both within the women's movement and outside of it, which pointed to the widespread nature of the problem.[32] In early discussions, sexual harassment was conceptualized as sexual violence. Women referred to incidents of sexual harassment as "little rapes,"[33] and the first group to develop confrontational strategies to end street harassment was the Community Action Strategies to Stop Rape (CASSR) project in Columbus, Ohio.[34]

At first, feminist activists used a variety of legal strategies to combat sexual harassment at work. They pressured unemployment agencies to recognize resignations following sexual harassment as constituting constructive discharge (coerced resignation). When they met with resistance, the WWU helped develop legislation that explicitly stated that sexual harassment is a reasonable cause for quitting one's job, so that the women who did so would qualify for unemployment benefits. Activists across the country also had local human rights commissions and commissions on the status of women intervene on behalf of sexually harassed women who were denied unemployment benefits.[35]

This legal remedy, as well as those available under criminal and tort law, proved inadequate, however. Earning the right to unemployment benefits individualizes the issue and does nothing either to punish the harasser or employer, or to prevent further incidents of sexual harassment. Criminal law applies only to instances involving serious physical harm[36] and must be proven "beyond a reasonable doubt." Moreover, prosecution relies on police and district attorneys who are often insensitive to complaints of sexual violence towards women.[37] Tort law, which is designed to address "offenses" (behavior that embarrasses, shames, disgusts, or annoys someone), tends to frame the harm as offending an individual women's "honor" rather than as reproducing gender inequality.[38] In light of these shortcomings, feminist activists began looking toward Title VII for an alternative solution.

The initial proposal of Title VII of the Civil Rights Act of 1964, which was designed to combat race discrimination, made no reference to sex discrimination. Through congressional debate, however, it was amended to address not only "race" and "color," but also sex, religion, and national origin.

The reason sex was added to Title VII is contested. Conventional wisdom maintains that Congressional Representative Howard Smith proposed the addition of "sex" as a protected class to Title VII as a ploy to sink the entire bill with a controversial measure, a big "congressional joke" that backfired.[39] Historians and legal scholars, however, have argued that feminists played an important role in lobbying for the amendment.[40] These accounts suggest that Howard Smith, who was a staunch opponent of the civil rights bill but a firm *supporter* of the Equal Rights Amendment (ERA), probably made the following calculation. With luck, his amendment would sink the entire bill, he thought. However, if that were to fail, he reasoned that it would be preferable to offer protection not only to blacks but also to white women. Though some liberal and feminist groups objected to the amendment, either because they preferred separate treatment of sex discrimination or because they feared the addition would sink the bill, others strongly supported it.[41] With their support, the sex amendment survived debate in the House and Senate, despite attempts to remove it.[42] In 1964, the incipient second wave women's movement thus gained in Title VII a powerful legal tool against sex discrimination.

The first sex discrimination cases focused on equal access to jobs, seniority, and pay;[43] it would be ten years before lawyers would think of using Title VII to combat sexual harassment. Beginning in the mid-1970s, however, early plaintiffs sought out (often through personal networks) optimistic young attorneys who had training in civil rights law and were not afraid to take risks, activist lawyers and organizations specialized in civil rights law, and feminist attorneys to represent them in sexual harassment cases.[44] Although women's organizations never sponsored a coordinated effort against sexual harassment, networks of activist attorneys discussed strategy, exchanged briefs, and gave each other moral support.[45]

In the late 1970s, feminists trained in the law thus began to formulate a case that sexual harassment constituted a form of sex discrimination.[46] Women's rights organizations also actively sought out attorneys and litigants handling sexual harassment cases that presented novel issues, offering them assistance with strategy, brief writing and coordination of amicus curiae briefs (legal essays urging the court to rule in a particular manner) to private practitioners handling these cases.[47]

In 1975, Catharine MacKinnon circulated a draft of her book *Sexual Harassment of Working Women*, in which she argued that sexual harassment should be considered a group-defined injury, suffered by individuals (usually women) because of their sex. This point, she maintained, was obscured in sexual tort cases, which stressed moralism and women's "delicacy."[48] According to MacKinnon, sexual tort cases are permeated with "the aura of the pedestal, more rightly understood as the foundation of the cage."[49] For instance, in one case that MacKinnon cites, a judge opined, "Every woman has a right to assume that a passenger car is not a brothel and that when she travels in it, she will meet nothing, see nothing, hear nothing to wound her delicacy or insult her womanhood."[50] Only antidiscrimination law, which was designed to *change the society* to prevent the reoccurrence of discriminatory behavior, clearly conveys the group-injury aspect of sexual harassment, MacKinnon contended.[51] In arguing that sexual harassment was a form of sex discrimination,

American feminists, like their 1960s predecessors, thus "bridged"[52] this new issue to that of racial discrimination, an issue whose social legitimacy was built by the civil rights movement. In so doing, they stressed the group-based discrimination component of sexual harassment.

In order to show that it should be addressed under Title VII, American feminists also framed sexual harassment as being about employment opportunity. Doing so, they built on ingrained American beliefs that the market should be fair. In a nation like the United States, where a low degree of "decommodification" and socialism is combined with a high degree of liberalism, there are particularly high expectations that markets should be "fair," since they are supposed to be a legitimate and efficient means of distributing wealth.[53] MacKinnon recognized this when she said:

> Legally, women are not arguably entitled, for example, to a marriage free of sexual harassment any more than to one free of rape, nor are women legally guaranteed the freedom to walk down the street or into a court of law without sexual innuendo. In employment, the government promises more.[54]

The belief that the market is or should be fair is stronger in the United States than in social democracies, like France. The latter are more likely to question the legitimacy of market-determined inequalities, regardless of the equality of opportunity, and seek to render human welfare at least partially independent of market mechanisms.[55]

Finally, Title VII was strategically appealing to feminists because it allowed victims of sexual harassment to sue their employers, who usually have deeper pockets than individual harassers. This combination of civil and market remedies has strong precedent in the American political tradition; in France, there is greater suspicion of the market and the state is seen as a more legitimate arbitrator.[56]

American sexual harassment law has been made primarily in the courts. It is here that feminists and feminist sympathizers have gained access into the law-making process and where they have also encountered legal opposition. In the early years, opponents argued that sexual harassment was not a form of sex discrimination because it was a personal, rather than group-based, behavior and/or because it had no serious implications for the victim's employment opportunities.[57] Since then, the precedent for treating sexual harassment as sex discrimination under Title VII is well established in case law, despite some challenges from legal scholarship.[58] Nonetheless, the limits of sexual harassment and employer liability continue to be debated in the courts and remain in flux. In what follows, I sketch some of the major moments in the making of current sexual harassment law in the United States.

The first feminist victory in the courts dates to 1977, when the three-judge panel on the case *Barnes v. Costle*[59] reversed the district court's decision and held that sexual harassment is sex discrimination in employment. The decision in this case was informed by an early draft of MacKinnon's *Sexual Harassment of Working Women*, which the author herself had given to a law clerk on the case.[60] The court reasoned that the plaintiff, whose job had been abolished because she refused to have sexual relations with the director of the Environmental Protection Agency's Equal Opportunity Division, was the victim of discrimination because "but for her womanhood . . . [the plaintiff's] participation in sexual activity would never have been solicited. . . . She was invited only because she was a woman subordinate to the inviter in the hierarchy of agency personnel."[61] In a footnote, the court further specified that this principle would also apply to a heterosexual woman who sexually harassed a man or a homosexual boss who harassed someone of the same sex: "In each instance, the legal problem would be identical to that confronting us now — the exaction of a condition which, but for her *sex*, the employee would not have faced."[62] This was also the year that two other federal Courts of Appeal held for the first time that sexual harassment constitutes sex discrimination under Title VII.[63]

In arguing that Title VII should not only apply to the quid pro quo type of sexual harassment but also to hostile environment sexual harassment, advocates appealed to existing race discrimination jurisprudence that recognized that an extremely hostile and discriminatory working environment could itself be found to be in violation of Title VII. One of the most important of these cases was *Rogers v. EEOC*,[64] in which a Hispanic woman complained that her employer, an optometrist, segregated his Hispanic and white patients. The Fifth Circuit held:

> The phrase "terms, conditions or privileges of employment" in [Title VII] is an expansive concept [that includes] the practice of creating a working environment heavily charged with ethnic or racial discrimination. . . . One can readily envision working environments so heavily polluted with discrimination as to destroy completely the emotional and psychological stability of minority group workers.[65]

In 1981, following the recommendations of feminists, the D. C. Circuit Court of Appeals extended the *Rogers* ruling to cases of hostile environment sexual harassment, ruling that:

> Racial slurs, though intentional and directed at individuals, may still be just verbal insults, yet they too may create Title VII liability. How then can sexual harassment, which injects the most demeaning sexual stereotypes into the general work environment and which always represents an intentional assault on an individual's innermost privacy, not be illegal?[66]

The court reasoned that unless a hostile work environment on its own could constitute a legal claim, "an employer could sexually harass a female employee with impunity by carefully stopping short of firing the employee or taking other tangible actions against her in response to her resistance."

The Court of Appeals for the Eleventh Circuit supported this ruling in 1982, in *Henson v. City of Dundee*,[67] ruling that the numerous and demeaning sexual "inquiries and vulgarities" suffered by the plaintiff from the chief of the Dundee Police Department, where she worked, themselves created a "hostile working environment" that constituted discrimination. In his opinion, the circuit judge quoted from MacKinnon's 1979 book to distinguish between "condition of work" (hostile environment) and "quid pro quo" sexual harassment.[68] Like MacKinnon, the court also made the connection between sexual harassment and racial harassment:

> Sexual harassment, which creates a hostile or offensive environment for members of one sex, is every bit the arbitrary barrier to sexual equality at the workplace that racial harassment is to racial equality. Surely, a requirement that a man or woman run a gauntlet of sexual abuse in return for the privilege of being allowed to work and make a living can be as demeaning and disconcerting as the harshest of racial epithets.[69]

Under pressure from feminist organizations, the High Court confirmed *Henson* in 1986 in *Meritor v. Vinson*. Mechelle Vinson claimed that her boss had fondled her in public, made requests for sexual relations (to which she succumbed out of fear of losing her job), and forcibly raped her on several occasions, but never conditioned concrete employment benefits on sexual relations (the definition of quid pro quo harassment).[70] Catharine MacKinnon joined Mechelle Vinson's lawyer on her brief; and several feminist organizations, including the Women's Bar Association of Massachusetts, the Women's Bar Association of New York, the Women's Legal Defense Fund, and the Working Women's Institute, filed briefs of amici curiae supporting Vinson.

While most of sexual harassment law was made in the courts, Congress intervened with the passage of the Civil Rights Act of 1991 (CRA 1991). This legislation was passed in the wake of the nationally televised senate hearings, where Anita Hill alleged that Supreme Court nominee Clarence Thomas had sexually harassed her when they worked together at the EEOC.[71] In fact, some have argued that public outrage over Hill's earlier treatment by Thomas and later treatment by the Senate made President George Bush (senior) more willing to sign the civil rights bill.[72] The CRA 1991 allowed courts to award plaintiffs punitive and compensatory damages for "future pecuniary losses, emotional pain, suffering, inconvenience, mental anguish, loss of enjoyment of life, and other non-pecuniary losses" in sexual harassment cases. The 1991 amendment also gave plaintiffs the right to a jury trial and, in general, strengthened sexual harassment law under Title VII.

The Supreme Court's 1993 ruling in *Harris v. Forklift Systems,* discussed above, expanded the category of hostile environment sexual harassment by clarifying that behavior need not have tangible economic consequences to fall under this category of wrong. Supported by briefs from the American Civil Liberties Union, the Feminists for Free Expression, the NAACP Legal Defense and Educational Fund, the National Conference of Women's Bar Associations, the National Employment Lawyers Association, the NOW Legal Defense and Education Fund, and the Women's Legal Defense Fund, the High Court ruled "Title VII comes into play before the harassing leads to a nervous breakdown."[73] In Justice O'Connor's opinion, issued on behalf of a unanimous court, she emphasized the debilitating effect that sexual harassment has on employment opportunities. She argued that even a discriminatorily abusive work environment that does not seriously affect an employee's psychological well-being often detracts from an employee's job performance, prevents career advancement, or leads the employee to quit entirely. While the court concluded that there is no precise test to measure a hostile environment, it did offer guidelines. It said that the plaintiff must establish two facts. First, she or he should demonstrate that the conduct objectively creates a hostile or offensive environment, so that a "reasonable person" (a legal term referring to a theoretical person of average sensibilities) would find it hostile. Second, the plaintiff should show that she or he personally found the behavior abusive.

In 1998 the Supreme Court delivered two decisions clarifying somewhat the conditions of employer liability for sexual harassment under Title VII. In *Burlington Industries v. Ellerth* and *Faragher v. City of Boca Raton,* the Supreme Court held that when harassment results in "a tangible employment action, such as discharge, demotion or undesirable reassignment," the employer's liability is absolute. When there has been no tangible action, an employer can defend itself if it can prove two things. First, the employer must show that it has taken "reasonable care to prevent and correct promptly any sexually harassing behavior," such as by adopting an effective policy with a complaint procedure. Second, the employer must demonstrate that the employee "unreasonably failed to take advantage of any preventive or corrective opportunities provided." This puts the burden of proof on the employer, who must prove each of these points.

The emphasis on corporate policies as a defense against liability has evolved over time and has its origins in the human resource professions and organizations, rather than in the courts. Faced with ambiguous federal mandates and legal liability, organizations and the professions have fashioned these policies by drawing on institutionalized accounts about appropriate responses to such mandates. By recognizing and legitimating these policies, as the High Court did in *Burlington* and *Faragher,* the courts confer legal and market benefits upon organizational structures that began as gestures of compliance.[74]

These decisions represented a gain for plaintiffs, who, according to some earlier decisions, had to demonstrate negligence on the part of the employer, or that the employer knew or should have known of the harassment but did not act.[75] In the case of sexual harassment among hierarchical peers, however, the plaintiff still has to demonstrate employer negligence. The courts argued that these rulings would help corporations limit liability by creating effective complaint procedures and training. For critics, these rulings put too much of a burden on employers to control workplace behavior that is already inconsistent with their interests. This was the position expressed by Justice Thomas, who, joined by Justice Scalia, argued that employers should only be liable for sexual harassment committed by hierarchical superiors in cases of quid pro quo: "Sexual harassment is simply not something that employers can wholly prevent without taking extraordinary measures — constant video and audio surveillance, for example — that would revolutionize the workplace in a manner incompatible with a free society."[76]

Human beings need categories, definitions, frames, or accounts (I am using these terms loosely, almost interchangeably) to make sense of the world.[77] Any given account, however, presents experience from a particular angle, making certain aspects of the phenomenon extremely clear, while obscuring others. In the case of sexual harassment, definitions that rely on a sex-discrimination frame focus on how sexual harassment can be motivated by and can contribute to gender inequality in employment, but are less useful for making sense of a sadistic boss who thrives on making life miserable for his subordinates, men and women alike.[78] A discrimination frame, which stresses employment repercussions, is also of little help in conceptualizing the denigration or fear many women feel in the streets when ogled or threatened by men. Nor is an employment discrimination frame very useful in understanding the sense of violation and betrayal a woman may feel when her psychiatrist abuses her trust and sense of vulnerability by initiating sexual relations.

Some of those who are unsympathetic to sexual harassment jurisprudence under Title VII appeal to the shortcomings of this frame to argue that sexual harassment should be addressed elsewhere, say, in state tort law. Those who support sexual harassment jurisprudence under Title VII prefer to work within an employment discrimination frame since, by definition, Title VII only applies to employment discrimination. For instance, Katherine Franke, a prominent feminist legal scholar and champion of Title VII sexual harassment jurisprudence, has argued in an influential law review article that the courts need to conceptualize sex discrimination differently.[79]

Franke has contended that the Supreme Court has not sufficiently theorized why sexual harassment is sex discrimination, and that feminist scholars and the lower courts have advanced three main theories for why sexual harassment falls under Title VII. The dominant view is that sexual harassment violates formal equality principles because members of one sex (usually women) are targeted for abusive behavior *because of their sex*.[80] Others have claimed that the sexism of sexual harassment lies in the fact that the conduct is sexual.[81] Finally, some have argued that sexual harassment is an example of the subordination of women by men.[82]

After showing how each of these theories fails to account for certain cases of sexual harassment, in particular those involving same-sex harassment, Franke offers an alternative analysis of why sexual harassment is a form of gender discrimination. She argues that sexual harassment is a technology of sexism, in that it penalizes gender non-conformity by humiliating and/or terrorizing "overly assertive" women or "effeminate" men. To date, few courts have applied Franke's reasoning.[83]

Franke's model does more easily account for certain kinds of male-on-male sexual harassment, particularly those that do not seem based on sexual desire but involve instead macho men humiliating or terrorizing their seemingly effeminate or weak (male) coworker(s).[84] However, her model of gender discrimination does nothing to compensate for the limitations of Title VII in dealing with the sadistic boss described above, abuse of authority outside of the workplace, or hostile environments beyond the office.

Moreover, some have argued that, in recognizing that sex discrimination can take the form of sexual behavior, the courts have become less sensitive to forms of sex discrimination that are *not* sexual in nature. According to legal scholar Vicki Schultz, women are more likely to lose their case when the harassment they suffered was not sexual in nature, even when the behavior, such as having their equipment sabotaged by male coworkers trying to prove that women cannot do manual labor, put their lives at risk.[85] Schultz's argument is that American sexual harassment jurisprudence equates sex with discrimination and discrimination with sex. In so doing, we are left little room for conceptualizing either nondiscriminatory sex or nonsexual discrimination.[86]

FRENCH LAW:
A PRODUCT OF ACTIVISM AND OPPORTUNITY

French sexual harassment law was also the product of feminist activism and legal, political, and cultural opportunity and constraint. The first important difference between France and the United States is that, in the former, laws are made strictly in Parliament through statutes rather than largely in the courts through case law. Penal code reform in 1991 opened a window of opportunity for feminists to propose a penal sexual harassment statute. French feminists were thus not forced to make sexual harassment fit under a preexisting discrimination statute. On the other hand, they did have to garner political support for their proposal. During parliamentary debates, they encountered resistance from some lawmakers who seemed intent on discrediting the bill by appealing to anti-American rhetoric, arguing that passing a sexual harassment law in France would have the undesirable effect of importing "American excesses" of litigiousness, puritanism, and the Battle of the Sexes. This is a common strategy in France for discrediting French feminist initiatives, such as affirmative action or antisexist legislation.[87] To salvage the bill from these critiques, the state-feminist sponsors of the piece of legislation argued before their socialist colleagues that, in fact, the bill defended traditional socialist values by denouncing the abuse of hierarchical authority. To prove their point, they revised the legislation so that it only targeted quid pro quo sexual harassment, where abuse of authority is involved. Once the penal statute was passed, an opportunity opened for the secretary of women's rights to propose a labor law statute to provide additional recourse for people who suffer employment retaliation linked to sexual harassment. The penal and labor codes then dictated the kinds of remedies that would be deployed.

Independent French feminist groups initiated the French sexual harassment laws that state feminists (that is, employees of the state-run women's rights office) eventually pushed through Parliament. The most important association was the Association Européenne Contre les Violences Faites aux Femmes au Travail (AVFT, European Association Against Violence Toward Women at Work), which was founded in 1985 to fight against all forms of workplace sexual violence including sexual harassment. The AVFT drew attention to this problem through the publication of its journal, *Cette violence dont nous ne voulons plus* (This violence that we want to end), and scholarly work published by its members, some of whom were also academics.[88] The situations the association grouped under the term "violence" included "sexual blackmail in hiring, battery, rape, psychological abuse, sexually vulgar environments, use of pornography, discrimination, [and] sexual harassment."[89] In 1989, the AVFT organized an international conference around the theme "Violence, sexual harassment, and abuse of power at work." Scholars from the United States (such as Catharine MacKinnon and Sarah Burns), Canada, and Europe presented work on the phenomenon of sexual harassment in their respective countries, and the AVFT published the collection of papers the following year.[90]

The Ligue du Droit des Femmes (LDF, League of Women's Rights), a feminist association founded in the mid 1970s, also helped politicize this issue in the early years. The rest of the women's movement vehemently criticized the LDF as "reformist" when the latter officially formed as an association.[91] Yet by embracing, rather than shunning, the political process, the LDF made a mark and, unlike most French feminist groups of the 1970s, survived into the twenty-first century. Having fought against rape and domestic violence, as well as fighting (in vain) for a law that would ban sexist images of women in the media, the LDF, led by Anne Zelensky, organized a conference on sexual harassment in 1985. Simone de Beauvoir presided and the minister of women's rights, Yvette Roudy, and the European Union sponsored the event. The colloquium speakers included representatives of the newly formed AVFT, who had quickly established themselves as leaders on the issue of sexual harassment in France. The LDF also cosponsored, with *BIBA* (a women's magazine for young professionals), a survey on sexual harassment.

Penal reform in 1991 provided an opportunity for French feminists to propose a law on sexual harassment for the penal code, which feminists recognized would send a strong message about the unacceptability of this act. The AVFT proposal defined sexual harassment as:

> Any act or behavior that is sexual, based on sex or on sexual orientation, towards a person, that has the aim or effect of compromising that person's right to dignity, equality in employment, and to work-

ing conditions that are respectful of that person's dignity, their moral or physical integrity, their right to receive ordinary services offered to the public in full equality.

This act or behavior can notably take the form of: pressure, insults, remarks, jokes based on sex, touching, battery [*coup*], assault, sexual exhibitionism, pornography, unwelcome implicit or explicit sexual solicitations, threats or sexual blackmail.[92]

The AVFT proposal suggested that this crime be punished by a maximum of two years in prison and a 200,000 F ($28,000) fine (twice the maximum jail term and fine of the bill that eventually passed). The AVFT proposal specified that the employer would be legally responsible for sexual harassment committed by his employees, clients, or suppliers, a provision that was not retained in the final version of the law. The AVFT made hierarchical authority an aggravating factor rather than a necessary element of sexual harassment, as in the statute that eventually passed. Marie-Victoire Louis, one of the AVFT leaders and founders, presented the proposal to lawmaker Jean Michel Belorgey, who was a personal friend of hers. He agreed to present and defend the proposal to about twenty deputies, including Yvette Roudy.

In June 1991, the Union des Femmes Françaises (UFF, Union of French Women), a feminist group within the Communist Party, published a report on sexual harassment and drafted a sexual harassment bill, which was reproduced in *Clara* magazine.[93] Similar to the AVFT recommendation, the UFF proposal defined sexual harassment broadly as any

pressure or constraint of sexual nature carried out through words, gestures, threats, promises, writing, drawings, sending of objects, blackmail, explicit or implicit sexual allusions, sexually discriminatory remarks, targeting a person during the hiring process, or while conducting their professional activity.

Note, however, that while the AVFT proposal targeted not only *sexual* behavior but also conduct that was "based on sex or on sexual orientation," the UFF bill, like the ultimate law, addressed only *sexual* conduct. Like the AVFT bill, the UFF bill called for longer prison sentences and higher fines when the sexual harasser was in a position of authority over the plaintiff. It further called for publication of the conviction and required employers to post the law in workplaces.

Because the AVFT and UFF were not working within the constraints of an anti-discrimination jurisprudence, like that under the CRA 1964 in the United States, they were not confined to an antidiscrimination analysis. Instead, they invoked a range of criteria for denouncing sexual harassment, including not only equal opportunity in employment, but also human dignity, moral and physical integrity, and consumer rights.

During these legislative debates, the European Union (EU) proved a valuable ally. In 1976, the EU issued a directive on sex equality at work.[94] In 1987, it commissioned a report documenting the existence of sexual harassment in member states.[95] In 1991, the EU issued a recommendation encouraging member states to take action against sexual harassment, stating that such behavior

> is unacceptable if: (a) such conduct is unwanted, unreasonable and offensive to the recipient; (b) a person's rejection of, or submission to, such conduct on the part of employers or workers (including superiors or colleagues) is used explicitly or implicitly as a basis for a decision which affects that person's access to vocational training, access to employment, continued employment, promotion, salary or any other employment decisions; and/or (c) such conduct creates an intimidating, hostile or humiliating work environment for the recipient; and that such conduct may, in certain circumstances, be contrary to the principle of equal treatment within the meaning of Articles 3, 4 and 5 of Directive 76/207/EEC.

The content of the recommendation was strikingly similar to the EEOC guidelines. Both described the behavior as unwelcome or unwanted from the victim's point of view. The two texts also recognized both behavior that has tangible employment repercussions and that which simply creates a hostile or intimidating environment. Both acknowledged that colleagues as well as hierarchical superiors can harass employees. Like the American lawyers, European Union officials justified the recommendation on sexual harassment by stressing the link to sex discrimination. As in the American case, there were strategic reasons for this emphasis; the EU only had the right to make recommendations to nation-states concerning the economic domain, under the equality clause in the Treaty of Rome. However, the EU also justified the intervention as a protection of "dignity," a theme not present in the American legal debates. Moreover, while the EEOC guidelines defined sexual harassment as "unwelcome sexual advances, requests for sexual favors, and other verbal or physical conduct of a *sexual nature*," the EU recommendation targeted not only "all behavior with a sexual connotation" but also "all other behavior based on sex that affects the dignity of men and women at work." The recommendation was not binding, but the AVFT, which was also subsidized in the early years by the European Union, found that it, along with the 1976 directive and the Rubinstein report, gave the association greater legitimacy in arguing before French lawmakers that sexual harassment was an important problem that necessitated legislative action.

State feminists, especially Deputy Yvette Roudy and the secretary of women's rights, Véronique Neiertz, played a crucial role in passing sexual harassment legislation. Not only did they sponsor penal and labor sexual harassment bills, respectively, but they also did some of their own consciousness-raising. Specifically, in 1991, Neiertz contracted a Louis Harris poll on the issue.[96] This was the first systematic survey conducted in France on sexual harassment and was an important tool in getting mainstream political support for legislation. One of the survey's major findings was that 19 percent of working women said they had at one point been sexually harassed in the workplace. As politicians, the state feminists also knew how to compromise, which, as in most legislative debates, would become necessary.

Globalization proved to be a mixed blessing during French parliamentary debates. On one hand, as we saw, French feminists found useful theoretical, empirical, and legal examples by looking to Europe and North America. On the other hand, opponents of the bill appealed to anti-American rhetoric in order to discredit the bill as an import that would replicate "American excesses" of litigiousness, puritanism, and the Battle of the Sexes in France. In the case of the labor law, which was debated later in the year, these fears were fed by French reporting of the Thomas-Hill debate, which portrayed Hill as a vengeful feminist and Thomas as a besieged male, caught in a "witch hunt."[97]

During penal reform in the National Assembly, Yvette Roudy proposed two amendments on sexual harassment. In both, abuse of authority was a necessary component. Why did Roudy thus restrict the scope of the law? According to her, this compromise was necessary to win over the male Socialist lawmakers she needed to vote for the bill. In her own words: "My amendment would never have passed without the support of certain men within the socialist group. I told them that sexual harassment, which is an abuse of power, is a form of exploitation. That's the language they understand."[98] In the newspaper *Libération*, Roudy was even more explicit about what the Socialists were ready to accept in the amendment:

> When I proposed it to the Socialist group, the first reaction was: 'You aren't going to prohibit flirting. We aren't in the United States.' I explained to them: sexual harassment in the corporation, abuse of power, exploitation. If there wasn't a hierarchical dimension, the group would not have accepted it, fearing that it would be penalizing flirtation.[99]

In other words, because Roudy realized that arguments about sexism and discrimination did not resonate among the members of Parliament, she shaped the amendment's definition of sexual harassment to fit with their concept of rights and injustice. Exposed to the AVFT and the larger women's movement, her cultural 'toolkit'[100] included concepts of sexism and discrimination. However, she put them aside when addressing her male colleagues, who did not think in terms of these categories.[101]

Once the National Assembly had approved Roudy's sexual harassment bill, it passed the bill on to the Senate for review, where it was modified. Then, in keeping with parliamentary rules, the Senate sent the modified bill to be examined by the commission of laws in the National Assembly and put before a second vote in the National Assembly.[102] Several changes were made to the statute during this process.[103] Most importantly, whereas the National Assembly had initially placed the sexual harassment statute in the section "Discriminations," the commission of laws moved the statute to the section "Sexual violence other than rape," under the logic that "the *délit* (misdemeanor) of sexual harassment does not appear to be discriminatory because it exists regardless of the sex of the victim or of the perpetrator of the *délit*. In reality, it is much closer in nature to sexual violence."[104] Indeed, as French legal scholar Françoise Dekeuwer-Defossez has demonstrated, the discrimination component of sexual harassment was essentially abandoned during the legislative process.[105] Neither is there any reference to sex discrimination in Article 222–33, which defines sexual harassment in the penal code, nor any mention of sexual harassment in Article 225–1 of the penal code, which condemns sex *discrimination*.[106]

Once sexual harassment was addressed in penal law, the secretary of women's rights, Véronique Neiertz, proposed a statute in the labor code that would complement the penal statute by allowing sexual harassment victims and whistle blowers to dispute employment retaliation linked to an incident of sexual harassment. Initially, Neiertz criticized the limits of the penal law and said she did not want to limit the definition of sexual harassment to abuse of authority.[107] Yet, the proposal she presented to the Council of Ministers ended up being similarly limited.

Like Roudy, Neiertz modified her position to appeal to the men she needed to convince. Faced with anti-American rhetoric that accused her of importing puritanism and gender warfare, Neiertz disarmed her adversaries by contrasting the "reasonable" character of the French initiative to American "excesses" and by limiting the content of the project.[108] Before the Senate, Neiertz described the project as pragmatic and modest, demonstrating her concern to "avoid falling into the excesses of a situation *à l'americain*, which leads to repressing all relationship of seduction between men and women."[109] The presenter of the bill before the National Assembly described it as "moderate" and corresponding to "French culture."[110]

French legal traditions put a high premium on consistency among the different legal codes. Yet the penal and labor statutes that were passed in the early 1990s varied slightly in how they defined sexual harassment. Whereas the penal law defined the harasser as one who uses "orders, threats, constraint," the labor law referred to "orders," "threats," "constraints," and "pressure of any nature." In 1997–1998, as discussed above, an amendment was proposed to the penal statute to add "pressure of any nature."[111] Twice the more conservative Senate rejected the amendment, arguing that the term "pressure of any nature" was too vague.[112] Finally, in a joint meeting between the Senate and National Assembly, Parliament approved the inclusion of "serious pressure" as a compromise.[113] Although the AVFT welcomed this amendment, they were not involved in its passage.

In the preceding narrative of the French legislative process, I have argued that (male) French lawmakers were more likely to condemn sexual harassment when presented as an abuse of hierarchical authority, rather than as a form of sex-based employment discrimination. Realizing this, state feminists restricted the content of the sexual harassment statutes and stressed themes of domination and abuse of authority rather than gender inequality. During legislative debates, the lingering analyses of sexual harassment as a form of sex discrimination were reduced further. In other words, during legal debates about sexual harassment, lawmakers appealed to and reinforced French political culture, in which social inequality is understood in terms of class struggle and abuse of power rather than in terms of ethnic group or gender conflict.

There are some historical reasons for this political tradition. To begin with, due to different histories, France did not have a civil rights movement, like the one that proved so important in the United States. By separating the church and state, the Third Republic hoped to confine customs and beliefs to the "private sphere," meaning both that the state should not segregate citizens according to these criteria and that citizens should not "politicize" these differences.[114] Consequently, and in accordance with republican principles, France's census does not gather information about race, ethnicity, or religion, which subsequently makes it difficult to measure racial discrimination.[115] Without an objective measure of racial inequality, it is difficult to make this a political rallying point. The lack of statistics in France on racial disparity can obscure discrimination and racism.[116] While certain social actors have tried to politicize ethnic identity in France, others have resisted by appealing to long political traditions of an assimilating model of nationhood.[117]

On the other hand, France has a long history of politicizing work-based group identities in its social policies, social theory, labor law, unions, and occupational-group representations, such as "*socioprofessionnels*," within the *Commissariat au Plan* committees.[118] The employee-boss (*employé-patron*) dichotomy is particularly well institutionalized in French political parties, French unions (which form to defend *either* workers or bosses), and French labor courts (which include an equal representation of employees and management). This employee-boss dichotomy is, in turn, linked to a long French tradition of critiquing the arbitrary use of power. Thirty-five years ago, sociologist Michel Crozier argued that many French workers conceive authority to be universal, absolute, and unrestrained.[119] Michèle Lamont more recently found that this general attitude persists; French workers are more likely than their American counterparts to believe that managers exercise power for their own benefit, while American workers are more likely to say that they use such power for the collective good or for the good of the company.[120]

Moreover, the particularly insidious combination of abuse of power and sexual violence has been both practiced and condemned in France for some time. According to historically contested rules of feudal tradition, lords had the right to sleep with their serfs' brides on their wedding night. This right, which was later waived in exchange for a tax, was referred to as *le droit de seigneur, le droit de cuissage,* or the First Night.[121] In the nineteenth century, the term "droit de cuissage" referred to overseers who, because of the enormous power they had over female factory workers, engaged in (sometimes consensual and frequently coerced) sexual relations with them, a practice that was condemned in several strikes and demonstrations.[122] The term "droit de cuissage" was reinvented in the late 1980s to raise consciousness about contemporary forms of sexual violence at work. Framing sexual harassment as a form of violence and an abuse of authority in France, where there exist deep-seated beliefs about the absolute and unrestrained nature of authority, thus proved particularly effective.

CONCLUSION

We have seen how, in mobilizing for sexual harassment laws, feminist groups in both the United States and France were successful to the extent that they were able to respond to the cultural, political, and legal opportunities and constraints before them. Variations in these national contexts necessitated distinct actions by feminists and others, which in turn resulted in dissimilar bodies of sexual harassment law.

In the United States, the courts offered feminists and others access to the law-making process. Having drawn on political and legal traditions of antidiscrimination, U.S. groups successfully built jurisprudence that condemned a wide range of unwanted sexual attention in the workplace as a form of sex discrimination under Title VII of the Civil Rights Act of 1964. Since Title VII addresses employment discrimination by employers, using the former to condemn sexual harassment imposed a discrimination frame on the situation. This frame made discriminatory intent or effect and employment consequences most salient. Violent or abusive behavior at work that did not appear discriminatory fell between the cracks of Title VII jurisprudence, as did behavior that did not occur in the workplace. Finally, some have argued that, in expanding the scope of *sexual* behavior that constitutes sexual harassment, the U.S. courts have overlooked other forms of nonsexual gender harassment.[123]

In France, penal law reform in 1991 provided feminists with a window of opportunity in the legislature, which they used to propose a sexual harassment statute in the penal code. They then argued that a labor code statute was necessary to complement the penal statute. Working within a political and legal context that recognizes class inequalities and abuse of authority more readily than race or gender discrimination, the state-feminist sponsors of the bill decided that they would be more persuasive if they could pitch their proposal in the vocabulary of their socialist colleagues, as abuse of power and exploitation. Framing their proposal as concerning an abuse of power rather than group-based discrimination (an approach associated with the United States) also made sense in a political climate of anti-American and nationalist sentiment. In so framing their bill, the state-feminist sponsors limited the scope of the proposed statute to target only sexual harassment involving abuse of authority, rather than the wider range of behavior addressed in earlier feminist proposals.[124] Informed by their own political and legal traditions, in which critiques of violence were more developed than analyses of discrimination, French lawmakers, during parliamentary revisions to the statute, recategorized the offense as sexual violence rather than sex discrimination. The penal law allowed for imposing penal (prison sentences and fines) and small civil remedies on the *harasser*. By also passing a labor statute, Parliament allowed victims of employment retaliation, linked to workplace harassment, to demand back pay and/or reinstatement from their employer.

Legal definitions are powerful symbols of social values, so legal definitions of sexual harassment provide an important measure of how a given society regards this issue. One would further expect that, once sexual harassment laws are enacted, they would inform more general views about this social problem. While laws are important, however, they are neither the only, nor necessarily the most influential, source of social meaning. Both French and American sexual harassment laws contain multiple and often contradictory meanings. Because of this, the impact of these laws on social consciousness is bound to be largely unpredictable and uneven, as well as mediated by the people and groups who apply them, such as lawyers, prosecutors, and judges. Understanding how and why American and French law define sexual harassment differently is essential for comprehending, more generally, how the social problem of sexual harassment has been conceptualized in these two countries. However, formal law is only a starting point, not the final word, for understanding the larger social meaning of sexual harassment. The next step involves examining the actual meaning these laws have in people's lives.

TWO

Sexual Harassment Law in Action
Legitimacy and Liability

What effect do the laws discussed in the preceding chapter have on people's lives? For "Nancy," a human resource manager at an American branch of an American multinational company known to be progressive in diversity and sexual harassment training ("AmeriCorp"), sexual harassment is one of the most important workplace issues facing the company. Although sexual harassment–related calls are rare, Nancy considers them so serious that she addresses them promptly when they do arise: "I have a lot of balls up in the air; when one of these issues comes in, everything else stops. Sometimes I just have to make a phone call to find out what happened [but I deal with it right away]." Moreover, what Nancy, like many human resource managers in American work sites, defines as "sexual harassment" includes a much wider range of behavior than that covered under U.S. sexual harassment law.

One of the cases in which Nancy intervened involved a male employee who brushed and kissed the cheek of a female employee during a lunch-time jog on the company property. The woman, who was married, was not romantically interested in her colleague and told him so. The advances did *not* continue but the atmosphere was tense between the two employees, who were no longer talking to each other. According to Nancy, "people around them were feeling [that] something was going on. . . . So it not only impacted those two individuals, and I'm sure it impacted their performance, but it impacted the people around them." A friend of the female employee encouraged her to call human resources.

When Nancy received her call, she asked the woman to come in and explain what happened. After hearing her story, she told the woman that "[AmeriCorp] management and HR now have knowledge of this incident and we have to respond to it. We have to keep it to its utmost high level of confidentiality," but that we "would need to at least investigate in determining the next step." Nancy assured the woman, who was agonizing over whether she was to blame in some way, that her colleague would not necessarily be fired. She also referred the woman to the Employee Assistant Program, which employs social workers and psychologists to help employees with personal issues, to "help her deal with the emotional part of that and help her deal with whether she's going to tell her husband, those kinds of things."

Nancy then called "the harasser [to] get his side of the story":

Finally, because I couldn't get a hold of him, I left him a message: "This is Nancy at HR, when you get a moment could you please give me a call." Well, [as I feared,] he did get alarmed, and he went over to his manager and said, "Would you know why Corporate HR is calling me?" And the manager was aware of the situation and said, "There have been some issues that have been brought to our attention regarding harassment and she needs to talk to you." And I think he used the word "sexual harassment." So, of course, this poor individual starts sweating bullets and [thinking to himself:] "Oh my God. What happened? What did I do?" . . .

So he called me back, and . . . I explained to him [that we would] only pull those who need to know into the process. . . . I said, "it doesn't [go into your file] until it becomes a point where we have to go down corrective action. We'll just give you a verbal warning, a written warning, and probation, or in case of misconduct, we'll walk you right out the door." . . .

[During our discussion, I asked him:] "Have you ever noticed any behavioral differences with [your female coworker, or changes] in how you're feeling or [in how you're] talking to each other?" He said, "Yeah, it's been a little on the quiet side." I said, "And people around you are probably observing this, too." So we talked through it and he said, "I won't ever do that again." . . .

After I met with him, [I informed the woman and asked her to] advise me if anything else occurred. . . . Shortly after that, I would say probably a month or so, I did send the female an email [that] said, "How are things going?" Just to follow up with her. She said, "Everything's fine. We're back on track. I've had to deal with this, but I'm ok and things are ok." So I do try to follow up and put closure [on such incidents].

Note that, even though the behavior described by this manager fell short of sexual harassment as legally defined, it was taken seriously in this American workplace. Although the woman questioned whether she had somehow caused her coworker's behavior, she received assurance from her friend and then the human resource department that she was not at fault and that her feelings were legitimate. The "harasser," in turn, was clearly told that his behavior was unacceptable and, if it were to continue, would be subject to disciplinary action. The human resource department thus "held court," independently of the American judicial system.[1]

In contrast, when asked if there were internal regulations governing sexual harassment in a French office of AmeriCorp, a French human resource manager responded:

Prevention? No. We have no specific action, keeping in mind that today sexual harassment is penalized in France, it's a law that applies outside and within the corporation. So, there isn't any additional internal regulation on sexual harassment, but it's one of those things that would be considered serious, very serious, and therefore [if an employee were convicted of sexual harassment in a court of law, that] could effectively lead to [his] dismissal . . . . But that doesn't mean [that] there needs to be [specific corporate action]. It's like theft, there is no [special training program to avoid theft at work]. . . . We don't make [the law]. The legislation applies to us, the corporation and each of us.

This respondent, like many of his French colleagues, rejected the notion that employers can "serve as a substitute" for the justice system; this would be overstepping their authority over employee disputes. Rather, companies, like individuals, should respect the law and the limits of the law.

These interview excerpts are indicative of the very different place sexual harassment law occupies in the United States and France. This chapter explores these differences. Drawing on interviews with feminist activists (from the AVFT in France and 9to5 National Association of Working Women in the United States), lawyers who have worked in this area, human resource managers, and union representatives (in France only because the American branches of AmeriCorp and Frenchco were not unionized), it discusses the legitimacy of sexual harassment law in each of these societies and the extent to which companies feel responsible for stamping out sexual harassment. More generally, this chapter explores the nature of the legal climate, corporate climate, and national cultural climate surrounding sexual harassment in the United States and France.

THE UNITED STATES

American firms take sexual harassment very seriously. In the United States, successful plaintiffs may receive significant compensatory and punitive damages from their employer.[2] The fear of lawsuits, which may be inflated by the media and human resource profession,[3] encourages firms to respond promptly to sexual harassment claims. In the words of one American defense lawyer:

> It might be to protect them from liability, but most of the employers that I deal with are very concerned about sexual harassment issues and are willing to take the action that they need to take. Whether it's training, you know, having the policies in place. And when they get complaints, taking them seriously.

According to the American lawyers interviewed, firms in the United States are quick to dismiss or otherwise sanction people accused of sexual harassment, even when the case would be questionable in court. As one female lawyer said bitterly:

> I had an employee [as a client], who made . . . a very off-color remark. The woman was very offended by it. She went to her superiors, and my guy was disciplined with the loss of his job. Now, he obviously made a comment that was out of line, but it was an isolated incident. He subsequently apologized for it; he went to training to get [his] consciousness raised. In my mind, you don't deserve to get fired for a mistake of that magnitude when you have a long-term relationship with your employer.

The American defense lawyers I interviewed play it safe by frowning on any behavior over which their client could potentially be sued. For instance, when asked whether or not they would consider it sexual harassment for a female employee to hound a female coworker, calling her a "slut" and a "whore," most American lawyers said that they would not. Nonetheless, they said they would be concerned about it and would advise management to intervene. The following response was typical of American lawyers:

> I haven't seen that, but I think she might be able to prove a case of hostile environment. I mean, it's the behavior of calling her a slut, and calling her names that are associated with that type of behavior . . . especially if co-workers are jumping on the band-wagon, and they're creating an environment so hostile that she's having difficulty working in it. As a management lawyer I would argue it's not sexual harassment/hostile environment. That's not what [the law] was designed to prevent. But, I think it could get there.
>
> *Q: So, you'd advise management to do something about the situation?*
>
> Absolutely. In all these cases, I advise them do to something about it . . . . There's always a court that might be willing to extend [the definition of sexual harassment].

In addition to American employers, individual American employees are increasingly likely to consult lawyers about potential sexual harassment claims.

While most people who have been sexually harassed do not seek legal action,[4] many of those who consult lawyers do not have actionable claims. The American lawyers I interviewed said that only 5 to 10 percent of the numerous sexual harassment complaints they receive are legitimate or actionable. According to an American lawyer doing mostly plaintiff work, some people

> think that they are gonna win the lottery and try to turn something into something that's much bigger than it is. [Others] genuinely feel that they have been harmed, but the harassment hasn't necessarily risen to the level that is actionable or that I think I can do something for them legally.

Behavior that American lawyers said did not rise to the level of actionable sexual harassment includes men who address female employees as "girl" or "honey," or abusive bosses who insult all workers, regardless of their sex. Lawyers also spoke of situations in which people were untruthful to "get someone [whom] they weren't particularly fond of."

Paradoxically, part of the appeal of sexual harassment law in the United States derives from the relative dearth of labor protection laws here as compared to European nations like France. One reason American employees increasingly look to sexual harassment law is that they have little recourse for dismissal *besides* discrimination law, in contrast with France where employers must justify any firing. As one American lawyer said: "A lot of people feel harassed, period. It might not be sexual: they don't feel they're treated correctly by their employer, . . . [but] if it's not based on their sex, if it's not based on their race, there's nothing they can do." According to another: "People are losing their jobs, being demoted, . . . and they want to ascribe it to something. So, they'll try and make it sexual harassment, they'll try and make it racial discrimination, they'll try and make it anything they can to see if they have a way out."

The heightened concern about sexual harassment among employers and employees alike makes it an interesting area of law for attorneys. Comments like the following were common among the American respondents: "It's just a fascinating area of law and the case law is actually evolving right now. It's an exciting area to be in. I enjoy it."

In the past fifteen years, "sexual harassment training" has proliferated in American workplaces.[5] American offices of both AmeriCorp and Frenchco had sexual harassment policies and training programs in effect when I conducted interviews in the spring of 1998. The managers that I interviewed cited expensive lawsuits as one reason why it was essential that their workplaces address the problem of sexual harassment. An HR manager in a New York office of Frenchco expressed a common sentiment among managers in American workplaces, when he said: "All suits are very expensive even if you haven't done anything, even if you are going to be found not guilty. . . . You [still] have to pay to defend yourself, and there is all the spin that you are going to put on it."

According to the human resource managers I interviewed, Frenchco USA began its training program in 1986, after *Meritor*, the first Supreme Court sexual harassment case. AmeriCorp began its program in 1994, after California passed its Fair Employment and Housing Act,[6] which established absolute vicarious liability for all harassment by supervisors, meaning that the employer was automatically liable for sexual harassment on the part of supervisors, regardless of whether the employer knew or should have known about it. This was fuller liability than that imposed by any of the federal court decisions at the time and more than that dictated by subsequent ones.[7]

At both Frenchco and AmeriCorp offices in the United States, sexual harassment complaints can be reported to one's own manager, another manager, or to a human resource manager or representative. Managers and representatives are supposed to listen to the complaint, offer support, and not criticize the person with the complaint. If necessary, and with the agreement of the employee, they investigate the situation.

The interviews with American human resource professionals suggest that in the United States, there exists a complex corporate system for translating court decisions into corporate practices. Internal constituencies — for instance, HR departments, affirmative action officers, diversity managers, and so on — strive to enhance their professional prestige by favoring the elaboration of civil rights protections because it is their job to handle these. Through their work, firms learn about and respond to even obscure court rulings. Media reporting that focuses on exorbitant sexual harassment awards or settlements can further raise employer concern about sexual harassment.[8]

These interactions are illustrated in Figure 1. The dependent variable, the enactment of American corporate policy, is at the center of the diagram. Above, employer liability is illustrated, as an independent variable contributing to the enactment of corporate policy. Arrows in the shape of funnels represent how the media and human resource managers inflate the risks of employer liability.

Below "American corporate policy" in Figure 1, we see that sexual harassment lawsuits exert further pressure on companies to enact sexual harassment policies. In other words, it is not only that employers can be held liable for sexual harassment; it is also employees' actual use of Title VII that pushes employers to take preventive action. Below "sexual harassment lawsuits" are several factors that make such lawsuits more likely, including the fact that there are few other avenues for legal redress for employees, that contingency fees lower the cost of suits for plaintiffs, and that employees too hope to be richly compensated, a hope that is fed by media reporting. Note that Figure 1 applies best to large companies; since their liability is often greatest, they have more active internal constituencies, and they tend to be most concerned about their corporate image.

In the United States, the legitimacy of sexual harassment laws and corporate policy is reinforced by increasingly feminist ideas of the role of women in firms. According to one American lawyer, times have changed in the United States, although there are still those who are behind the times: "I think that some men just don't get it yet: that that's not appropriate anymore. That you don't just go and put your arm

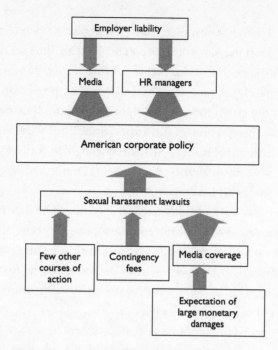

Figure 1.   Factors Feeding American Sexual
Harassment Corporate Policy

around somebody." In the words of another American attorney: "[Expectations that women should have to sleep their way to the top are] gone; that's absolutely gone, and no one should have to do that." The deep-seated American belief that the market is or should be fair makes instances of discrimination, including those involving sexual harassment, repugnant. The general acceptance that civil awards are an effective and fair way to both punish offenders and compensate victims further legitimizes American sexual harassment law.

FRANCE

In contrast to the situation in the United States, sexual harassment law has been poorly implemented and largely discredited in France. In the French legal system, punitive damages do not exist and compensatory damages are typically low, especially for moral or psychological harm. The French lawyers interviewed reasoned that the high costs and low benefits of sexual harassment lawsuits in France discourage victims of even egregious sexual harassment and battery from pressing charges. Without the specter of expensive lawsuits, they said, employers do not address the problem.

The fact that sexual harassment is a penal offense in France carries a powerful symbolic message that sexual harassment is a serious infraction. However, this viewpoint is out of step with common French assumptions about the gravity (or lack thereof) of sexual harassment. According to the French lawyers interviewed, many people do not think sexual harassment is serious enough to warrant prison time, which makes them reluctant to appeal to the sexual harassment penal statute. According to one, "Because you have to choose between penal court or nothing, you choose nothing because penal court is too serious in people's lives. Here, [many forms of sexual harassment are] not considered serious enough to risk being condemned before a penal court."

Several French lawyers said they would like to see employers develop internal grievance procedures as an intermediary solution for dealing with, say, sexist jokes or the display of pornography. However, because employer liability is so limited in France, employers have few incentives to do so. Unions have generally not mobilized against sexual harassment, which French feminist activists attribute to their predominantly male (and sexist) leadership.[9]

French respondents emphasized the obstacles facing lawyers in this field, who have no financial incentives for representing sexual harassment plaintiffs or advising employers. Moreover, some lawyers said their colleagues denigrate them for representing sexual harassment plaintiffs. A feminist female lawyer affiliated with the AVFT explained:

> When you are the AVFT's lawyer, you feel a bit as if you were representing the SPA, the Société Protectrice des Animaux (the Association for the Protection of Animals). Everyone laughs. It's morally trying. I do it out of conviction.

Another lawyer who works with the AVFT said: "You rarely hear a lawyer accused of having a particular interest in bad checks because he works on this type of case. On the other hand, a lawyer interested in sexual harassment is said to be personally obsessed with sex." These respondents said that most of their colleagues consider sexual harassment litigation to be a fad or a pretext used by employees who will not take responsibility for bad job performance.

According to members of the AVFT, French lawyers are reluctant to invoke the relatively recent sexual harassment laws, preferring instead to use more traditional claims like wrongful discharge. The French lawyers I interviewed said that sexual harassment cases are particularly difficult to win because the problem lacks legitimacy among French judges. Moreover, they said that even when they do prevail, judges often rule according to other, more established statutes like wrongful discharge.[10] This effectively stymies the evolution of sexual harassment jurisprudence. In 1999 and 2000, the AVFT found it had greater success in court when its own employees (trained as lawyers), rather than external lawyers, began representing plaintiffs. They attributed their success to their familiarity with the specific women's situations, their feminist analyses, and their willingness to depart from traditional French legal argument.

As a direct consequence of the fact that French law entails limited or no employer liability, the financial stakes of sexual harassment are minimal for employers. Not surprisingly, sexual harassment prevention is low on the list of priorities in French workplaces. Among the twenty-three representatives of French branches of large multinational corporations I surveyed during the summer of 1997, every one reported that sexual harassment was not a major concern in their company at the time.[11] Though the labor law *requires* all French employers to include sexual harassment in their internal regulations, according to the survey, only seven of the twenty-three firms — six of which were French branches of American companies — did so. When I told the director of human resources at a French multinational that I was surprised that her company did not address sexual harassment in its internal regulations, considering that French law requires it to do so, she snapped: "The law is all well and good, but I'm not going to add a hundred pages to the internal regulations!"

Even the relatively progressive firms that did discuss sexual harassment in their internal regulations (usually by reproducing the labor statute) said that they had no particular programs or initiatives in place and that, moreover, they did not consider sexual harassment to be a serious problem. For instance, the "director of social issues" at a French branch of AmeriCorp explained that her business had added sexual harassment to its internal regulations to comply with French law. Nonetheless, she insisted that sexual harassment was not an object of reflection in her firm:

> There isn't the same psychosis here that exists in the United States. The law says that we have to include sexual harassment in the internal regulations. When I told our internal regulations committee that, it made them laugh. Because I said that we were required by the law to adopt [the new internal regulation] we all voted yes, but it was considered a big joke. Here, we haven't had this type of problem. We haven't had such worries to make us think [about the issue].

According to discussions with members of the AVFT as late as October 2002, this perspective had changed very little since the survey was conducted.

The French AmeriCorp human resource manager, quoted at the beginning of the chapter, explained that sexual harassment is

> not yet something that has really entered [popular consciousness, perhaps because] we haven't yet had big sexual harassment cases in France [like in] the U.S., with huge sums of money accorded to the plaintiff. So it's not yet something that has entered public debate [*est venu sur la place publique*]. So maybe it's like it used to be for rape when people didn't dare [file a complaint].

A French (male) union representative at Frenchco also likened sexual harassment to rape, arguing that victims often do not speak about it because they feel ashamed and largely responsible for the harassment:

> It's like with rape, the women don't talk about it. . . . I have never intervened in a case of sexual harassment as a union representative. In general, the women try to work it out on their own when it comes to that topic. . . . Since an unhealthy relationship is involved, people often interpret it as being either the woman's fault or that she is not completely innocent, like with rape. Because [the victims] don't dare talk about it, people assume that it's their fault. That's well known. . . . So the women ask little, nothing really, of the unions.

Moreover, while this particular union representative was very concerned about women's rights, he said that his colleagues were less so:

> Every year we have a meeting, which the Labor Code requires, on the comparative situation of men and women [at work]. There are about twenty elected union representatives at this meeting and I often intervene, and I am basically the only one, to defend the situation of women in the company: their relationship with management, promotions, and a whole bunch of things. So I have colleagues in the session and when we are about to begin [a discussion on this topic], they say, "Ah, you are going to give us your great speech! That's good, your big speech."

These patterns are presented in Figure 2. Lack of French corporate action, the dependent variable, is shown in the middle of the diagram. Independent variables contributing to the dearth of corporate action in France are illustrated above and below. For instance, French law does not impose employer liability for sexual harassment, which means that French employers do not have the same incentives as their American counterparts to adopt sexual harassment policy. In addition, there do not exist in France internal constituencies equivalent to American affirmative action officers or diversity managers, whose job is to elaborate and execute civil rights protections in corporations.

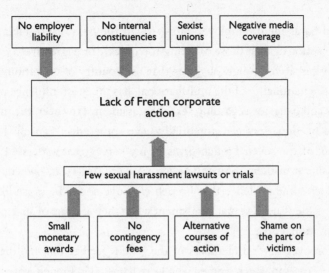

Figure 2. Factors Discouraging French Sexual Harassment
Corporate Policy

The way the French media represent sexual harassment as an American issue of little concern in France, explored in detail in the next chapter, further contributes to discrediting this problem. Most unions, which are otherwise active in defending employee rights in France, have done little to address this issue. With their weak record on women's rights, unions often come to the defense of the alleged harasser, rather than the alleged victim.[12]

French corporations are also unlikely to take action because there are few sexual harassment lawsuits or trials in France, a point evoked by the French AmeriCorp manager above. Several factors, listed at the bottom of Figure 2, impede sexual harassment victims from appealing to the law in France, including the small monetary awards typically granted, the fact that the high cost of lawyers cannot be offset by contingency fees, the fact that French labor law provides several alternative courses of action for workers, and the shame and guilt most victims feel about the harassment. Because the French labor code provides employees with considerable protection from wrongful discharge, faced with a charge of sexual harassment, employers must weigh the risks of not taking adequate action against those of acting too quickly or aggressively.

My research strongly suggests that the country of operation, rather than the nationality of the multinational, has the most influence on attitudes and behavior regarding sexual harassment. However, the international headquarters can potentially have some effect as well. For instance, of the seven French firms in my survey that addressed sexual harassment in their company policy, six were American-owned, which provides some evidence that French employers may be more likely to address the issue of sexual harassment when they are part of an American multinational firm.

Moreover, several members of the AVFT further told me that they knew of cases in which women who were harassed in French work sites of American-owned companies got immediate relief after bringing their complaint directly to the American CEO. American management, they argued, is more likely than French management to act promptly to resolve an issue of sexual harassment, even when it occurs in an office overseas. Employees of French offices of American multinationals may consider appealing to the American CEO as a last resort. Indeed, one (female) respondent in the French office of AmeriCorp spontaneously said that if she were sexually harassed and could not herself put a stop to it, she would not hesitate to bring her problem to the (American) CEO, whom she perceives as highly accessible, despite his lofty position in the corporate hierarchy. This suggests that American employers' motivation for disciplining incidents of sexual harassment in their workplaces is not solely driven by the threat of lawsuits. Rather, it is likely that they are concerned with the reputation of their firm, which is revealing of the increasing social rejection of sexual harassment, or even that the employers have internalized the idea that sexual harassment is morally or at least economically undesirable.

Persistent sexism contributes to the minimization of the problem of sexual harassment in France. A male French lawyer with high status in the French legal establishment explained that, in his mind, sexist comments were simply not comparable to racist or anti-Semitic remarks:

In France, we have a fundamental liberty: freedom of expression. As long as one is expressing an opinion, one has the right to express it. I understand that [a sexist joke or comment] can annoy, distress, or shock a young woman, but, after all, one has the right to think this way, right or wrong, as long as the words are not racist [or] anti-Semitic, which are forbidden.

Q: Sexist comments are different from racist comments?

Ah! For me, it's very different. It is not at all the same cultural notion. [Anti-Semitism] is an ideology that is completely unacceptable as such. And then there is . . . a legal text, that reprimands it; the legislature has taken a stand because of the whole history behind anti-Semitism. I cannot see how one could compare a sexist comment with anti-Semitism for the simple reason . . . that it is natural [*le droit naturel*] that man is made one way and woman another. There was Adam and Eve and they have the right to discuss what is in their eyes sexuality, with all that that implies. In contrast, anti-Semitism is an ideological approach that goes against nature.

This respondent begins by arguing that sexist comments are protected under legal principles of freedom of expression, but he then undermines his own argument by pointing to the substantial restrictions that French law puts on freedom of expression, as in the case of racism or anti-Semitism. In contrasting sexism with anti-Semitism; the respondent reveals that he considers sexism, which he conflates with sexuality and sexual difference, natural, inevitable, and thus justified.

In my sample, which included many female and feminist French lawyers, this man's view was extreme. Those who condemned sexism, however, said that they were in the minority in France today. One female French lawyer, affiliated with the AVFT, said that women who denounce sexist behavior, like misogynist jokes or comments, are considered: "in need of a good fuck [*mal-baisées*]. [French people] don't consider such things to be a sexist attack. They consider it very French. It's awful but I don't think I'll see that [change] in my lifetime." Another female French lawyer said: "[Men] think that a woman is always lucky when a guy [notices and comments on her]. That shows that she is considered beautiful, desirable, that you like her, you'd like to do her. That should honor her." In other words, it is not just that French law does not address such sexist behavior and sexual objectification of women; to many French men and women, such behavior is culturally acceptable and even desirable.

The interviews further suggest that different national attitudes and behavior concerning money influenced how French and American respondents approached sexual harassment. Since the passage of the Civil Rights Act of 1991, U.S. courts assign significant monetary compensation, including compensatory and punitive damages, for sexual harassment. In France, this is not the case, and the concept is offensive to many. As the following lawyer explained:

> There is a kind of prudery, or reserve, or denial, call it what you will,
> about money. When we go to court, it's not about a financial
> request. It's about an attack on public order or on an individual.
> Therefore, there is this feeling that you have to know how to avoid
> this individual attack. And the best way might be by not dramatizing
> a situation, which will make someone more violent.

The general uneasiness that French people feel with monetary equivalence for moral suffering is supported by previous research that shows that the French, compared to Americans, do *not* perceive the economic market to be an essentially fair arbiter of human worth and interpersonal disputes.[13]

This approach to money, however, does not explain judges' reluctance in applying heavy penal sentences for sexual harassment, nor the fact that so few sexual harassment victims press penal charges. To understand this, the second part of the respondent's comment is key. In saying that sexual harassment victims should be able to avoid or minimize the gravity of what they suffer, this respondent reveals the extent to which sexual harassment is still trivialized in France. This was made strikingly clear in a 1992 French survey, conducted by Ipsos–*Le Point*, which found that 47 percent of female and 45 percent of male respondents did not think it would be sexual harassment if a woman seeking a promotion was asked by her supervisor to take an overnight trip with him to "discuss it." Twenty percent of female respondents and 24 percent of male respondents did not consider it sexual harassment if a male employer asked a female candidate if she would be ready to undress before him.[14] The idea that women should be able to deflect sexual harassment without appealing to the courts or even management is still prevalent in France, even among French lawyers. As one feminist female lawyer put it: "Sometimes a well delivered slap in the face of an adversary might have an even greater effect than a court hearing."

French respondents actively accentuated cultural differences between the United States and France. The following response of the director of human resources at a French multinational consulting firm was typical: "I have to admit, mores and ideologies are not anything alike in France and the United States. . . . We have a large branch in the U.S. I know that that [sexual harassment] represents a different problem there, but over there, they're more on top of the problem than we are."

With no prompting from me, the French respondents criticized the approach the United States has taken in terms of sexual harassment. They were particularly critical of American "puritanism," "litigiousness," and the alleged codification of social relations in the United States.

Rather than confined to the political right, as is generally the case in the United States, such views are widespread in France. In fact, the two public figures that have been among the most vocal skeptics of sexual harassment law are neither right-wing nor opponents of women's rights. On the contrary, Françoise Giroud is politically center and a former secretary of women's rights. Elisabeth Badinter is a prominent intellectual, a self-identified and press-identified "feminist," and closely affiliated with the French Socialist Party (her husband, Robert Badinter, is a prominent Socialist politician). In fact, E. Badinter's views on this issue are quite consistent with the dominant rhetoric of the Socialist Party, which is both hostile to radical (American) feminism and very critical of the United States, particularly for its *capitalism sauvage* (wild, unchecked capitalism and small social safety net).

Françoise Giroud and Elisabeth Badinter praised the French sexual harassment law for its exclusive focus on abuse of power and criticized the broader reach of American regulation. In defending the French penal statute, Giroud and Badinter drew symbolic boundaries against Americans and, more specifically, against American feminists. They presented American society as seized by gender warfare and France as a place of harmonious relations between the sexes. Giroud explained:

> Two big centuries ago, the French invented a way of speaking
> amongst each other, of loving each other — I'm talking about men
> and women — and of making conversation, of having relationships
> that are a lot softer and sweeter than American relationships. There
> is no comparison. And that's felt in the whole history of these last
> years.

In this context, Giroud and Badinter argued that French women can negotiate most situations well on their own.[15]

Likewise, Badinter described American society as typified by asexual and distant social relations:

> Do you see what kind of ideal [of relationships between men and
> women] shines through your vignettes? The comrade. Do you see
> what that means in French? It's a very asexual relationship between
> men and women. It's a bit like the model in Nordic society. In
> Sweden, it's like that. I find it terrifying, just terrifying!

Badinter juxtaposed this image with that of the French workplace, which she described as a place of pleasant flirtation and playful seduction. She argued that this atmosphere should be preserved:

> You know it's at work that people meet their lovers, their mistresses,
> who sometimes become their wives or husbands and sometimes
> don't. . . . So if you start saying, 'Oh, but a gaze that is a bit insistent
> or an off-color remark is harassment,' that's going to rule out the

possibility that couples will form, that people will date, court, have flings [*aventures*]. It'll all be over.

There are people in the United States who also criticize sexual harassment policies as threats to "sexual freedom." However, in France, such arguments are often framed in opposition to the United States.[16] Some French journalists and intellectuals contrasted alleged French respect for *la vie privée* (a personal sphere outside of state control) to American disregard for this principle, which they see manifested in American articles about politicians' sex lives and in "overzealous" sexual harassment laws.

Other French respondents, like members of the AVFT, have contested this portrayal of "French character." Rather, they have criticized the "narrowness" of French sexual harassment law and the uneven protection of privacy among the powerful (men) and the powerless (women). One French study of Mitterand's presidency, for instance, has described how the French press targeted female French politicians' physical appearance and sexual behavior.[17] Likewise, French feminist scholars (like their American colleagues) have denounced the fact that courts rarely respect rape victims' privacy, but rather, scrutinize their sexual past for signs that they welcomed the assault.[18] Activists at the AVFT expressed similar concerns about the privacy of sexual harassment plaintiffs.

Many of the French respondents further argued that social relations, particularly between the sexes, are overly codified in the United States. As one (female) French lawyer put it: "Everything [in the United States] seems codified. . . . I'm a bit for the liberty of desire, its expression. . . . I say to myself, it's crazy this notion of codifying social relationships. . . . I need more freedom." Or, in the words of one (male) Frenchco union representative: "You get to the point [in the United States] where guys are afraid to have professional contact with women because they are afraid of being accused of sexual harassment. Well, I think that is going too far because . . . we are French; maybe it's not the same culture."

Another union representative at Frenchco criticized what he perceived to be American litigiousness and large monetary awards for moral harm: "We wonder if it's not only for economic reasons that all of these [sexual harassment lawsuits] take place." Referring to an accusation of child molestation involving pop artist Michael Jackson, he continued:

> These stories about Michael Jackson: for 16 million dollars, he
> solves his problem. I think . . . if there was abuse . . . [the victim]
> should have gone all out and then not touched a penny. I mean,
> [Michael Jackson might pay] a fine, but you don't settle. And to the
> humble [*petits*] French people that we are, what goes on in the U.S.
> strikes us as excessive.

In other words, while in the United States it has become moral to draw explicit monetary equivalencies for nonpecuniary losses because the award is seen not as replacing, but assuaging a sentimental loss,[19] this has not happened in France to the same degree. French respondents consider any financial compensation to the plaintiff as undermining her claim. For this respondent, settling out of court completely undermines the plaintiff's legitimacy. By rejecting American approaches to money, this respondent discredited the United States and American plaintiffs, affirmed and reinforced a particular version of French culture, and discredited French plaintiffs who seek monetary compensation for sexual harassment.

Likewise, the image of the United States as a frightening extreme in feminism or the "Battle of the Sexes" may serve as a warning to French feminists not to go too far in challenging gender arrangements in France.[20] As a male union representative at AmeriCorp said: "The employees do not dare to openly say, "He's bothering me." And the boundary is [the term] sexual harassment. . . . We have images of the United States where you can't even touch someone's shoulder without being called an awful, mean person."

According to one penal lawyer in France who collaborates with the AVFT, French judges' image of American justice paralyzes them. He said:

> The judges think first of the excesses in the United States, [which
> constitute] the pole of repulsion for the French judge. That is, [they

reason:] "See the excesses in the United States?" Therefore, to not fall into the same excesses, they do nothing at all, . . . a type of institutional block and denial.

In both my interview and a recent article, Marie-Victoire Louis said negative caricatures of American feminists provide a way to disqualify and intimidate French feminists.[21] Other AVFT activists and many of the French plaintiff lawyers I interviewed concurred that myths about "American excesses" were often used to discredit their work. The need to dissociate themselves from such negative images reinforces national differences in approaches to sexual harassment. One young AVFT activist explained in 1995 how such a social climate led her to avoid the term "sexual harassment" altogether when describing her work:

> I prefer to talk about violence to women at work. . . . Because of this trend [that consists of saying that] women make up things, women invent things, the movie *Disclosure*, Demi Moore . . . — you can't imagine the damage that [movie] did to mentalities. ["Sexual harassment"] is a totally discredited term. When people ask me what I do, I don't mention sexual harassment. I'm sure they would burst out laughing: 'Oh but women make up stories, oh but sexual harassment, it's like in the United States. It's anything goes. It's all about making money in court cases.' No, I say that I work on violence towards women at work.

CONCLUSION

In sum, American lawyers described a legal climate in which sexual harassment laws are taken seriously and where working in this area of law is valued. American human resource managers similarly said that sexual harassment is an important concern for their employers. Several factors lead employers to adapt sexual harassment policy in the United States, including employer liability — which is exaggerated by the media and human resource profession — and sexual harassment lawsuits — which are made more likely by the fact that there exist few other courses of action for aggrieved employees — contingency fees, and the expectation of large monetary damages (also exaggerated by the media). The growing belief in gender equality and the persistent view that legal harm can be effectively remedied with monetary compensation, further legitimizes sexual harassment law among Americans.

In contrast, French lawyers said that the French sexual harassment statutes still lack legitimacy and that plaintiffs and their lawyers are largely discredited and stigmatized in France. French human resource managers and union representatives said that sexual harassment is not a major concern for French employers or for the French population at large. Several factors contribute to the lack of corporate action in France, including the fact that employers are not held liable for sexual harassment, media stories discredit sexual harassment victims, unions tend to be male-dominated and sexist, and there are few sexual harassment trials. Legal action is thwarted by the fact that in France, there are only small monetary awards for sexual harassment victims, no contingency fees, and that other available courses of action exist for aggrieved employees. Persistent sexism and rejection of the idea that monetary awards can compensate for moral wrongs further undermine sexual harassment law in France. Finally, the French respondents reinforced Franco-American cultural differences by drawing rigid symbolic boundaries between France and the United States, particularly against American feminism, "puritanism," and "litigiousness."

Throughout this chapter, as well as in the previous one, the mass media has emerged as a powerful producer of accounts regarding sexual harassment. These accounts have shaped how people conceptualize sexual harassment as well as the content of sexual harassment laws. Yet so far we have not discussed the factors shaping media reporting on sexual harassment. It is to this very important piece of the puzzle that we now turn.

THREE

Sexual Harassment in the Press
National Scandal, Pride, or Superiority?

In 1991, the nomination of Clarence Thomas to the United States Supreme Court met an important obstacle when Anita Hill, a law professor and one of Thomas's former employees, publicly affirmed that Thomas had sexually harassed her when they worked at the Equal Employment Opportunity Commission (EEOC), the governmental agency responsible for enforcing Title VII of the Civil Rights Act of 1964.[1] The mass media was key in publicizing Hill's accusations. Beyond the question of Thomas's guilt or Hill's credibility, the mass media's discussion of these proceedings led people to talk about this relatively new concept of "sexual harassment." "What was it and why was it wrong?" they asked and, in searching for answers, they began to learn about the phenomenon of sexual harassment and sexual harassment law.

We have already seen evidence that mass media reports have influenced laws and attitudes governing sexual harassment. Via the Hill-Thomas scandal, the mass media raised American public consciousness about a problem that, despite existing jurisprudence, was little known among the American public. As the scope of sexual harassment law expanded to include a wider range of behavior and to give plaintiff lawyers greater freedom to search the background of accused harassers, it generated further sexual harassment scandals. Most notable were those involving President Bill Clinton and Paula Jones (who accused him of sexually harassing her while he was governor of Arkansas) and the president and Monica Lewinsky (a White House intern, who, Jones's lawyers discovered in their research, had engaged in sexual acts with Clinton during his term as president of the United States). The way the press has, in turn, reported on these subsequent scandals has had its own consequences.

Foreign presses also picked up the Hill-Thomas story, but generally with different social implications. In France, as we have already discussed, Thomas's confirmation hearings, and particularly the discussion of Hill's grievances during those hearings, were largely presented as a "witch hunt" in which Thomas was the victim.[2] Rather than raise consciousness about sexual harassment, the French press used the event to warn the public about the dangers of falling into "American excesses" in prosecuting sexual harassment and to highlight the advantages of showing restraint in addressing this social problem. Indeed, as we saw in Chapter 1, there is strong evidence that the French press's reporting on the Hill-Thomas scandal led lawmakers in 1991 to limit the scope of behavior legally defined as sexual harassment. The revised law applied only to cases in which a person in a position of hierarchical authority uses his power to coerce a subordinate into having sexual relations with him or a third party.[3] Subtle forms of sexist or sexual behavior were not included in the revised legal definition. Neither were any forms of sexual harassment among hierarchical peers.

Because of the important role the press has played in shaping the meaning of sexual harassment and sexual harassment law in the United States and France, it is important to examine press representations more closely. This chapter analyzes three components of coverage: volume of articles, topic of articles, and media "frames." The volume of American and French reporting on sexual harassment is *not* correlated with the timing of landmark court decisions (in the case of the United States) or with major legislation (in France) but instead, *in both countries*, closely shadows *American* scandals involving high-profile American politicians or political institutions. Rather than reporting primarily on sexual harassment as a legal category, the media in both countries have focused on sexual harassment as *American* political sex scandals.

Because of the focus on these types of stories, much of the media sample in both countries framed the sexual harassment incident at hand as political and as scandalous. Both presses also featured consciousness-raising articles that framed sexual harassment as a social problem and/or as a women's issue. Though legal frames of sexual harassment did *not* dominate media coverage, the American press was more likely to frame sexual harassment as a form of discrimination — the dominant American legal frame — than in terms of competing legal frames such as violence or dignity. The French press, in turn, was more likely to frame sexual harassment as a form of violence — the dominant French legal frame — than as a form of discrimination or an attack on dignity. The French press was more likely to frame sexual harassment as an abuse of power, a social problem, and a women's issue *when reporting on France* but as a political scandal about morality and greedy plaintiffs trying to get rich in lawsuits when reporting on the United States. This type of representation of the United States has provided important ammunition for French lawmakers, judges, and others in their claims that the United States represents the excesses that France needs to avoid by exerting prudence in this arena.

AMERICAN REPORTING

Figure 3 shows the volume of coverage of sexual harassment in the United States and France. The most striking feature of these graphs is that coverage of this issue in the United States dwarfed that of France. This is true whether one examines coverage in terms of the total number of articles or as a proportion of all articles published in a given year in the surveyed publications. Note that there seems to be a slight increase in French coverage over time, particularly in 1998 and 2000. U.S. coverage of sexual harassment, on the other hand, spiked in 1991, 1992, 1994, and 1998 and was relatively high in all of the years between

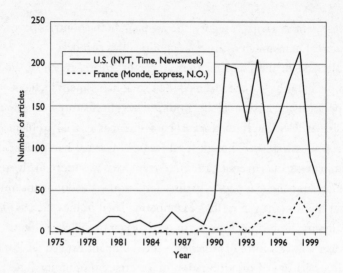

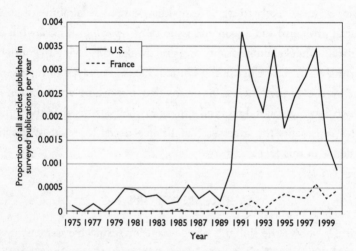

Figure 3. Coverage of Sexual Harassment in the American
and French Press, 1975–2000 (N = 1889). (Articles selected
contain the term "sexual harassment" in the heading or leading
paragraphs.)

1991 and 1998. In 1999 and 2000, however, it fell precipitously. These patterns are similar when we examine coverage as a proportion of all articles published that year.

Political scandals erupted throughout the 1990s and specifically in 1991 (Anita Hill's accusations against Supreme Court justice nominee Clarence Thomas), 1992–1994 (accusations against Senator Bob Packwood), 1991–1995 (scandal over the assault of twenty-six women at the 1991 Tailhook Association, a private group of retired and active-duty U.S. Navy aviators), and 1994–1998 (Paula Jones's accusations against President Bill Clinton). As is illustrated in Figure 3, coverage of sexual harassment was much higher between 1991 and 1998 than in the years preceding or following this period. Moreover, as is shown graphically in Figure 4, volume in reporting on these four scandals closely shadowed reporting on sexual harassment more generally. This is true when we compare the sample of all coded American articles with those articles that *focused* on one of these four scandals and, even more so, when we compare all the coded American articles with those that *mentioned or focused* on one of these four scandals. In sum, American press coverage of sexual harassment has tended to focus on cases involving high-profile political figures and institutions (such as Clarence Thomas, the EEOC, the Supreme Court, and the Senate; Bob Packwood and the Senate; Bill Clinton and the presidency; and Tailhook and the U.S. military).[4]

Considering what we know about the disproportionate focus given by the publications surveyed to sexual harassment allegations involving high-profile political figures like Supreme Court Justice Clarence Thomas, Senator Bob Packwood, and President Bill Clinton, it is not surprising that a large proportion of the press articles focusing on sexual harassment framed the issue as about politics and/or scandal. These frames, which are not mutually exclusive, were present in 40 percent and 35 percent of the American sample, respectively. An article published in *Time* magazine during the aftermath of the Hill-Thomas scandal provides an example of the politics (and women's issue) frame:

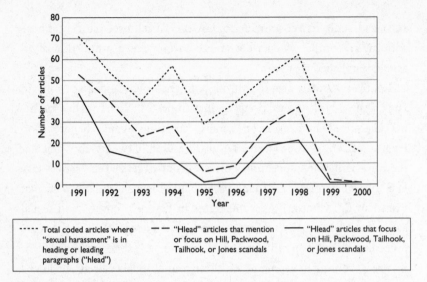

Figure 4.   U.S. Press Coverage of Sexual Harassment and Sexual Harassment Scandals, 1991–2000 (N = 443)

Harriett Woods predicts that the lingering image of the all-male Senate panel sitting in judgment of Anita Hill will prompt large numbers of *female voters to back women candidates because of their sex.* "They're going to go to the voting booth," she says, "and literally try to change the face of American politics." Ruth Mandel, director of the Center for the American Woman and Politics at Rutgers University, predicts that this year may go down in the books as the one "in which women voters joined with women candidates."[5]

Notice how the focus was on the *political implications* of Clarence Thomas's Senate confirmation hearings, rather than on the fact that Hill's testimony revealed that sexual harassment was a serious social problem (social problem frame).

An article published about the Tailhook scandal in the "Week in Review" section of *The New York Times* and entitled "Aftermath of Tailhook; The Pentagon's Accountant Takes Over a Troubled Navy" exemplifies the scandal frame:

With the Navy reeling from the military's worst sexual harassment *scandal*, Defense Secretary Dick Cheney last week tapped one of his closest aides, Sean O'Keefe, the Pentagon comptroller, to clean up the mess.

As Acting Navy Secretary, Mr. O'Keefe, a 36-year-old former staff director for the Senate Appropriations Committee's Subcommittee on Defense, will have to deal with the fallout from a scandal involving the assault of 26 women at last year's convention of the Tailhook Association, a private group of retired and active-duty aviators. Lawrence Garrett 3d resigned in June as Navy Secretary over the incident.[6]

Note that the journalist focused on the implications of this "sexual harassment scandal" for the Navy, rather than, say, on how the incident affected the women assaulted or was evidence of a larger social problem.

Several frames can coexist in one article. This is especially likely given American journalistic standards of presenting conflicting viewpoints. The politics and scandal frames, however, were particularly likely to coexist,[7] as in the following article:

Mr. Clinton's reputation as a womanizer is already an important element in the relatively *poor showing he makes in the polls* on "the character issue." Bob Dole's late surge in the 1996 *campaign* came when he switched his attacks on the President from economic policies to questions of personal probity.

But the Jones case has the potential to amplify whispers of *scandal* into shouts. In a media age, that would *damage Mr. Clinton and the Presidency.*[8]

This article framed Jones's lawsuit as a sex scandal with important political implications. The prevalence of the scandal and politics frame peaked in 1991, 1994, and 1997/1998, years marked by one of the four major high-profile sexual harassment scandals, three of which involved political figures: Supreme Court Justice Clarence Thomas, Senator Bob Packwood, and President Bill Clinton.

Notwithstanding the focus on sexual harassment as scandal, the

American press was *un*likely to frame sexual harassment in terms of morality (5 percent) or to discredit sexual harassment victims by suggesting that they were motivated by economic greed (5 percent). In fact, statistical analysis revealed that the scandal frame was *not* positively correlated with either the morality or greedy plaintiff frames. Likewise, despite such a focus on high-profile political scandals and despite the fact that neither the scandal nor political frames were positively correlated with either the women's issue or the social problem frame, 34 and 42 percent of American articles focusing on sexual harassment still presented sexual harassment as a social problem and a women's issue, respectively. Moreover, the women's issue and social problem frames were positively correlated with each other.[9] The following excerpt from a *Newsweek* article published in 1980 provides an example of an article that framed sexual harassment as a social problem that affects women (and as an abuse of power):

> It may be as subtle as a leer and a series of off-color jokes, or as direct as grabbing a woman's breast. It can be found in typing pools and factories, Army barracks and legislature suites, city rooms and college lecture halls. It is fundamentally a man's *problem*, an *exercise of power* almost analogous to rape, for which *women pay with their jobs*, and sometimes their health. It's as traditional as underpaying women — and now appears to be just as illegal. Sexual harassment, the boss's dirty little fringe benefit, has been dragged out of the closet.
>
> *Authorities can only guess how widespread sexual harassment on the job really is*, but the number and nature of reported episodes form an ugly pattern. In Los Angeles, supermarket checker Hallie Edwards walked into a storeroom and found a manager exposing himself and groping for her breasts. After Edwards complained, the chain promoted her boss and transferred her. In Cambridge, Mass., college freshman Helene Sahadi York went to her Harvard professor's office looking for research help. She found an instructor determined to kiss her. In New York, typist Doreen Romano's boss offered her a raise if she would sleep with him. When she refused, he fired her.[10]

The prevalence of the social problem and women's issue frames falls steadily between 1992 and 1997 following the Hill-Thomas hearings, and rises somewhat towards the tail end of the Clinton scandals and their aftermath in 1998–2000. I speculate that there are two reasons for this pattern. First, over time, the issue of sexual harassment has become institutionalized, making it less novel and therefore less newsworthy to argue that this is an important social problem. As the issue becomes more legitimate, the concept of sexual harassment may be broadened to include not only sexual harassment of women by men but also sexual harassment of men by other men or by women, through a process of "domain expansion."[11] However, to fully evaluate this hypothesis, it would be necessary to track the prevalence of these frames in media reporting in the next decade or two.

An alternative explanation is that the pattern in these frames is due to specific traits of the Hill and Jones scandals, in that the press was more likely to stress the seriousness of sexual harassment when discussing Hill's accusations against Clarence Thomas than when discussing Jones's allegations against Bill Clinton. Indeed, compared to articles on the Jones scandal, articles focusing on the Hill scandal were significantly more likely to present sexual harassment as a social problem[12] and/or women's issue.[13] This points to the fact that not all sexual harassment scandals are created equal by the mass media. While the American mass media (partly or largely) used the Hill-Thomas incident, and the Packwood and Tailhook scandals as well, to raise public consciousness about the problems of sexual harassment, American journalists spun Paula Jones's lawsuit against Bill Clinton primarily as a case of sexual harassment laws gone amuck.[14] This image was reinforced during the late 1990s with (mis)reports on other extreme cases of mostly institutional regulation of sexual behavior at work or at school, such as the incident in which a man was fired for allegedly recounting an episode of the popular television situation comedy "Seinfeld" (although he had a longer history of sexual harassment, not discussed by the press); a six-year old boy was made to miss an ice-cream party and coloring one day ("suspended from school," according to the press) for having kissed a classmate; or a professor was reprimanded for having told a sexual story from the Talmud.[15] Indeed, at least one legal scholar has argued that media reporting in the late 1990s, particularly before Jones's lawsuit was dismissed, constituted a "backlash against feminism" and weakened the legitimacy of American sexual harassment law.[16]

As Figure 5 illustrates, coverage of new laws and court rulings accounted for a tiny proportion of all U.S. media coverage of sexual harassment. Moreover, volume in coverage of new sexual harassment laws and court rulings was a poor predictor of total coverage of sexual harassment. In 1986, the small increase in coverage of sexual harassment laws or rulings (due to the Supreme Court decision *Meritor v. Vinson*[17]) did mirror the small increase in total coverage of sexual harassment by the American presses surveyed. The year 1998 was the only other period when an increase in reporting on three new court decisions coincided with a rise in the total number of sampled articles. However, these years were exceptions. Furthermore, the volume of coverage on new laws or rulings in 1998 represented a tiny fraction of total coverage for that year, suggesting that something else was also drawing the attention of journalists to the topic of sexual harassment (such as the sexual harassment scandals involving President Bill Clinton and culminating in his impeachment). Finally, note that in 1991, when American press coverage of sexual harassment soared, only two of the 71 articles coded for that year pertained to new laws or court rulings.

While the American press has not focused on landmark legal decisions, the influence of the law was still apparent in press coverage of sexual harassment. For instance, 61 percent of the American articles discussed legal remedies (such as lawsuits) and 23 percent of articles quoted one or several lawyers. Although only a minority of articles framed sexual harassment as a form of discrimination (23 percent), this dominant American legal frame was more common in American articles than the competing legal frames of violence (12 percent) and dignity (8 percent). The following quote provides an illustration of the discrimination frame:

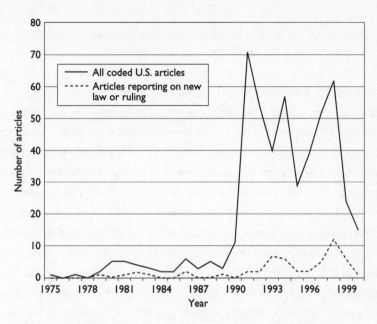

Figure 5. U.S. Press Coverage of Sexual Harassment and Sexual Harassment Laws or Rulings, 1975–2000 (N = 496)

Legal experts cite the enactment of Title VII of the 1964 Civil Rights act as the legal basis for preventing sexual harassment. The law now views sexual harassment as a kind of *employment discrimination*.[18]

The power frame was almost as common in the American press as the discrimination frame. Sometimes the focus was on hierarchical power, as in the following quote from *Time* magazine:

Sexual harassment is not about civility. It is not about a man making an unwelcome pass, telling a dirty joke or commenting on someone's appearance. Rather it is an *abuse of power* in which a worker who depends for her livelihood and professional survival on the goodwill of a superior is made to feel vulnerable. "This is not automatically a male-female issue," says Wendy Reid Crisp, the director of the National Association for Female Executives, the largest women's professional association in the country. "We define this issue as economic intimidation."[19]

Other articles, however, also stressed male power over women. An excerpt from a 1992 *Time* article provides an example of this framing: "Most men do not sexually harass their co-workers. Those who do are engaging in a *power trip* that plays on sex; work-related strings are attached."[20] The analysis of sexual harassment as abuse of power is consistent with both American law and arguments proposed by American feminists.[21] Likewise, consistent with the courts' disproportionate focus on sexual harassment *at work*, 66 percent of the American articles discussed sexual harassment occurring in the workplace, compared to less than 30 percent that discussed sexual harassment occurring in any of the following other places: the military (12 percent), K—12 schools (7 percent), colleges (7 percent), military schools (1 percent), housing (.8 percent), transportation (.4 percent), streets (.4 percent) or prisons (.4 percent).

FRENCH REPORTING
AND A CROSS-NATIONAL COMPARISON

French press coverage of sexual harassment has been quite low, never surpassing fifty articles per year in the three surveyed publications combined. As in the United States, only a small proportion of the French sample (11 percent) have focused on new sexual harassment laws. However, unlike American reporting, French reporting has not been dominated by domestic sexual harassment scandals remotely comparable to the Hill-Thomas or Jones-Clinton scandals.

Moreover, as is illustrated in Figure 6, only 43 percent of the full French sample were about France. (In contrast, 97 percent of the American sample focused on the United States.) The disparity between the number of articles on France and the number of articles on other countries (primarily the United States) was particularly high after 1994. Of the articles in the French sample focused on a country other than

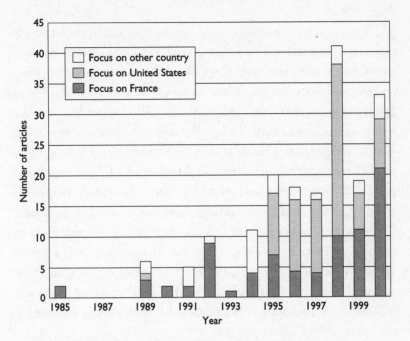

Figure 6. French Press Coverage of Sexual Harassment (N = 185)

France, 83 percent were about the United States. Of those, 56 percent mentioned or focused on one of the top four American sexual harassment scandals (Hill-Thomas, Tailhook, Packwood, or Jones-Clinton). In other words, French coverage of sexual harassment has tended to focus on the United States, and specifically, on the same scandals that have preoccupied the American press. Because of this trend, it is necessary to distinguish between three sub-samples, including: (1) all French articles focused on sexual harassment; (2) articles that focus on sexual harassment in the United States; and (3) those that focus on sexual harassment in France.

Compared to American articles, the full French sample of articles (sub-sample 1) were more likely to frame sexual harassment as about power, violence, morality, and plaintiffs making money in lawsuits, while they were less likely to present it as a scandal or as a women's issue.[22] Among all French articles focusing on sexual harassment, 31 percent framed the incident as a scandal and 29 percent as a political issue. Ten percent suggested that sexual harassment plaintiffs were driven by monetary greed.

French articles focusing solely on sexual harassment in the United States (sub-sample 2) were significantly *more* likely to use frames such as politics, scandal, morality, or plaintiffs' desires to make money in lawsuits as compared to French articles on France (sub-sample 3).[23] The scandal and politics frames accounted respectively for only 18 and 13 percent of French articles on sexual harassment in France, compared to 51 and 54 percent of French articles reporting on the United States.[24] These patterns are consistent with the fact that the French press has focused on *American* scandals, rather than French ones. Only 4 percent of the articles that reported on sexual harassment incidents in France suggested that sexual harassment lawsuits were motivated by the plaintiff's economic greed, while the figure for French articles reporting on the United States was 23 percent.[25]

While almost a third of the French sample presented sexual harassment incidents as about scandal or politics, a greater or equal proportion also framed sexual harassment in social justice terms. Most strikingly, a full half of these articles framed sexual harassment as about power. Most of these articles depicted sexual harassment victims as women in vulnerable economic and social positions who are exploited by men in positions of authority, a scenario in which the power dynamic is particularly salient. Thirty percent of the French articles focusing on sexual harassment also framed it as a women's issue and 26 percent framed it as a social problem. French articles reporting on France were even more likely to employ these frames. Sixty-two percent of the French articles reporting on France framed sexual harassment as about power; this proportion was half as much for French articles that reported on the United States.[26] Thirty-three percent of French articles on France (but 14 percent of French articles on the United States) framed sexual harassment as a social problem.[27] Thirty-one percent of French articles on France framed sexual harassment as a woman's issue.[28]

In other words, the French press has portrayed sexual harassment as a more serious problem when reporting on domestic compared to American events. An article about Bob Packwood's resignation, published in *Le Monde* in 1995, exemplifies how the French press has reported on American sexual harassment scandals in a way that ends up trivializing the problems of sexual harassment and suggesting that American concern over this problem is exaggerated:

> Accused of sexual harassment, the president of the Finance Committee of the American Senate, Robert (Bob) Packwood, decided to *resign* Thursday September 7 . . . . Between 1969 and 1990, this sixty-year-old made unwelcome sexual advances to seventeen women, most working in Congress and often under his orders.
>
> The man in question, who admits that he stole a few kisses, some a bit too ardent, has confronted a process of *inquisition* that did *not allow him to confront the witnesses* . . . . His departure *allows [the Republicans] to limit the consequences of a scandal* that threatened to grow in proportion.[29]

This article considered only the political repercussions of Packwood's behavior on his own career and on the fate of the Republican Party more generally. By describing his behavior as "stolen kisses," the author trivialized the complaints of the women who claimed to have been sexually harassed by Packwood.

Many of the French articles on France, in the style of editorial journalism, contrasted France with the United States, describing Americans, American women, and particularly American feminists as extreme, puritanical, and hysterical. A 1994 article in the *Nouvel Observateur* entitled "Here, in law, we [women] have it all," consisted of an interview with the public intellectual Elisabeth Badinter, who criticized the American feminist movement. According to her:

> American feminism has flourished in an environment completely different from ours . . . that of a radical puritanism that makes the tranquil understanding of one's body and the other's body almost impossible. . . .

[An American] woman must not give a man — and vice versa — the idea that she would want to seduce him in the workplace. Feminine flirtation is experienced by [American] women as already an admission of submission; masculine seduction is experienced by men as the expression already of a desire for domination. It's stupefying: what seems to us to be a game, a sweetness of life, even the expression of nature, to them is perceived as a threat to equality! We don't want the separation of the sexes. That's not our pleasure, our happiness, or, even less so, our objective.[30]

By discrediting American feminists as hysterical man-haters, French journalists and the people they quote dismissed "their issues," including sexual harassment, at least to the extent that they take place in the United States.

One reason why French reporting on American scandals tended to be more dismissive of the problem of sexual harassment is that the French press accorded proportionately more coverage to Paula Jones's lawsuit against Bill Clinton than to Clarence Thomas's confirmation hearings. Forty-one (out of 166) French articles mentioned or focused on the Jones case, compared to twelve for the Hill case. Since both American and French reporters were less likely to frame the Jones lawsuit, compared to Hill's accusations against Thomas, as a social problem or a women's issue and more likely to frame it as about politics, scandal, morality or making money on lawsuits, the disproportionate focus of the French press on this issue explains some of the difference in treatment. However, the fact that the French press did focus so overwhelmingly on this case is part of what needs to be explained. A large part of its newsworthiness stems from the fact that the lawsuit was jeopardizing the American presidency, but this scandal was also attractive to the French press, I would argue, because it lent itself well to the narrative of "American excesses."

Moreover, even when reporting on these very same scandals, the French and American presses have presented them in different ways. Among French articles on Thomas's confirmation hearings, for instance, half of the French articles, compared to only 12 percent of the American articles, framed the issue as about morality,[31] and 33 percent of French articles, compared to only 3 percent of the American sample, stressed that American plaintiffs were motivated by economic greed,[32] even though Hill never sued Thomas and never stood to earn any money by her accusations. When reporting on this incident, a smaller proportion of the French articles, compared to American articles, framed sexual harassment as a social problem, although this difference is not statistically significant.[33] When reporting on Jones's lawsuit against Clinton, the social problem and women's issue frames were infrequent in both national presses, and the idea that plaintiffs, Jones in particular, are motivated by economic greed was relatively common. Nonetheless, at 28 percent, the French press was still significantly more likely than the American press, at 4 percent, to frame the Jones case as about morality.[34]

As in the United States, the effect of the law on media reporting has been mixed. Though the French penal statute is not limited to the workplace, French jurisprudence has been heavily concentrated at work. Seventy-two percent of French articles focused on France discussed sexual harassment in the workplace, compared to 0.5 percent of articles that discuss sexual harassment in any of the other following places: K–12 schools, colleges, the military, military schools, prisons, housing, transportation, or the streets.[35]

Rather than French lawmaking, it is American scandals that have dominated French reporting, yet, among legal frames, the French press was more likely to employ the dominant national legal frame of violence. With 27 percent of the French articles framing sexual harassment as a form of violence, the French press was also significantly more likely than the American press to employ this particular frame.[36] For instance, an article published in 1999 by the *Nouvel Observateur* discussed sexual harassment as one of the many "forms of *violence* that strike women."[37] Other forms of violence mentioned in this article included domestic violence, rape, and female genital mutilation. Another article, published in *L'Express* in 1999, suggested that sexual harassment was a form of violence at work by saying: "In a study on *violence* at work, conducted in 1996 and published by the International Bureau last year, almost 20% of French women complain that they have been sexually harassed."[38]

Although French law does not frame sexual harassment as a form of sex discrimination, this frame appears in French articles at a rate (16 percent) comparable to that of American articles. This can be explained by the frequency of French reporting on the United States. Compared to French articles reporting on France, however, American articles reporting on the United States were significantly more likely to frame sexual harassment as a form of discrimination.[39] In other words, though legal frames of sexual harassment dominate in *neither* country, American and French articles that *reported on domestic affairs* were more likely to frame sexual harassment in terms of the dominant national legal analysis: discrimination in the United States and violence in France.

Eleven percent of French articles focusing on sexual harassment framed it as a question of human dignity, of which the following article, published in *Le Monde* in 2000, provides an example. It reported that a European Community sexual harassment directive, passed two days prior (on 7 June 2000) defined sexual harassment as "unwelcome sexual behavior that has the goal and effect of violating a person's dignity or creating an intimidating, hostile, offensive, or upsetting environment."[40]

While the law has had some influence on media reports, the converse is also true. In France, for instance, as we saw in Chapter 1, the French press's negative portrayal of the Hill-Thomas debate, as an instance of American excesses in the repression of sexual harassment, was important in restricting the scope of French law. Specifically, media reports of sexual harassment played a determining role in the French National Assembly debates in 1991–92 that preceded the passage of sexual harassment statutes in the penal and labor codes. In response to French media reporting that presented Clarence Thomas's Senate confirmation hearings as a modern-day "witch hunt" of which Thomas was the victim,[41] French lawmakers were concerned about casting the sexual harassment net too broadly. In other words, the French mass media shaped legislative debates by informing lawmakers' perceptions of the issue, particularly in terms of how it was being dealt with in the United States. The official Senate report on the labor code reform summarized such concerns:

> Recent press articles report that in [the United States] the simple act of holding the door open for a woman can elicit a severe reprimand, and that most men admit to being much more precautionary in their dealings with women in the workplace. Sometimes this resembles a caricature and can even turn against women by leading to segregation, fatal for equilibrated gender integration and normal work relations.
>
> This conclusion can, in particular, be drawn from the manner in which Supreme Court candidate Mr. Clarence Thomas's judgment played out after he was accused of sexual harassment by one of his former employees, Anita Hill.[42]

The fear of falling into "American excesses" was sufficient to seriously jeopardize the bill. In response to this threat, state-feminist proponents of the legislation revised the labor code statute so that sexual harassment would be defined more narrowly than originally conceived. It, like the penal code statute, was ultimately limited to abuses of hierarchical authority, not addressing any forms of coworker harassment.[43] The new legal definition was further restricted to cases in which the harasser uses his or her position of authority to try to coerce the victim into having sexual relations, excluding more general sexist or sexual behavior, like that alleged by Anita Hill and referred to in the United States as "hostile environment sexual harassment." In other words, media reporting of sexual harassment did not only mirror social representations in other fields but had an independent effect on the construction of this social problem.

MEDIA ROUTINES AND REPORTING

To some extent, differences in American and French reports on sexual harassment reflect actual discrepancies in how this social problem is treated in each country. For instance, much of American reporting has covered sexual harassment litigation, and there have been more sexual harassment suits to cover in the United States than in France. Furthermore, the fact that American courts have condemned a broader range of behavior, including conduct among peers and "hostile environment" harassment, and ruled on sexual harassment over fifteen years before French lawmakers passed sexual harassment legislation, has made American politicians more vulnerable to sexual harassment scandals. The conduct of which Anita Hill accused Clarence Thomas was arguably illegal under Title VII of the Civil Rights Act of 1964, a statute that Thomas had been hired to defend in his job at the EEOC. Paula Jones was suing Bill Clinton for sexual harassment. Because of their legal status, both of these women's claims were legitimate news. In contrast, Hill's and Jones's claims would have lacked any legal standing under French law, making them less newsworthy in France. Crucially, during the time that the articles in the media sample were published, French law prohibited the media from reporting on legal allegations before prosecution.[44]

Press coverage of sexual harassment has been informed by legal realities in other ways as well. For instance, in both countries, the bulk of reporting has focused on the workplace, just as most litigation has. To take another example, when framing sexual harassment as a legal issue, each press was more likely to employ the dominant national legal frame than competing legal frames.

However, it is important to note that the influence of the law on media reporting was limited. Only a fraction of articles in either country involved in-depth legal analysis or reported on landmark decisions or legislation. Instead, the bulk of American reporting consisted of sensationalist coverage of sexual harassment scandals involving high-profile political figures and institutions. Rather than a function of national law, these trends reflect mass media routines that favor simplification, individualism, symbolism, and "gotcha journalism."[45] As media scholars have shown, in the United States, pressures to make a profit in an industry controlled by business, dependent on advertising revenues, and facing ruthless competition, lead mass media organizations to cut down on rigorous and costly investigative journalism and to focus instead on scandals and human melodramas.[46] In the case of sexual harassment, this has meant a focus on high-profile sexual harassment scandals, rather than on sexual harassment as a larger societal problem. Such stories are cheaper to produce and sell but do a poor job of educating the American public. In some ways, market motives actually lead to misleading reporting, such as when American presses are much more likely to report on unusually large monetary awards or settlements than on the smaller ones that are more common. As we discussed in the preceding chapter, this reporting bias heightens concern among American employers.

People generally assume that the French press is less likely to report on the private sex lives of politicians because of more sophisticated and less "puritanical" attitudes about sex. There are other factors that discourage French journalists from delving into the sex lives of their politicians, such as the fact that they are more constrained than their American counterparts by greater legal restrictions to certain kinds of information and by more broadly drawn libel laws prohibiting personal criticism of political officials.[47] Moreover, the French mass media are less dependent on advertising revenues and at least historically have not been expected to attain the same profit levels as American media organizations, which might lessen the tendency toward sensationalism and the personalization of politics.[48]

In fact, the French press has reported quite eagerly on *American* sexual harassment scandals. These scandals were even cheaper to report on in France, as French journalists could gather all the facts directly from American media reports. French journalists wrote their own accounts of the scandals in the "political-literary" tradition. In contrast to devalued investigative reporting, the "political literary," which consists of commentary, editorial writing, and the mixing of reporting and commentary in news stories, is the dominant and most prestigious journalistic tradition in France.[49] This style of reporting was used to interpret the American scandals as morality tales of the importance of avoiding "American excesses" in sexual and gender matters, tales that had important implications for domestic struggles over these issues. By associating sexual harassment with the United States, the press has conveyed the message to French employers that this is not a problem with which they should be concerned, while it has suggested to French women that it is risky to complain about sexual harassment.

CONCLUSION

Sexual harassment is a problem faced by many women (and some men) in both the United States and France.[50] There is no reason to believe that the behavior itself is fundamentally different in these two countries. Yet, as we have seen, the American and the French presses have portrayed this issue quite differently. Due to institutional pressures and media routines, both the American and French presses have also framed sexual harassment differently from national laws and jurisprudence.

Rather than simply mirroring some underlying reality, in both countries press reports on sexual harassment have had an independent effect on the construction of this social problem. American reporting on Thomas's confirmation hearings arguably led to stronger sexual harassment laws, while reporting on the Clinton scandals may have weakened existing laws and their legitimacy. The French media's focus on "American excesses" in regard to sexual harassment repression has been used to limit the scope of French sexual harassment laws (see Chapter 1), and it has served to stigmatize the work of French feminist activists and plaintiff lawyers engaged in fighting sexual harassment at home (see Chapter 2).

Frames are important in that they draw attention to certain aspects of problems and away from others, shaping the overall perception of issues in often-dramatic ways. This chapter and Chapter 1 have explored how the press and the law have framed sexual harassment, respectively. The next chapter examines how feminist activists, lawyers, public figures, human resource managers, and union representatives have drawn on these public accounts as well as other cultural resources to frame sexual harassment in ways that both overlap with and differ from the press and the law.

FOUR

Discrimination, Violence, Professionalism, and the Bottom Line

How Interview Respondents Frame Sexual Harassment

What is sexual harassment? According to Nancy, the United States–based AmeriCorp manager cited at the beginning of Chapter 2:

> Sexual harassment is any unwelcome or unsolicited behavior that makes an individual feel uncomfortable. Sexual harassment generally is more focused around the way that someone looks at somebody [or] the way that someone touches somebody. And I haven't seen this, but it could [also refer to when a supervisor says to a subordinate], "if you sleep with me [I'll give you certain job benefits]," the *quid pro quo* [variety].

Note that, unlike American law, Nancy did not say that the behavior must offend not only the individual but also a "reasonable person" (person of average sensibilities). Nor did she say that the behavior must be sufficiently severe or pervasive to alter the employee's job conditions, as the U.S. courts have ruled. Rather, like other American managers I interviewed, Nancy defined sexual harassment very broadly and saw it as her responsibility to intervene well before the conduct rises to a level at which it would be considered sexual harassment in a court of law.

In contrast, Géraldine, a personnel representative at a French branch of the same American multinational (AmeriCorp) explained that for her sexual harassment was a "very strong term" used to designate only the most egregious behavior:

> We laugh a bit about sexual harassment here because we have an image, in fact, of the U.S., where you are puritans. Holding a door open for a woman is practically considered an attack [in the United States], while in France, I think we have a different culture, that of French gallantry. . . . In French "harassment" is a very strong term. It means it's constant; you don't have an instant to breathe. . . . . I can't say that I have really suffered, in my professional life, harassment to the point of being obligated to give in. . . . It's true that we're pestered; it's true that there are men in the elevators who take advantage of the situation to "put their hand in the basket" [touch a woman's rear], as we say in French, but [that is not strong enough to constitute sexual harassment]. . . . At AmeriCorp, I was never in a situation in which someone said to me, "If you say no, you're fired; I'll make your life impossible." . . . I would only truly feel threatened if someone put a knife to my throat and told me that if I didn't [give in to his sexual demands], I would lose my job . . . or he'd hurt my son, [blackmail so bad that] the person eventually makes you give yourself physically or touches you. For me, in harassment, there is the notion of touching or being taken against your will.

Géraldine clearly defined sexual harassment more narrowly than did her American colleague. Note that Géraldine also defined sexual harassment even more narrowly than does French law. Not only must the harasser be in a position of authority over the person he or she harasses but, according to her, the pressures must successfully lead to coerced sexual relations or involve physical touching. As we saw in Chapter 1, according to French law, the sexual coercion need not be successful; if a woman quits her job rather than submit to sexual relations with her boss, she still has a legal claim. If groping or other forced touching is involved, the victim can bring not only charges of sexual harassment but those of sexual battery as well, a legal distinction that Géraldine does not address.

These interview excerpts reveal that American and French individuals conceptualized sexual harassment very differently from each other and from their national laws. To more systematically evaluate how American and French respondents defined sexual harassment, during the interviews I presented respondents — including feminist activists from 9to5 (United States) and the AVFT (France), public figures (such as Catharine MacKinnon, Phyllis Schlafly, Camille Paglia, Marie-Victoire Louis, Françoise Giroud, and Elisabeth Badinter), lawyers, human resource managers, and union representatives — with a series of vignettes that described different sorts of workplace behavior. I then asked them if the behavior described was sexual harassment and why or why not.

Table 2 gives the proportion of respondents who thought that the behavior described in a given vignette was a form of sexual harassment, breaking the respondents down by country of origin and by profession or activity (activists, lawyers, managers/union representatives). Table 2 also provides the difference between the proportion of Americans and the proportion of French who thought that a given behavior was sexual harassment and the level of statistical significance of this difference.[1] Table 3 provides the full vignettes from Table 2.

As is shown in Table 2, for six of the eleven vignettes, the difference between the proportion of American and French respondents who thought the behavior constituted sexual harassment was *not* significantly different.[2] The vast majority of American and French respondents agreed that a boss who makes employment conditional on sleeping with him (Vignette 1) or a boss who undresses a saleswoman with his eyes, compliments her body, asks her if she ever cheated on her husband, suggests they go out on a date, and puts his hands on her buttocks (Vignette 3) is engaging in sexual harassment.

About half of the American (57 percent) and French (64 percent) respondents thought that a boss who pestered an ex-girlfriend, making her life miserable but not changing her duties or responsibilities (Vignette 8), was sexually harassing her. About half of the American (57 percent) and French (38 percent) respondents also thought that a coworker who pestered an ex-girlfriend was sexually harassing her (Vignette 9). Less than twenty percent of American (17 percent) and French (13 percent) respondents labeled as "sexual harassment" the conduct described in Vignette 11, in which a female employee incessantly insults a female coworker by calling her a "slut" and a "whore."

As is shown in Figure 7 (see page 104), the American respondents were significantly more likely than the French respondents to think the remaining five vignettes described incidents of sexual harassment. For instance, all of the American respondents thought that a salesman who pestered his *coworker* daily by undressing her with his eyes, commenting on her body, asking her about her sex life, asking her out, and patting her rear (Vignette 4), was sexually harassing her. Only 67 percent of the French respondents thought that this conduct constituted sexual harassment. The American respondents were also significantly more likely than the French respondents to label as "sexual harassment" the conduct of a boss who gives one of his employees special treatment because he is having an affair with her (Vignette 5), although many of the American respondents (73 percent), especially the lawyers (90 percent), rejected the "sexual harassment" label for this behavior. The American respondents were also significantly more likely than their French counterparts to think that displaying pornography in the workplace (Vignette 6), non-sexual sexist jokes (Vignette 7), or a male boss's nonsexual verbal abuse toward a female employee (Vignette 10) constituted sexual harassment.

In many ways the respondents echoed the national legal definitions of the time. For instance, American respondents were more likely than French respondents to label as sexual harassment forms of hostile environment harassment, harassment among hierarchical peers, and nonsexual forms of gender harassment. Lawyers were particularly likely to reproduce legal definitions. While some of the lawyers distinguished between sexual harassment that is or is not legally actionable, others sug-

Table 2. *Proportion of Respondents Who Labeled Selected Vignettes as "Sexual Harassment"*

	U.S. Activists	U.S. Lawyers	U.S. HR	French Activists
1. Weekend with boss for job	1.00 (N=6)	1.00 (N=10)	0.80 (N=5)	0.83 (N=6)
2. Sex for hire, men and women	1.00 (N=6)	0.70 (N=10)	NA (N=0)	1.00 (N=6)
3. Boss harasses saleswoman	1.00 (N=5)	1.00 (N=10)	0.83 (N=6)	1.00 (N=6)
4. Colleague harasses saleswoman	1.00 (N=4)	1.00 (N=8)	NA (N=0)	1.00 (N=5)
5. Boss's mistress gets special treatment	0.50 (N=6)	0.10 (N=10)	0.67 (N=3)	0.00 (N=3)
6. Porn	1.00 (N=6)	0.70 (N=10)	1.00 (N=5)	0.67 (N=3)
7. Sexist jokes	0.50 (N=6)	0.20 (N=10)	0.60 (N=5)	0.17 (N=6)
8. Bad breakup with boss	1.00 (N=6)	0.40 (N=10)	0.60 (N=5)	0.67 (N=6)
9. Bad breakup with colleague	NA (N=0)	0.50 (N=10)	0.75 (N=4)	NA (N=0)
10. Boss insults female employee	0.17 (N=6)	0.30 (N=10)	0.60 (N=5)	0.00 (N=6)
11. Employee insults coworker	0.17 (N=6)	0.10 (N=10)	0.20 (N=5)	0.00 (N=6)

NOTE: The responses of the "public figures" are not shown separately but are included in the country totals.

French Lawyers	French HR/Union	Total U.S.	Total France	U.S.– France
0.90 (N=10)	1.00 (N=9)	0.92 (N=24)	0.89 (N=27)	0.03
0.89 (N=9)	NA (N=0)	0.83 (N=18)	0.88 (N=17)	-0.05
0.80 (N=10)	1.00 (N=9)	0.96 (N=24)	0.92 (N=28)	0.04
0.44 (N=9)	NA (N=0)	1.00 (N=13)	0.67 (N=15)	0.33*
0.00 (N=9)	0.00 (N=9)	0.27 (N=22)	0.00 (N=27)	0.27**
0.00 (N=10)	0.44 (N=9)	0.83 (N=24)	0.29 (N=28)	0.54***
0.10 (N=10)	0.00 (N=8)	0.33 (N=24)	0.07 (N=27)	0.26*
0.50 (N=10)	0.78 (N=9)	0.57 (N=23)	0.64 (N=28)	-0.07
0.22 (N=9)	0.75 (N=4)	0.57 (N=14)	0.38 (N=13)	0.19
0.00 (N=10)	0.25 (N=8)	0.35 (N=23)	0.07 (N=27)	0.28*
0.00 (N=1)	0.17 (N=6)	0.13 (N=24)	0.06 (N=16)	0.07

***p<.001; **p<.01; *p<.05; statistical significance is based on a Chi-Square test.

Table 3. *Vignettes*

1. During a job interview for a position as sales representative, the boss invites the applicant to spend the weekend with him in San Francisco. He says he'll make his hiring decision after the weekend.

2. What if this boss makes the same proposal to men and women? (Sexual relations are indeed expected in exchange for hire, from both men and women).

3. A saleswoman complains that her boss calls her by her first name, often undresses her with his eyes, compliments her body, has asked her if she ever cheated on her husband, suggests they go out on a date, and puts his hands on her buttocks.

4. A saleswoman complains that her *coworker* calls her by her first name, often undresses her with his eyes, compliments her body, has asked her if she ever cheated on her husband, suggests they go out on a date, and puts his hands on her buttocks.

5. The boss has been dating one of his subordinates. She is entirely consenting. But the other employees complain that the boss's mistress has privileges. They decide that they are penalized because they are not sleeping with the boss.

6. Truck drivers have pornographic posters hanging in their break room. A newly hired female truck driver finds the posters offensive and has asked her coworkers to remove them, but they refuse. In fact, they have begun teasing her about the posters, telling her to "loosen up," that they would like to see her in some of the positions portrayed in the posters and could "show her a good time." (Activist version:) Pornographic posters hang behind the desk of an executive. One of his colleagues complains that she feels very uncomfortable every time she walks in his office. However, no other employee has ever complained.

gested that sexual harassment must be, by definition, legally actionable. For instance, several of the American lawyers insisted that the behavior in Vignette 4 only becomes sexual harassment after the employee has asked the harasser to stop his behavior and he continues. These American lawyers further maintained, consistent with American jurisprudence,[3] that if the harasser is a coworker the employee must tell management about the behavior. In the words of one lawyer: "It's not actionable

Table 3. *(continued)*

7. Chris often jokes about "dumb blondes," bad women drivers, or "bimbos." Despite these jokes, he claims to love women. He says they are closer to nature, more tender, give life. He sometimes says, in the tone of a joke, things like "It's up to the women to save the firm." Most of his colleagues laugh at his jokes, but Sue finds them unbearable. She says that even his supposed compliments are generalizations that confine women to very limited roles and sees this a form of sexual harassment. She expresses her point of view but is not taken seriously because she is considered a "feminist."

8. A woman has been dating her boss. The relationship was completely consensual but now the woman wants to break up. She lets him know, but he does not want to end the relationship. He calls her several times a day on the phone, sends her letters, and stops her in the hallway to discuss his suffering. She says that she can't work under these circumstances.

9. A woman has been dating a *colleague*. The relationship was completely consensual but now the woman wants to break up. She lets him know, but he does not want to end the relationship. He calls her several times a day on the phone, sends her letters, and stops her in the hallway to discuss his suffering. She says that she can't work under these circumstances.

10. A woman complains that her boss calls her "stupid," "incompetent," and "slow." He doesn't make any sexual propositions, but she says that he does not have this attitude with male employees.

11. A male boss breaks off a romantic relationship with one employee to date another of his employees. The ex-lover is hurt and constantly insults and humiliates the new one in front of their colleagues: "You slut, you whore, you'd do anything to get ahead, wouldn't you?"

between coworkers until she goes into a supervisor and complains in person. The company isn't liable until they know or have reason to know about the harassment and either take action or don't take action."

In other ways, the respondents departed significantly from national legal definitions of sexual harassment. For instance, despite the fact that U.S. courts require that harassment serve to discriminate against a person "because of sex," which makes same-sex sexual harassment and "bisexual" sexual harassment difficult to prove in the United States,[4] the

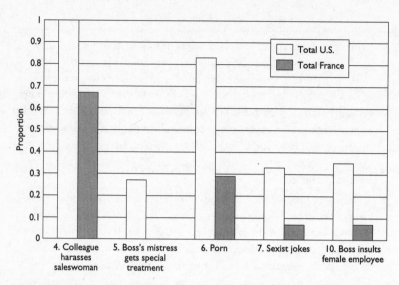

Figure 7.   Proportion of Respondents Who Labeled Selected Vignettes as "Sexual Harassment"

vast majority of American and French respondents also thought that a man who conditions employment, *for women and men,* on sleeping with him, is guilty of sexual harassment (Vignette 2).

Many of the French respondents, including many of the French lawyers, said that the physical touching in Vignette 3 was an instance of sexual harassment when, in fact, sexual harassment as legally defined in France involves only verbal coercion and not physical touching, which transforms the behavior into *agression sexuelle,* or sexual battery. On the other end of the spectrum, 29 percent of the French respondents — including 67 percent of the activists and 44 percent of the managers and union representatives — considered pornography, as described in Vignette 6, to be a form of sexual harassment, even though this belief is contrary to French law. Likewise, while French law at the time the interviews were conducted dictated that there must be an abuse of official authority for there to be sexual harassment and that sexual harassment among coworkers could not exist by definition, all of the French activists and 44 percent of the French lawyers *did* label these kinds of behavior, as described in Vignette 4, sexual harassment. Some of these respondents, especially the activists, said that they disagreed with the legal definition and thought that the law should penalize sexual harassment among coworkers. In fact, as we saw in Chapter 2, this has been the official position of the AVFT since the early 1990s, during legislative debate.

Others, especially French lawyers, said that although they considered this behavior to be a form of sexual harassment, they thought that it should be handled informally rather than through legal mechanisms. As one (female) French lawyer said in response to sexual harassment among coworkers:

> One could conceptualize that as harassment but one returns to the question that I evoked at the beginning of this interview: Should we make a penal infraction out of this or rather should we reserve the penal infraction for the heaviest cases, which have the most serious consequences for women? I [favor] the second [solution].

In other words, this French lawyer, like many of her colleagues, did not fully embrace the legal definition of sexual harassment. However, she did accept the implicit boundaries that the law established between what is and is not legally actionable.

It would be very difficult to convince a U.S. court that the conduct described in Vignette 5, in which a boss gives job perks to his mistress, constitutes sexual harassment, unless it could be shown that the boss in question routinely rewarded sexual services with job benefits, which is *not* suggested by the vignette. Rather, the relationship described is ongoing and exclusive. Nonetheless, half of the American activists, 10 percent of the U.S. lawyers, and 67 percent of the American managers were willing to extend the concept of sexual harassment to this vignette. The following interview excerpt with an American activist is representative of these respondents:

Q: Do you consider the conduct in Vignette 5 to be sexual harassment?
Yes.

Q: And how's that?
Because they've been treated perhaps unfairly because they were not.

Q: Because they were not dating the boss?
Uh, huh. Or having a relationship or whatever.

Q: But someone could say that the boss isn't making any sexual propositions to the other employees; he just has this personal relationship with one of the other employees.

And I would say "Yes, [it is sexual harassment]," based on a personal opinion, and I don't really know what the law says on that. I had a case similar to that a few days ago, and I really didn't have an answer to that, and I have to look that up.

For this American respondent, the conduct described in Vignette 5 was sexual harassment because the boss treated his employees in an unfair or discriminatory way, due to the fact that he was romantically involved with one of them.

FRAMING SEXUAL HARASSMENT

The ways in which American and French respondents framed sexual harassment partly echoed and largely departed from national laws. As we have seen, American respondents were more likely than the French to consider vignettes involving nonsexual jokes and nonsexual verbal abuse targeted at women by men to be sexual harassment. These patterns are consistent with national legal differences, and provide evidence that the Americans were more likely than the French to conceptualize sexual harassment as a form of sex-based discrimination. Those Americans who did not think that these vignettes described sexual harassment said that the behavior was not sufficiently severe or pervasive to alter the employee's working conditions. Alternatively, they said that the behavior was an instance of "gender harassment" or "sex discrimination," illegal under Title VII but analytically distinct from sexually tinged behavior. While a few of the French respondents spoke about sex discrimination, most said that the behavior in these vignettes was simply due to "bad character" and was not legally actionable or that it was only actionable as (non sex-based) insults.

None of the French respondents thought that the behavior described in Vignette 5, in which a boss extends preferential treatment to one employee because he is romantically involved with her, was sexual harassment. In the words of one French lawyer, when asked if this vignette constituted sexual harassment: "Absolutely not, because she's consenting. For me, in harassment . . . there is clearly the absence of the person's consent. Otherwise, everything is harassment." In other words, for him, sexual harassment had to target an individual and involve coercion, key elements of the French legal definition of sexual harassment as sexual violence that was in effect at the time the interviews were conducted.

Likewise, a French lawyer explained why he thought the conduct in Vignette 3 constituted sexual harassment:

> Sexual harassment is one type of sexual violence among other kinds of sexual violence. Sexual violence should be prosecuted so as to preserve the moral and physical integrity of people, [because] we should never accept that a person be forced to do something they do not wish to do.

This respondent employed a sexual violence frame to argue that only the most egregious forms of *coerced* sexual conduct constituted sexual harassment. By focusing on the coercive and violent nature of the act, he further designated responsibility for punishing this behavior to the state, via the penal courts. The most obvious sanctions, in this context, are penal ones, including fines and/or prison.

In many ways, however, the respondents framed sexual harassment differently from national laws, by alternatively rejecting, ignoring, or innovating upon legal definitions or by creating new sexual harassment frames. For instance, French activists from the AVFT innovated upon the sexual violence frame by widening the category of what is normally considered "violence" to include, for instance, pornography, and by discussing gender-specific forms of violence, such as "violence against women." Many of the American respondents bracketed the discrimination frame to argue that the boss who makes sexual relations with him a condition of employment for male and female candidates (Vignette 2) was sexually harassing both men and women, even if he was not practicing gender discrimination. In other instances, American respondents, especially those employed in human resources, did not frame sexual harassment as a form of group-based discrimination at all, but instead used what I call a "business frame" to argue that sexual behavior is undesirable *at work* because it is unprofessional and detracts from the bottom line. The multiple ways in which respondents employ the discrimination, business, and violence frames are reviewed further below.

The Discrimination Frame

The American respondents appealed to antidiscrimination principles to argue that behavior described in the vignettes constituted sexual harassment. In response to Vignette 1, in which a potential employer asks a female job applicant to spend the weekend with him in San Francisco, an American activist said the conduct described was sexual harassment because romantic relations with the employer were made "a condition of her employment." When probed about why it is wrong to make sex a condition of someone's employment, this respondent laughed and said: "Well I thought that was one of our basic rights, freedom from gender discrimination."

The American lawyers also relied heavily on a discrimination frame by, for instance, emphasizing the adverse effect sexual harassment has on the victim's working conditions. According to one American lawyer: "The conduct or behavior you're complaining about has to interfere with your ability to do the work." The American lawyers further stressed the discriminatory basis of the behavior. One explained why he thought the behavior in Vignette 10, in which a boss constantly makes (nonsexual) sexist comments to a female employee, is sexual harassment: "It's sexual harassment because he is making this distinction based on sex." Likewise, many of the American respondents insisted that sexual harassment is driven by "stereotypical ideas of what the role of a woman is."

As was discussed in Chapter 1, according to American law, sexual harassment is one form of sex-based discrimination. While all (Title VII) sexual harassment is sex discrimination, not all sex discrimination is sexual harassment. Other forms of sex discrimination include not hiring women or paying women less than men for the same job. Some of my respondents and some of the U.S. courts label as sexual harassment behavior in which a supervisor or coworker creates a hostile environment for women by targeting them with sexist but not sexual abuse (such as saying that women should be at home barefoot and pregnant).[5] Others distinguish sexual and nonsexual harassment, labeling the latter "sex discrimination" or "gender harassment."

According to one American lawyer:

> People say sexual harassment when what they mean is sex discrimination. And of course there's a difference, with sex discrimination meaning not being given equivalent job opportunities or equivalent pay just because they're female, but there's no sexual conduct of any kind.

This respondent said that a boss who systematically insulted female but not male workers would be guilty of sex discrimination but not sexual harassment. According to him: "If you treat disparately people of protected classes, like Whites and Blacks, or men and women, or whatever it is, then that is discrimination. But, in order for it to be sexual harassment it has to be treatment that's sexual in nature, either physical or verbally." According to a New Jersey lawyer, however: "In New Jersey [sexual harassment] doesn't have to be sexual in nature. It just has to happen because of the person's sex."[6] However, all of the American lawyers agreed that, sexual or not, sex discrimination was reprehensible and illegal under Title VII.

The American activists frequently combined antidiscrimination arguments with more general concern over the sexual harassment victim's well-being. For instance, in response to Vignette 4, in which a coworker pesters a saleswoman, one New Jersey activist said:

> Her whole career is threatened. She can't work in that environment. It's a hostile environment. I don't care who's doing it to her. If it's the janitor . . . . It's a hostile environment. The impact will be the same. She'll go home and she'll be the same way with her husband, her children; she'll not feel good about herself. You can't work like that.

This respondent thus stressed both the threat this behavior poses for the woman's continued employment and the strain it creates in her personal and family life.

The American respondents used the discrimination frame strategically to strengthen their positions. However, many disregarded this frame when it did not provide a resource for condemning a given behavior. For instance, all of the American activists and 70 percent of the American lawyers labeled "sexual harassment" the conduct in Vignette 2, in which a boss makes employment *for men and women* contingent on having sexual relations with him, despite the fact that, according to American law, for there to be sexual harassment there must be discrimination on the basis of sex.[7] Since, in this vignette, the boss treats male and female candidates identically, it is difficult to argue that he discriminates against either men or women. Yet this did not seem to faze the American respondents. As an American activist said, "It doesn't matter if he'll sleep with anyone. To insist on that as an aspect of your employment is sexual harassment." Another activist concurred: "It's sexual harassment for all of them." According to a third activist, "As far as I understand, it's still unwanted, offensive, usually repeated behavior of a sexual nature." One (male) lawyer said of Vignette 2: "It's discrimination against someone who won't put up with sexual harassment. I don't think it's necessarily on the basis of your sex. It's on the basis of sex." This respondent thus played on the ambiguity between sex as a social category and sex as activity, twisting the established legal meaning of sex discrimination.

Among the three lawyers who did not think the behavior in Vignette 2 constituted sexual harassment, two were unsure about how a court would rule in such a case. The third said that, unfortunately, such a case would not be sexual harassment under Title VII even though "it's inappropriate to condition employment on that kind of behavior."[8] In other words, while respondents were quick to use anti-discrimination arguments when useful, many disregarded the discrimination component of sexual harassment when it would have limited protection for employees. In addition to legal conceptions of sexual harassment, respondents drew on more popular concepts of right and wrong, coercion, abuse, and power, to go beyond the definition of sexual harassment as discrimination.[9]

Rather than simply bracket the discrimination requirement of Title VII in the case of the bisexual harasser, Catharine MacKinnon pointed out that the courts that have addressed this question have, in the main, ruled that a situation in which a person sexually harasses both men and women in a way that is entirely indiscriminate regarding gender is not actionable under Title VII because such behavior is not discriminatory. MacKinnon, however, said she disagrees with this reasoning, arguing that because sexuality is part of what defines gender, gender is usually socially implicated even if a single perpetrator sexually harasses both men and women. The women are harassed sexually as women, the men as men. Therefore, so-called bisexual harassment is still sex-based discrimination.

In other instances, respondents used the logic of discrimination or the market to extend legal definitions. The most striking example of this was the frequent condemnation of discrimination against homosexuals. In one of the vignettes, I described a woman who taunts a young gay man about his sexual preference. Five of the six American activists said that this type of behavior should be considered sexual harassment. The sixth preferred to label it "discrimination on the basis of sexual orientation." All treated homosexuals as members of a protected group, even though sexual orientation was not covered under Title VII or any other Federal discrimination law at the time the interviews were conducted.[10] As one activist explained, "That is sexual harassment. She's discriminating against him. She's calling him a fag. She's saying that he's like one of the girls. She's calling him derogatory names because of his sexual orientation." Although only one of the American lawyers thought the behavior in this vignette was sexual harassment under Title VII, three thought that this should be considered "discrimination on the basis of sexual orientation," although they all recognized that sexual orientation was not (yet) a protected category under federal law.

While American respondents used a discrimination frame more often than the French, some of the French respondents, notably AVFT activists, did use elements of a discrimination frame. Although French discrimination law only applies to hiring or pay and not to any forms of hostile environment, half of the French activists labeled the nonsexual sexist insults in Vignette 10 "discrimination," and the other half called them "sexist." While the French activists recognized that their position was not legally sound, they used antidiscrimination arguments to critique the limits of French discrimination law.

The French activists drew on their exposure to international feminist scholarship and networks to think outside of the French legal model. They spoke often of their ties to feminist intellectuals and activists across the globe, with whom they share written texts, oral presentations, and personal ties. These ties are fostered by national, international, or foreign conferences and workshops organized by the United Nations, universities, or various associations, and influence the French activists' perspectives. This influence was evident in the following quotes, where activists described ideas that they explicitly attributed to such international influences: "[The primacy of the woman's viewpoint] is a position defended by American feminists." "As the Canadian women say, 'For guys, it's clear. . . . A woman is there to be pretty, made up, in a short skirt, even fondled.' . . . It's because she's a woman that she is treated like that. So if that's not discrimination, I don't know what is!"

One of the French activists, who is trained as a jurist, was particularly skillful in drawing on American, Canadian, and European legal concepts and French legal categories. For instance, in response to Vignette 3, in which a saleswoman is propositioned by her boss, who "undresses her with his eyes, asks if she has ever cheated on her husband, and puts his hands on her buttocks," she said:

> If we took out the physical touching and only kept the language, one could consider that this creates a sexist environment. It's the type of environmental harassment that would not at this moment be pursued by [French] law, narrowly conceived. But, in my opinion, that could change because you have to be logical. . . . I don't see what [the victim] can think besides: 'If I don't smile, if I don't laugh when he says these stupid things, I could be fired at the next downsizing.' One must be realistic. In my opinion, there is constraint. And . . . if she says yes, he won't say no. So, implicitly his remarks aim at obtaining sexual favors.

The term "environmental harassment" refers to the category of hostile environment sexual harassment in American law. However, because existing French law did not recognize hostile environment sexual harassment, this respondent expanded explicit components of French law — "constraint" and "sexual favors" — so they could accommodate the behavior described in this vignette. Largely due to the influence the AVFT has had on the courts via their work with plaintiff lawyers, some of the courts have evolved in this direction.[11]

Some French lawyers affiliated with the AVFT or other feminist groups also used elements of a discrimination or gender inequality frame to discuss sexual harassment. For instance, one French lawyer recognized that sexual harassment is facilitated by patterns of gender inequality in the workplace: "It is rare that women are at the head of a corporation. . . . If the guy were to tell his version in the firm, everyone would laugh at her and she would be more vulnerable in the end than the man." However, the French lawyers interviewed typically shrugged off sexist behavior that did not involve physical violence or coercion, such as that described in Vignette 10, as "societal," "human," or otherwise outside of the law.

Likewise, the French human resource managers and union activists did not frame sexual harassment as a form of gender discrimination, and most had a narrow understanding of discrimination that did not extend to the sort of hostile environment described in Vignette 10. Nonetheless, there were some exceptions. One (male) French union activist at Frenchco, who had a reputation for defending women's rights, said in response to Vignette 10:

> That enters into the intellectual approach to not treat women differently [from men]. . . . So that's an instance of discrimination that, intellectually, I would put with sexual harassment but, typically, in terms of the law and in the terms that are generally felt, it's not sexual harassment. . . . In any case, it's a situation that is unacceptable.

Likewise, in response to this same vignette, a French AmeriCorp manager said, "To some extent it's harassment. Sexual harassment? I don't know. . . . It's discrimination in regards to a woman." He did not think that this kind of behavior could or should be pursued in a court of law but he did conceptualize it as discriminatory, a perspective that he attributed to the (American) influence of AmeriCorp: "We're at [AmeriCorp], so it's a bit different because, on some level, we are after all impregnated by, I would say, Anglo-Saxon culture and mentality. So we are French but in an international environment. . . . I don't know if you would get similar responses in a different company."

Elisabeth Badinter and Françoise Giroud dismissed gender-based hostility as human behavior that should be dealt with informally. They each condemned quid pro quo sexual harassment because it involves coercion of individuals by others in positions of authority. While they recognized that women are harassed more often than men, they did not understand the harassment as customarily legitimized by sexism or as a form of employment discrimination. Rather, they stressed the abuse of hierarchical power involved. For instance, when I asked Giroud how she defined sexual harassment, she said:

> It's generally an attitude of supervisors [*petits chefs*] in offices, in factories, who think they can do anything because the employees are defenseless. . . . There are even [*laughter*] cases of sexual harassment of men by women. There was one last year, I don't know if you saw that, who was absolutely persecuted by a woman. Still, that's very rare.

While emphasizing the formal power of the boss and the institutional vulnerability of the employee, Giroud did not analyze the power men have over women by virtue of being men.[12] She did not discuss situations in which, for example, female managers and professionals are sexually harassed by colleagues who perceive them as a threat and use sexuality to "put them in their place."

For Giroud and Badinter, sexual harassment was necessarily sexual. They did not consider sexual harassment to be an instance of gender discrimination. In response to Vignette 10, which describes a boss who insults his female, but not male, employees by calling them "incompetent and slow," Giroud said: "That's just someone with a bad character. You can't condemn him for sexual harassment." When I then asked if this person could be condemned for anything, she replied: "I don't think so. That's the case of lots of supervisors [*petits chefs*]. The hierarchy needs to be changed. That's something else!"

I then tried to make the insults more specifically discriminatory (such as "dumb broad!"). Giroud repeated that what I was describing was not sexual harassment and finally said that it could be considered an insult and that he could be "condemned for insults." I pointed out that there is a French law against racist insults and asked if there should not also be a law against sexist insults.[13] Giroud replied: "I don't believe there is a need to be specific. It should be recognized simply as an insult . . . because it's an insult regardless of whether or not it is sexist. An insult should be condemned." In other words, after much prodding, Giroud agreed that the behavior should be tempered, but refused to group it with either sexual harassment or gender discrimination.

Similarly, Badinter resisted the idea that certain supervisors are verbally abusive to female employees because of their gender, making Vignette 10 particularly frustrating for her: "Listen, this is one of the most unbelievable cases [*cas de figure*] because why would he hire her then? Knowing that she's a girl and he can't stand women? I don't know. I can't answer." Badinter thus dismissed the findings of empirical studies that show that many women workers are targeted for abusive behavior precisely because their colleagues and/or supervisors resent working with women.[14]

The Business Frame

While American law frames sexual harassment as a form of sex discrimination, American respondents often used a "business frame," in which any sexually-tinged behavior *at work* is considered undesirable because it detracts from productivity or is not "professional." American managers distinguished between what behavior was permissible at work as compared to a "bar," "party," or "country club." For instance, according to one American human resource manager at FrenchCo:

> [A] sexual advance is harassment, as far as I am concerned. And if it is done at a party, when everybody is drinking and having fun, I think it's natural. I think it's going to happen if you go to the country club and no employees are there and there's someone there, of the same or opposite sex, that's attracted to you. I don't have a problem with that; I think that's where it should be done. But I don't think it should be done in the workplace, I like to work in a professional environment.

For this American respondent, sexual conduct that might be perfectly acceptable in another social situation becomes unacceptable when it occurs in the workplace. By including in the rubric of "sexual harass-ment" all workplace sexual advances, American managers defined sex-ual harassment significantly more broadly than does American law. At the same time, they disregarded the original point of Title VII, as it applies to gender, which is to combat gender inequality rather than sanitize the workplace of all sexual innuendo. In fact, some of their practices, like firing one member of a dating or married couple, actually hurt women, as women are more likely to be more professionally expendable.

Respondents also used the business frame to justify corporate pre-ventive and remedial action because, insofar as sexual harassment jeop-ardizes the bottom line, it is management's responsibility and right to stamp it out. I was struck by how little American managers spoke about the law and liability and how much they stressed respect and creating a comfortable working environment. I asked a human resource manager at AmeriCorp about this, to which he replied:

> Financial liability is always an issue. . . . Nobody wants to see their name in headlines. But my perception is that we're really moving toward ownership, personal ownership, of standing up and saying that's not right. . . . If you walk by somebody's computer and you see this porno queen on there, that's not appropriate. What if you have customers coming through there? *What value does that add to the work environment?* . . . It's not that we're trying to control people's lives. *It's more that it adds no value, it does not bring our company any revenue. That's not what we hired you here for* [emphasis added].

Rather than argue that sexual harassment was wrong or that it perpetu-ates gender inequality, this American manager, like his colleagues, con-demned sexual harassment as *bad business*, thereby justifying corporate action. This supports what previous research has shown: managers do not deny that the law affects them, but they develop efficiency rationales for how they respond to the law, via corporate regulation.[15]

The business frame is consistent with corporate rationality writ large and is not limited to human resource professionals, or even the business world per se. Rather, the business frame seemed to have seeped out of the corporation, shaping how Americans more generally, including activists and lawyers, conceptualize sexual harassment. So American lawyers argued that sexuality is inappropriate in the workplace and antithetical to productivity. The overwhelming majority of American lawyers said that it is best not to date people at work, especially across levels of hierarchical authority. According to one:

> [I] advise supervisors that [dating at work] is not something that's favorably looked upon, because of the problems that can arise from it. And if [they] arise, the supervisors [are] not only placing the employer in jeopardy from a lawsuit, but they're placing their job in jeopardy.

Many French respondents, in contrast, argued that prohibiting all sexual relations at work would transform the workplace into a drab, impersonal environment. Only one of the ten American lawyers expressed this concern. On the contrary, the following comment poignantly expressed the general sentiment among American lawyers:

> I don't think we'll ever get flirtation out of the workplace, not in my lifetime. But, I don't think it would be a bad thing if we did. I'd love to see that. . . . We want to create an environment where anyone who comes into work can do the best kind of work possible. In most instances, that [means] removing all the nonsense that's going on around them and the harassment so that they can focus on their work.

American feminist activists also drew on the business frame. When probed about the risk that overzealous employers might stamp out playful and harmless flirtation in the workplace, one American activist asked: "Why do people have to . . . ? Really they don't have to have everyday seduction and flirtation in the workplace. . . . Has it been proven that that helps productivity?" Similarly, Catharine MacKinnon said in her interview: "Somebody ought to worry that no work is getting done. The workplace is not essentially a place for sexual recruitment. People are mostly supposed to be working." American activists argued that one should be "professional" at work. This means being productive and maintaining social distance with coworkers. As one American activist said: "As a professional, I think about going to work and getting my work done and having a relationship with a colleague as a professional relationship. But to even go over that line into a real personal relationship, I think that can be dangerous and not wise."

Of course, American feminists are not concerned about sexual harassment only because of its effects on industrial productivity. In a discussion with Catharine MacKinnon about the way I used the above citation in an earlier draft of this chapter, she pointed out that even if it were shown that sexual harassment improves productivity, it would still be a form of sex inequality. Indeed, the common goal among people who identify as feminists is gender equality, not industrial efficiency. Such use of a business frame by many American respondents reveals that arguments about professionalism and productivity are especially effective in legitimizing particular positions in the American context. However, this line of reasoning can be dangerous if it leads to a double standard in which abusive behavior is condemned at work but not in more "private" spheres like the family.

Phyllis Schlafly said that current American sexual harassment law has gone "overboard," in that "a woman can make a charge against an employer and, whether it's true or not, a company lawyer will tell them to pay up because it's too costly to fight it." Echoing American conservative critiques of "big government," even though in reality it is employers who police themselves to preempt legal complaints, Schlafly said: "I just don't think we should have a government inspector at every water cooler to catch some man who's a slob." As a different kind of efficiency argument, such a point of view is consistent with the (fiscally) conservative movement in the United States, in which it is thought that the labor market should be unhampered by state intervention. For years, however, the American government has regulated the labor market out of concern for both employees and employers. In France, of course, where the market is expected to be more restricted by social considerations,[16] state intervention in the market enjoys even greater public support.[17] Despite Schlafly's political rhetoric, when asked to respond to the vignettes describing specific behavior, she categorized a wide range of behavior as constitutive of sexual harassment, including conduct that would be considered hostile environment sexual harassment by the U.S. courts.

A self-identified libertarian feminist, Camille Paglia lobbied for the adoption of "moderate" sexual harassment guidelines at the University of the Arts in Philadelphia, where she is a Professor of Humanities, after evaluating sample academic codes in her "Women and Sex Roles" class in 1986. While she expressed support for laws and rules against quid pro quo sexual harassment, Paglia has insisted that the "hostile environment" clause is "reactionary and totalitarian" because it "imposes a genteel white lady's standard of decorum on everyone, and when blindly applied by management, imperialistically exports white middle-class manners, appropriate to an office, into the vigorously physical and more realistic working-class realm."[18]

Paglia has argued that mainstream feminists are naïve about the harsh realities of sexuality and aggression. According to her, women, particularly sheltered American middle-class white women, need to learn to be more "street smart," so that they can defend themselves with words and, if need be, force, to get ahead in the harsh reality of the workplace. According to Paglia, "*Every* workplace is hostile, as any man who has worked his way up the cutthroat corporate ladder will testify . . . . 'Transformative feminism,' . . . which imagines a pleasant, stress-free work environment where the lion lies down with the lamb, is unreachably utopian."[19] Rather than see broad sexual harassment guidelines (including hostile environment harassment) as empowering to women because they provide additional tools with which to fight back, Paglia has said that such rules promote dependence and reliance on authority figures and produce "young women unable to foresee trouble or to survive sexual misadventure or even raunchy language without crying to authority figures for help."[20]

It should be noted that, while many employers have interpreted hostile environment sexual harassment very broadly to include such things as raunchy language, this is not true of the courts, which have established much stricter standards of severity. Not only must the individual woman find the behavior offensive but it must be determined that the behavior would be offensive to a "reasonable person" and that it would alter that person's conditions of employment and create an abusive working environment.[21] Indeed, as we saw in Chapter 1, Mechelle Vinson, whose sexual harassment claim in the 1986 Supreme Court decision *Meritor v. Vinson* first established that hostile environment sexual harassment violates Title VII, claimed that her boss had fondled her in public, made requests for sexual relations (to which she succumbed out of fear of losing her job), and forcibly raped her on several occasions. His behavior was determined to be hostile environment rather than quid pro quo sexual harassment only because he never conditioned concrete employment benefits on sexual relations.[22] Contrary to Paglia's assertion, condemning his behavior does not seem to impose a "genteel white lady's standard of decorum," especially given that Mechelle Vinson, like many of the early sexual harassment plaintiffs, was an African-American woman.

Despite major political differences with Schlafly, Paglia affirmed in an interview that she "strongly believes in private property and the importance of the profit motive in social development." According to her, "women's modern economic liberation and feminism itself were made possible by capitalism and the industrial revolution." Paglia likened small businesses to fiefdoms and said that a small owner should be free to hire whom he chose and, in her characteristically provocative style, said he could even have a "harem of women that he wants to sleep with." On the other hand, middle managers, who are accountable to public interests, should not, according to Paglia, "sexualize their jobs." To do so would be "unprofessional." Paglia explained that while a family firm is "private" and should be free from government intervention, large firms "have evolved economically into public institutions," so that outside intervention is appropriate there.

Shocking as Paglia's statement about business fiefdoms may appear, her personal demarcation of the public and private, in which smaller enterprises ("the mom-and-pop companies") are "private" but larger ones are "public," is consistent with American political traditions, in which smaller businesses are less accountable to federal control. For instance, as mentioned in Chapter 1, Title VII only applies to businesses with fifteen or more employees, although many states have their own sexual harassment statutes that cover businesses with fewer than fifteen employees.[23]

The Violence Frame

According to the sexual violence frame, sexual harassment is a form of violence that is physically, psychologically, and/or morally harmful and violates the victim's free will. The *unusual* use of force and coercion distinguish it from "normal" social interactions. As described in Chapter 1, this is the dominant perspective of French law. The violence frame was also widely accepted by French lawyers. As the lawyer quoted above said, "Sexual violence should be prosecuted so as to preserve the moral and physical integrity of people, [because] we should never accept that a person be forced to do something they do not want to do." French respondents used the sexual violence frame to distinguish sexual harassment, defined as a personal attack on a particular individual, from sexism, said to denigrate women as a group. As one French feminist lawyer put it: "I consider sexual harassment to be an individual attack, but sexism is an attack on the group."

For these French lawyers, the concept of sexual harassment as a "hostile environment," diffused rather than aimed at one person in particular (such as a display of pornography or sexist jokes) was meaningless. The response of the following lawyer to Vignette 6 was typical:

For it to be sexual harassment, you would have to show that the [pornographic] posters were put up after [the] arrival [of the female truck driver]. If they were there before she arrived, you cannot say that they are directed at her . . . and therefore, you cannot say that there was sexual harassment.

Several French lawyers used a violence frame to condemn physical touching or explicit quid pro quo proposals, where the aspects of physical and/or moral violence are evident. However, they excused requests for dates and sexual comments entailing no economic threats, which they did not consider violent or coercive. As one said, "To the extent that such comments are not accompanied by a real apparent blackmail or clear coercion, it's borderline." Or, according to a French feminist lawyer, "I think we must not confuse harassment, which is an assault against one's will, with rules of seduction, which normally assume that there is an exchange, equality, and consent." In other words, these respondents used the sexual violence frame to limit the scope of the law to extreme situations of violence or coercion, making more subtle forms of sexual inequality "private," or outside public control.

Another lawyer explained that he did not think one should ban pornography in a truck driver's break room just because it offended a newly hired female truck driver. According to his reasoning, this would begin a dangerous trend of infringement on personal freedom. As he said: "Imagine . . . that this woman puts on lipstick and the men say, 'I want her to remove her lipstick because we consider it a form of seduction that shocks us.'"

As we have already seen in the previous chapter, the focus on violence is also institutionalized in the European Association against *Violence* Toward Women at Work (AVFT). It is therefore not surprising that the AVFT activists were more likely to discuss sexual harassment as an act of violence than as an impediment to equal opportunity in employment. Yet they used the concept of violence more broadly than either French law or many French lawyers. One French activist explained why she thought sexual harassment among colleagues is wrong by saying: "For me, that's an act of violence. To be constantly behind someone harassing them, that's a kind of violence." Another said that she considers pornography an "agression sexuelle," or sexual battery.[24]

Moreover, like their American counterparts, the French activists often mixed several rationales in their arguments about sexual harassment. In the following citation, a French activist explains why sexual harassment is wrong:

> Sexual harassment is a denial of [women's] right to work, but what [harassers] try to do more profoundly is to dominate [women] by denying their word. In fact, we find that women often say no, maybe implicitly initially and then very explicitly, but the [harassers] do not hear the 'no.' Refusing to hear what another says is like saying: 'You don't exist.' So it's really destruction. 'You don't exist and I destroy your intimacy, your personality, the psychological and physical barriers that you have constructed.' I think that for many women this has a certain resonance in a patriarchal society that continually tries to oppress them with violence.

This woman skillfully weaves arguments about employment opportunity, psychological harm, violence, and systematic oppression of women into a few sentences.

As we have seen, French employers were not especially concerned about sexual harassment, especially compared to their American counterparts. This is not particularly surprising considering they faced limited to no liability under existing French law. Not having to justify preventive or remedial measures, French employers have not emphasized the impact that sexual harassment has on the bottom line or on standards of professionalism. Instead, the respondents from the French branches of AmeriCorp and Frenchco framed sexual harassment much like French lawyers and activists, as a form of sexual violence that can occur in the workplace or elsewhere; the place is incidental. According to them, employers should respect both the law and the *limits* of the law by not going beyond it to create their own rules in this area. In other words, they considered sexual harassment legislation and enforcement a matter for lawmakers and national courts rather than for private employers.

As a French-based AmeriCorp personnel director explained, "We apply [the law]. I mean, we don't create [it]. The legislation applies to the firm and to each of us individually." One Frenchco union activist was particularly adamant that corporations should not do the work of the justice system, which should be responsible for determining, evaluating, and punishing instances of sexual harassment. According to him, "The firm should not substitute itself for the responsibility of the society. I'm not against creating greater criminal penalties [for sexual harassment], but that's a decision for society." He made an analogy to how AmeriCorp dealt with an employee who attacked another with a knife and a second employee who stole:

> [All of these are] problems for the justice system. If one day someone attacked another with a knife — that has happened here by the way — . . . that is a problem for the justice system. A guy who steals something, as has happened here, that's a problem for the justice system. But after the court ruled, [Frenchco] fired the person because he violated his labor contract [by stealing]. I think that's logical. It's not for the corporation to say, "I fire you because you attacked someone with a knife." It's "I fire you because you have been condemned by the justice system, [and] your labor contract was violated."

This is not to say that the French respondents thought that the corporation had no responsibility regarding sexual harassment. All of them said that management should deal seriously with clear cases of harassment. A personnel manager at a French branch of AmeriCorp explained how he would respond to a "serious situation" of sexual harassment (meaning, according to him, quid pro quo harassment or physical touching): "I think we would take immediate measures to sanction [the harasser]. So there we would rely on the labor and penal law. We would ask the person to file a [legal] complaint and we would eventually help her do that."

The lower profile of French management, as compared to American management, in sexual harassment cases is largely a result of cross-national legal differences. Not only are French employers not held liable for sexual harassment occurring in their workplace, but they may also be penalized for disciplining an alleged harasser with less than compelling evidence of his guilt. This is because the alleged harasser could appeal to France's more effective labor laws against wrongful discharge and sanctions.[25] However, the interviews further suggest that these national legal differences are tightly interwoven with distinct conceptions of the role of the employer versus the state in governing workplace intersocial behavior.[26]

CONCLUSION

In sum, this chapter has shown that American and French people who are considered "specialists" in sexual harassment (that is, activists, public figures, lawyers, managers, and union representatives) conceptualize this social problem fundamentally differently. Moreover, these distinct understandings of sexual harassment are not the mere product of their country's particular legal traditions. While the respondents' conceptualizations of sexual harassment are influenced to varying degrees by national legal approaches, they also depart from the latter in important ways. Indeed, the business frame used by so many of the American respondents, in which sexual conduct *at work* is condemned because it impairs productivity and compromises standards of professionalism, is absent from American sexual harassment law. Likewise, even though French respondents, like French law, chiefly framed sexual harassment as a form of sexual violence, French feminist activists drew on foreign law and scholarship to argue that sexual harassment is also a form of sex-based discrimination. They spoke about gendered violence or violence toward women, thereby innovating on the violence frame.

These findings suggest that people pick and choose from cultural repertoires, which are limited by national contexts but are still sufficiently varied to provide ample opportunity for innovation. This chapter further demonstrates how the salience of particular elements of cultural repertoires varies according to the individual's social position. Thus both American and French lawyers were more influenced by legal definitions than were nonlawyers. Likewise, American human resource managers were more likely than other American respondents to frame sexual harassment as bad business.

Institutions, Framing, and Political Power

In 1998, a French psychiatrist and psychoanalyst published a book that captivated the nation.[1] Entitled *Harcèlement moral*, or "moral harassment," it drew on clinical cases involving bosses who use their authority to humiliate subordinates or coworkers who gang up on an individual. *Harcèlement moral* documented the abuse and often tragic implications "moral harassment" had for employees. Though the author, who studied in the United States (and France), referred to American discrimination laws in her book, she framed "moral harassment" as a form of interpersonal violence and perversion, as the subtitle, "Perverse everyday violence," reveals. Presented in such individual terms and devoid of any discussion of discrimination, sexism, or sexuality, the concept seemed to resonate with the French public, who turned *Harcèlement moral* into a best-seller and formed associations like Harcèlement Moral Stop (HMS) to fight for moral harassment legislation. The mass media discussed the implications of the book and lawmakers proposed new laws to specifically address this problem.

After the publication of *Harcèlement moral*, the AVFT, a French association that deals specifically with *sexual* harassment, saw a surge, unparalleled in its previous thirteen years of existence, in the number of calls received by its hotline. Often women said they were being morally harassed but, upon examination of the facts, AVFT members deduced that they were being sexually harassed. AVFT members came to understand that it was easier for French women to label the behavior "moral harassment" than "sexual harassment," since this term was less stigmatized.

The AVFT considered the increased awareness of the problem of moral harassment to be a double-edged sword. On the one hand, more women felt comfortable denouncing the abuse they suffered, albeit as "moral harassment" rather than as "sexual harassment." On the other hand, the concept of moral harassment, which was not gender-specific, further diluted the claim that women are more likely to be targeted and that they are mistreated in ways that are gender-specific.

Given the way in which the discrimination aspect of sexual harassment has been downplayed in legislative debates, media reporting, and individual accounts of sexual harassment in France, it is not surprising that the concept of moral harassment, which avoids all discussion of sex and gender inequality, would be a more popular cause in France.

No such trend has occurred in the United States. The concept of "sexual harassment" as a form of group-based discrimination has strong support in American legal and political traditions. Moreover, it fits well into a host of other concerns, such as civil rights, affirmative action, and diversity, which are also established agendas for American corporations. Internal corporate constituencies, like affirmative action and diversity officers, further stress the importance of these issues.

THE EFFECT OF INSTITUTIONAL LOGIC

The difference in salience of sex-based discrimination for how inequality is conceptualized and institutionalized in the United States and France has shaped how sexual harassment is understood and addressed in these countries. Of course, group-based discrimination is but one concept, albeit a very important one, that has informed approaches to sexual harassment in the United States but not in France. Ideas about hierarchy and authority, money, sexuality, and the right of employers to control employees' behavior have also shaped national understandings of sexual harassment.

Ideas are not free-floating, however. Rather, they are imbedded in individual and collective consciousness[2] and behavior. As such, they are further constrained and enabled by distinct institutional structures. For instance, sexual harassment lawmaking has been constrained and enabled by national legal systems. In the United States, much of sexual harassment law was created in the courts rather than in the legislature. American sexual harassment laws were thus shaped both by the rules governing legal reform via case law, such as those that require lawyers to show that the conduct at stake (in this case sexual harassment) violates a preexisting statute. In the case of sexual harassment in the workplace, lawyers built sexual harassment case law predominantly on Title VII of the Civil Rights Act of 1964, which prohibits discrimination on the basis of several group identities, including gender.[3] Preexisting laws, especially Title VII, thus also shaped American sexual harassment law. The fact that sexual harassment was defined as a violation of Title VII in the United States accounts for a great deal of its character, including how it frames sexual harassment as a form of group-based discrimination and how it holds employers liable for sexual harassment among their employees.

In contrast, in the French legal system new laws are made in Parliament, not the courts. Rather than having to argue that sexual harassment violated a preexisting statute, independent and state-feminists had to convince French lawmakers that a new statute was needed to address sexual harassment. They too were constrained and enabled by preexisting laws. In France, employment discrimination laws only addressed situations in which there was discriminatory *intent*, rather than simply discriminatory *impact*, and were poorly enforced, making them a less compelling model than Title VII had been for sexual harassment in the United States. On the other hand, French penal laws concerning sexual violence seemed well suited to popular understandings of sexual harassment as a form of sexual coercion. Once the sexual harassment statute was added to the section on sexual violence, the rules of this body of penal law applied to the sexual harassment statute as well. Sexual harassment was thus legally defined as a form of sexual coercion, involving the abuse of hierarchical authority. Sexual harassers, rather than employers, could be ordered to pay state fines and/or be sentenced to jail or, more commonly, receive suspended jail sentences.

In the United States, corporate approaches to sexual harassment have been informed by the existence of internal constituencies, such as affirmative action and diversity officers, whose job it is to respond to civil rights laws, including those concerning sexual harassment. These groups, who have no equivalent in France, have inflated the legal risks of sexual harassment to American employers, making it more likely that they would take preventive and remedial action.[4]

American litigation or legal claims involving high-profile politicians and institutions have provided the American mass media with stories that are particularly appealing in light of media routines, as they "can be easily recognized and interpreted as drama," and involve individuals who are certifiably newsworthy.[5] Due to institutional pressures to sell copy, the American presses have focused on such profitable scandals or stories of multi-million-dollar lawsuits, rather than report on a more representative sample of litigation or provide in-depth legal or social analysis. Because of more recent and narrow sexual harassment laws in France, French politicians and institutions have not yet been accused of sexual harassment. On the other hand, French presses found that American sexual harassment scandals also sold in France. The status of the United States as the sole global superpower made it likely that France would report on American sexual harassment scandals. The French mass media's embrace of anti-Americanism made it even more likely that they would use such scandals as an opportunity to point to American excesses and French superiority.

INTERACTIONS AMONG INSTITUTIONS

Interactions among the legal, corporate, and media spheres further shaped responses to sexual harassment in each country. For instance, there is evidence that American media reports on Anita Hill's account of sexual harassment at the hands of Supreme Court nominee Clarence Thomas and on the Senate's treatment of her testimony facilitated President George Bush's signing of the Civil Rights Act of 1991, which greatly strengthened American sexual harassment laws.[6] In contrast, some have argued that media reporting on Paula Jones's lawsuit against Bill Clinton and other scandals in the late 1990s instigated a backlash against sexual harassment law in the United States at the end of the twentieth century.[7]

By holding employers liable for sexual harassment and providing only ambiguous guidelines about how to protect themselves from liability, American law prompted extensive corporate action. Employers' perception of their liability has been further inflated by media reports focusing on the most costly lawsuits and settlements and by human resource departments. In response to ambiguous federal mandates, human resource professionals urged employers to protect themselves by adopting corporate training programs and regulations before such policies had any legal significance. However, over the years, the courts followed employers' lead and ruled that the existence of corporate training programs could be used as an "affirmative defense" to protect employers from liability in certain cases of sexual harassment.[8]

Likewise, as we saw in Chapter 3, American press articles were more likely to frame sexual harassment as a form of (group-based) discrimination, the dominant American legal frame, than as a form of sexual violence or a violation of human dignity, the competing legal frames. Individual respondents drew from a range of perspectives when discussing sexual harassment but were more likely to be influenced by the institutions with which they were most closely aligned. American lawyers were thus more likely to echo national legal definitions of sexual harassment by framing it as a form of group-based discrimination. American managers were more likely to invoke business arguments about professionalism and productivity.

French reporting on the Hill-Thomas scandal, which presented Thomas as the victim of a feminist "witch hunt,"[9] in contrast, led to revisions of the pending labor code statute that excluded from the law instances of "hostile environment" sexual harassment or any instances of sexual harassment among hierarchical equals.[10] In the absence of legal liability for sexual harassment, French employers have done little to address this issue. Like the American press, the French press was also more likely to employ the dominant legal frame — in its case, that of sexual violence — than competing legal frames, such as employment discrimination or human dignity. Likewise, French lawyers were inclined to frame sexual harassment as a form of sexual violence and to apply French legal definitions of what does and does not constitute sexual harassment. Although some of the French feminist activists used elements of the discrimination frame to condemn sexual harassment, the violence frame was incontestably dominant among French respondents. French human resource managers did not frame sexual harassment as bad business. In the French context, where employers are not at risk of being sued or even publicly shamed for tolerating or condoning sexual harassment at work, there is less of a business incentive to address sexual harassment. Moreover, the idea that social relations or personal (including sexual) expression should be curtailed for the sake of productivity or efficiency is less legitimate in France.

Finally, the preceding chapters provide ample evidence that the United States and France have not defined sexual harassment in isolation from each other. France in particular has been influenced by American approaches to sexual harassment. While French feminist activists have drawn on American (and European) models, French lawmakers, journalists, lawyers, managers, union activists, public figures, and many others have represented the American example as an anti-model. By ridiculing "American excesses," these French groups and individuals have raised concerns about going too far in prohibiting sexual harassment. As has been demonstrated throughout this book, such discourse has discredited both sexual harassment as a social problem and also French sexual harassment victims and their advocates.

DEFINITIONS OF SEXUAL HARASSMENT

The different national contexts, described above, led to distinct approaches to sexual harassment in American and French law, corporations, and mass media, and by activists, lawyers, and human resource managers in the two countries. These are summarized in Table 4. In the United States, sexual harassment is addressed in employment law, and employers are held liable for sexual harassment occurring in their workplaces. Sexual harassment has been legally defined to include not only quid pro quo forms of sexual harassment, in which an employee's sexual cooperation or lack thereof is used as a basis for employment decisions, but also hostile environment sexual harassment, in which sexual or sexist behavior or language is sufficiently severe or pervasive to alter an employee's conditions of employment. American lawyers and employers consider sexual harassment law to be an important body of law and take it seriously. American law frames sexual harassment as a form of group-based discrimination.

In American corporations sexual harassment is a major concern, and it is considered a responsibility of the employer to address and prevent instances of sexual harassment in the company. The American press has reported extensively on sexual harassment, focusing particularly on domestic scandals involving high-profile political individuals and institutions. This focus explains why a large proportion of the articles in the American sample framed the incident at hand as a scandal or as political in nature. Equally prevalent, however, were articles that framed sexual harassment as a social problem or a women's issue.

American respondents framed sexual harassment as either a form of employment discrimination, consistent with American sexual harass-

Table 4. *Major National Trends*

	U.S.	France
Law	• Employment law • Employer liability • Quid pro quo and hostile environment • Important body of law • Discrimination frame	• Penal and labor law • No employer liability • Quid pro quo only (until January 2002) • Devalued body of law • Violence frame
Corporations	• Major concern • Responsibility of employer	• Minor concern • Responsibility of the state
Press	• Substantial coverage • Focus on American high-profile political scandals • Scandal, politics, women's issue, social problem, and discrimination frames dominate	• Little coverage • Focus on *American* high-profile political scandals • More likely to trivialize the problem when reporting on the United States by framing as political scandals and greedy plaintiffs • When reporting on France, power, social problem, violence, and women's issue frames dominate
Activists	• Discrimination and business frames	• Violence and discrimination frames
Lawyers	• Discrimination and business frames	• Violence frame
Human resource professionals	• Business frame	• Violence frame

ment law, or as "bad business," in that it detracts from professionalism and productivity. The activists and lawyers tended to draw on both of these frames; the human resource professionals favored the latter.

In France, sexual harassment has been addressed in both penal and labor law. There is no employer liability, and before legal reform in January 2002, only quid pro quo sexual harassment was targeted.[11] Moreover, sexual harassment law has been devalued in France and sexual harassment victims and their advocates stigmatized. French law frames sexual harassment as a form of sexual violence. Sexual harassment is not a major concern in French corporations; the state, rather than employers, is generally considered responsible for addressing this issue.

There has been comparatively little coverage of sexual harassment in the French media, and a large proportion of the French press reporting on this issue has focused on American scandals, typically involving high-profile politicians or political institutions. Such reporting has tended to focus on "American excesses" in addressing sexual harassment rather than on the problems of sexual harassment itself. In fact, when reporting on the United States, as about half of the French media sample did, the French press has been more likely to frame the incident at hand as a political story, a scandal, a story about money-hungry plaintiffs, or a morality tale. When reporting on sexual harassment in France on the other hand, the French press has framed the problem as about power, as a social problem, as a form of violence, or as a women's issue. French interview respondents tended to frame sexual harassment as a form of sexual violence, although the French feminist activists also employed elements of a discrimination frame.

BORROWING POLICY FROM OTHER NATIONS

While social scientists use cross-national research to better explain social processes, policy-makers look abroad for useful models for policy reform.[12] Policy-makers might be tempted to use this book as a source of new policy ideas for the United States or for France, but a careful reading suggests that exporting public policy across national boundaries is a tricky enterprise. Since national public policy is built into local legal and political institutions, divorcing it from those institutions entails transforming it into something quite different. In order to learn policy lessons from other nations, it is therefore important to understand the larger legal, political, and cultural context of a given policy.

The U.S. federal government and each of the fifty states can look to France for ideas, but basic differences in legal structure will make replication of French law in the United States difficult. Passing penal sexual harassment laws could prove useful as a complement to the sexual harassment jurisprudence under employment law. However, even existing rape and sexual assault laws are notoriously difficult for victims to use, particularly because of the high burden of proof that exists in American criminal courts and the narrow way in which these crimes are generally defined.[13] The fact that victims cannot receive any kind of compensation in American criminal court, unlike in France, is another drawback of criminal court for many victims (and their lawyers) in the United States. Finally, because criminal laws target the sexual aggressor rather than the employer, they do little to encourage employers to take preventive or remedial action.

On the other side of the Atlantic, people are likely to denounce any adoption of American approaches to sexual harassment, arguing that this will serve to import the "American excesses" of litigiousness, feminism, and "puritanism." This book suggests that these fears are largely unfounded. Even if the French Parliament were to revise the sexual harassment penal statute to hold employers liable for sexual harassment in the workplace, this would still not result in the infamous million-dollar verdicts of the United States. Bracketing the way in which the American media and human resource managers exaggerate the occurrence of these lucrative verdicts in the United States, French awards would be even smaller, in keeping with the rules of French penal law. French penal law, in general, allows for jail sentences and state fines, but only small compensatory damages and no punitive damages. Moreover, even if employers were to be held liable for incidents of harassment among hierarchical peers and hostile environment forms of sexual harassment, they would have to take into account labor protections before hastily dismissing an employee for sexual harassment, as sometimes occurs in American workplaces, where labor protections are much weaker.

These facts could prove handy in rejecting French arguments that by imitating any aspect of American sexual harassment law, France runs the risk of reproducing "American excesses" of litigiousness. Rather, this study suggests that even if some aspects of American law were replicated in France, French sexual harassment law and its ramifications would remain very different from their American counterparts.

SOCIOLOGICAL LESSONS

There are several lessons to be drawn from this study that go beyond sexual harassment and beyond the United States and France. First, while states are gendered, this study illustrates that particular states are gendered in different ways, providing distinct openings for influence by women's movements. Second, while national cultural differences exist, they are mediated by institutional structures.[14] A complete cultural account therefore needs to study how institutional context, which varies cross-nationally and over time, shapes social meaning. On the other hand, this book suggests that structural differences cannot determine everything. Rather, national cultural differences concerning how inequality is conceptualized, attitudes toward money or sexuality, and so on have real implications for policy debates independent of institutional effects.[15]

Finally, we have seen that there are limits to globalization. The globalization of culture means that ideas circulate broadly, but it does not mean that they take hold everywhere they circulate. Ideas are selected and changed in interaction with political regimes (for example, French resistance to the United States), institutional factors (the French legal system), and cultural repertoire (ideas about inequality). For example, the French mass media reported quite extensively on American sexual harassment scandals. However, they generally represented these stories as demonstrative of "American excesses" of feminism and litigiousness. Lawmakers, in turn, drew on the French media's version of American sexual harassment scandals to argue that French law should only recognize the most egregious forms of sexual harassment involving abuse of authority to coerce an employee into having sexual relations. They further buttressed their claim by appealing to French traditions of critiquing the abuse of (hierarchical) power. In turn, the state-feminist sponsors of sexual harassment law limited the scope of their proposals so as to insure the support of their colleagues. In other words, American ideas informed debates about sexual harassment in unexpected ways, depending on how local actors and institutions responded to these ideas and to each other.

The interviews further demonstrate that, for French individuals, attitudes and behavior regarding sexual harassment have been informed by ideas about what it means to be French versus American. Thus female French employees who have felt sexually harassed at work have hesitated before condemning the behavior out of fear of being associated with American feminism. Likewise, in an effort to avoid falling into "American excesses," French judges have been reluctant to rule against sexual harassers at all. To distinguish themselves from American feminists, some French feminist activists have even rejected terms associated with the United States, such as "sexual harassment," favoring instead others like "violence towards women." These are instances of the surprising ways in which increased exchanges and communication across national boundaries have changed the nature of cognition, the practice of law, and political mobilization.

Some have argued that anti-Americanism and antifeminism have made for a "politically successful marriage" in France.[16] However, anti-Americanism is not limited to gender issues. As is demonstrated by research on race politics in France and Britain, whereas Britain has emulated American antidiscrimination policy, France's race policy has also been articulated in opposition to the American model.[17] Likewise, French political leaders and journalists have rejected multiculturalism by appealing to anti-American rhetoric.[18] While France tends to be most vocal in its criticism of the United States, it is not alone in its suspicion of American hegemony. The impact of globalization on national identity and national cultural repertoire remains an understudied and promising topic for cultural sociologists.

NAMING SEXUAL HARASSMENT AS POLITICAL

In exploring how sexual harassment has been defined in the United States and France, this book has shed light on how social problems are defined in distinct national, institutional, and temporal contexts. The career of sexual harassment has thus provided a useful prism for understanding larger issues of how cultural meaning is created, how laws are made, and how laws shape society. However, it is important not to lose sight of the fact that the act of naming sexual harassment and the particular way this conduct is defined, as say, a social problem, a form of group-based discrimination, an act of violence, inappropriate behavior in certain places, or as a pretext for greedy plaintiffs to make money on lawsuits, has vast political implications. Indeed, it is because of these political implications that so many people care so deeply about how this issue is defined or if it is defined at all.

Before 1975, the behavior we now call "sexual harassment" had no name. As such, it was difficult to denounce. Rather than see themselves as victims of illegal behavior, most women, American or French, who lost their job because they refused to sleep with their boss or to tolerate sexist or sexual workplaces considered their situation unfair but inevitable. Today, American women in similar situations are more likely to feel that they have been wronged and to condemn the behavior. Few will go to court but many more will confront their harasser, speak to their friends, or report the behavior to management. Of course, many American women continue to suffer in silence or quit their job rather than stay and fight, but they have more options than they would have had thirty years ago. Potential harassers and employers are also more likely to censure themselves or their employees due to heightened concern about sexual harassment.

In France, where sexual harassment is less of a concern, victims face greater obstacles than their American counterparts in defending themselves against unwanted sexual advances and in denouncing sexist and sexually-tinged work environments. The fact that, until very recently, French sexual harassment law only prohibited situations in which a boss uses his authority to coerce an employee into having sexual relations with him or a third party has made it difficult for French women to condemn the kind of sexual or sexist innuendo that has fallen short of sexual harassment as legally defined. Nonetheless, French women also have more resources today than they had twenty years ago.

Debates over what constitutes sexual harassment and how it should be addressed are fed by disagreement over more general issues, such as the role of women and men at home and at work, the relation of sexuality to power, the place of sexuality in the workplace, and the lines between public and private spheres. As long as these topics continue to be the object of heated debate, sexual harassment is likely to remain contested. As people and institutions take a stand on sexual harassment, defining it in particular ways and not others, these more general issues of concern are also clarified. In both the United States and France, the trend documented in the preceding pages has been to affirm that women do indeed have the right to work outside the home in an ambiance free from violence or discrimination. In both countries, sexual harassment laws and regulations strive to prevent powerful men from leveraging their professional authority to obtain sex, while American employer policies also attempt to limit hierarchically subordinate women's ability to translate their sexual appeal into professional advantages. In the United States, but not in France, employers have increasingly decided that sexuality has no place in the workplace and that employees' behavior is subject to a high level of surveillance.

One should expect future changes to build upon the legal, political, and cultural trends documented here. In the United States, sexual harassment will continue to be debated as a form of workplace discrimination, while in France it will be conceptualized in terms of sexual violence. However, as we have seen, these legal definitions are inherently multivalent and ambiguous, which provides the potential for social change. Thus, for instance, the list of groups that are protected from discrimination in the United States may grow or become more limited; and the concept of violence in French law may be extended to a wider range of emotional violence or restricted to a more narrow range of physical assault. While future trends will be largely shaped by existing legal institutions and traditions, they also will be fashioned by other institutions and key individuals, like the media, corporations, and social movement activists.

Plus ça change,
plus c'est la même chose

As this book was going to press, French lawmakers modified French sexual harassment statutes, which previously limited sexual harassment to sexual coercion from professional hierarchical superiors, to apply also to sexual pressure from coworkers. Around the same time, the first student mobilization on sexual harassment and the first lawsuit in higher education generated a series of articles in the French press. At first glance, these events seem to signal that French and American approaches to sexual harassment are converging and, indeed, in some ways they are. However, upon closer examination, these developments also reveal persistent national differences in legal and popular conceptions of sexual harassment.

The legal reforms further emphasized sexual harassment as a form of interpersonal violence rather than as a product of structural gender inequality or discrimination, as in the American legal frame. They left intact a legal system in which the harasser can be fined, imprisoned, and/or made to pay small compensatory damages to the victim but in which employer liability is limited.

As far as the developments in the university, the press reported quite extensively on a petition against sexual harassment in higher education and a criminal charge of sexual harassment and retaliation brought by a graduate student against her former dissertation advisor. The extent of press coverage these events generated is indicative of the centrality of intellectuals — particularly Parisian intellectuals — in French politics. The specific details of the student mobilization provide further evidence that international networks aid feminist political activity but that French feminist politics are local, as I argued in Chapter 1. This group of students seems to have been successful precisely because they had a sophisticated understanding of French political opportunities and constraints.

French media reporting on these events revealed that, unlike in the United States, where many universities no longer permit professors to have sexual relations with the students they supervise, French universities do not prohibit this practice. In fact, if French journalists are at all representative of popular opinion, many French still condone professors sleeping with their graduate students. French reporting on the petition and legal case also revealed that, although the media are now free to report on sexual harassment charges before initiation of prosecution, many French people still see this as an infringement on the defendant's "private life." Press reports on these events demonstrate that, despite legal reform, abuse of professional hierarchical power is still a central component in French popular understanding of sexual harassment. In fact, recent events suggest that for many French sexual harassment in graduate school is merely a product of underlying problems regarding professors' exorbitant power over their doctoral students. Finally, these events have shown that, as in 1992, anti-American discourse in 2002 remained a powerful rhetorical device for discrediting sexual harassment victims and their advocates in France.

FROM SEXUAL VIOLENCE TO MORAL HARASSMENT

The elimination of abuse of authority as a necessary condition for sexual harassment is remarkable when one recalls the resistance, only three years prior, with which certain lawmakers responded to attempts to add "pressures of any nature" — a more inclusive term than "orders," "threats," "constraints," or even "serious pressure" — to the penal code.

Surprisingly, while feminist activism was important to the story of the original French sexual harassment law, enactment of the 2002 amendment had little to do with feminist mobilization. French lawmakers passed the amendment as part of the larger modernization law *(la loi sur la modernisation sociale)*, which primarily concerned downsizing. More specifically, the sexual harassment amendment fell under Chapter II (Combat Against Moral Harassment at Work) of Title II (Work, Employment, and Professional Training) of this law. The main object of this chapter, as its title suggests, was to prohibit the newly conceptualized problem of *"moral* harassment."

Marie-France Hirigoyen coined the term "moral harassment" in her best-selling book of the same name, as was discussed briefly at the beginning of the Conclusion. The subtitle, "Perverse Everyday Violence," revealed the psychological perspective of the author, a practicing psychiatrist, psychoanalyst, and family psychotherapist, with French and American training in victimology (a subdiscipline of criminology that seeks to understand the process of victimization). The author framed moral harassment as a form of interpersonal violence, much as sexual harassment has been framed in French law and is understood by the French public:

> I deliberately chose to use the terms aggressor and aggressed, because violence is at stake, even if it is hidden, which tends to attack the identity of another person, and to take from him his individuality. It is a real process of moral destruction, which can lead to mental illness or suicide. I will also keep the denomination "perverse" because it clearly evokes the notion of abuse, which is the case with all perverse people. It begins with an abuse of power, continues with a narcissistic abuse in that the other loses all self esteem, and can sometimes lead to sexual abuse.[1]

Hirigoyen makes a persuasive argument, supported by excerpts from clinical cases, that emotional or psychological violence can be just as destructive as physical violence, thereby expanding the notion of violence itself. She then uses the term "moral harassment" to speak of this kind of abuse in its most general terms, arguing that "sexual harassment" is but a subset of "moral harassment."[2]

Hirigoyen defines moral harassment at work as "all abusive conduct, notably manifesting itself by behavior, words, acts, gestures, or writing that can harm *[porter atteinte à]* the personality, dignity or physical or psychic integrity of a person, put their employment at risk, or degrade their work climate."[3] These sorts of behavior would fall under the American notion of "hostile environment," if and only if one also showed that they were discriminatory based on race, color, religion, sex, or national origin, and constituted a condition of employment. However, as Hirigoyen does not frame moral harassment as a subset of discrimination, these conditions are not necessary for there to be moral harassment in her terms.

By lumping together sexual harassment with "perverse everyday violence" rather than with sex discrimination, violence against women, or even *sexual* violence, Hirigoyen effectively minimizes the sexual and gender component of sexual harassment, as she simultaneously reinforces the violence and interindividual component. While she focuses on moral harassment at work, she also discusses this phenomenon in the home. In other words, while Hirigoyen discusses how moral harassment can impair job performance, she does not make negative impact on job performance a prerequisite for moral harassment, as it is for sexual harassment under American law.

For Hirigoyen, moral harassment (and thus sexual harassment by extension) is a psycho-dynamic between individuals or between a group and an individual, not a product of structural inequalities. She notes, drawing on American literature, that employees often harass women and minorities precisely because they are women or minorities, but explains that this is because groups do not tolerate difference or that the individual target makes others jealous.[4] Her analysis is thus fundamentally psychological and interindividual rather than structural. For her, harassers are perverse rather than bigoted people.

The reception of *Harcèlement moral* is, of course, distinct from the book itself. The French press focused on Hirigoyen's conceptualization of moral harassment as a form of interpersonal violence, particularly in the workplace. On the other hand, it largely ignored Hirigoyen's specific discussion of *sexual* harassment, which draws heavily on American feminist and social scientific analyses. For instance, Hirigoyen states that sexual harassment "is not about obtaining sexual favors but marking one's power, considering the woman as a (sexual) object,"[5] thus contradicting French legal definitions of sexual harassment as being precisely about obtaining sexual favors. Likewise, drawing on American research in social psychology,[6] Hirigoyen talks about six different categories of sexual harassment, including "gender harassment, which consists of treating a woman differently because she is a woman, with sexist remarks or behavior,"[7] which is clearly not covered by French law. She also includes sexual assault as a type of sexual harassment, even though, according to French law, sexual harassment and sexual assault are two separate criminal offenses, the first involving verbal coercion and the second physical force. By noting that sexual blackmail is the only form of sexual harassment reprimanded in France, she reveals that she does not ground her conception of sexual harassment in French law.[8]

Under the influence of the media buzz generated by Hirigoyen's book, French lawmakers inscribed the following moral harassment statute into the penal code:

Art. 222–33–2. — The act of harassing another with repeated actions having as object or effect a degradation of work conditions susceptible to undermining that person's rights and dignity, altering that person's physical or mental health, or compromising their professional future, is punished by [a maximum of] one year of imprisonment and [a maximum] fine of 15,000 euros.

The moral harassment statutes in the labor code now state:

Art. L. 122–49. — No employee shall suffer repeated actions of moral harassment that have as their object or effect a degradation of work conditions susceptible to affect [the employee's] rights and dignity, to alter his or her physical or mental health, or to compromise his or her professional future.

No employee can be sanctioned, fired, or be the object of a direct or indirect[9] discriminatory measure, notably in matters of salary, training, change of title *[reclassement]*, position *[affectation]*, qualification, title *[classification]*, professional promotion, transfer, or contract renewal for having submitted or refusing to submit to acts defined in the preceding paragraph *[alinéa]* or for having witnessed such acts or having reported them.

Any rupture of the work contract that would result from [such harassment] or any contradictory disposition or act is void *[nul de plein droit]*.[10]

Art. L. 122–50. — Any employee having violated article L. 122–49 may face disciplinary sanctions.

Art. L. 122–51. — It is up to *[il appartient au]* the head of the company to take all dispositions necessary to prevent the actions targeted by article L. 122–49.

Art. L. 122–52. — In case of litigation relative to the application of articles L. 122–46 [Labor law on sexual harassment] and L. 122–49 [Labor law on moral harassment], the employee in question presents factual elements suggesting the existence of harassment. In light of these elements, it is incumbent on the defendant to prove that his acts do not constitute such harassment, and that his decision is justified by objective elements having nothing to do with harassment. The judge forms his conviction after having ordered, if needed, all measures of instruction that he considers useful.

In many ways, the rules outlined by these statutes look very similar to those developed in American sexual harassment jurisprudence. Unlike in the case of sexual harassment, the labor code penalizes moral harassment itself and not just retaliation following moral harassment. It also discusses disciplinary sanctions and employer liability and puts the burden of proof on the employer, as did the American High Court decisions in *Burlington Industries v. Ellerth* and *Faragher v. City of Boca Raton*.[11]

However, the moral harassment labor statutes, L. 122–50 and L. 122–51, copy word-for-word the language used to address employer liability for sexual harassment, which has proven to be very weak in practice. Only time will tell if, through legal practice and/or pressure from the European Union,[12] plaintiff lawyers are able to actually hold employers liable in labor court for moral harassment or for retaliation linked to moral or sexual harassment. Without the particular system of tort remedies involving high compensatory and punitive damages, however, sexual harassment is unlikely to become as costly to French employers as it has been for many American companies. For the moment, it is safe to say economic incentives for internal regulations and sexual harassment training remain low in France. Moreover, sexual and moral harassment are also criminal infractions for which the individual harasser is held responsible and for which the courts alone (and not employers) are seen as legitimate arbitrators in France. This will probably continue to undermine employer responsibility for workplace harassment.

Finally, the modernization law adds a labor code statute (Art. L. 122–54) that allows employees who feel they are being harassed to bring in an outside mediator instead of going to labor court. The mediator's job, according to this statute, would be to gather information about the "state of relations between the two parties," to "try to reconcile" the harasser and the harassed person, and to "offer written suggestions for ending the harassment." If this fails, the mediator is to inform both parties of the possible sanctions and the procedural guarantees in the victim's favor. By treating sexual harassment as an interpersonal conflict rather than as an illegal assault, this statute minimizes the gravity of harassment and undermines the sexual violence frame of French penal law, as Catherine Le Magueresse, the current president of the AVFT, has pointed out.[13]

The moral harassment laws were modeled largely after French sexual harassment laws. To the extent that they differed from the latter, they spurred lawmakers to revise the sexual harassment laws. Most notably, lawmakers expanded the sexual harassment penal statute to apply to coworkers as well as hierarchical superiors, as was the case with the moral harassment law. According to the National Assembly Report (Terrier 2001):

> This article [on sexual harassment], adopted by the National As-
> sembly in the second round, aims to make the dispositions relative
> to sexual harassment consistent with those relative to moral harass-
> ment. Sexual harassment today is limited to behavior of a hierarchi-
> cal superior. This restrictive condition is eliminated.

The amendment thus reinforced the framing of sexual harassment as a form of interpersonal violence — rather than, say, group-based employment discrimination — as it simultaneously enlarged the scope to include harassment among coworkers. It appears that Hirigoyen's best-selling book was powerful enough to lead to a reconfiguration of the category of violence so that it could henceforth accommodate hostile environment harassment. Once the moral harassment law, clearly modeled on the sexual harassment law, was passed, the Cartesian logic of the French legal system "kicked in," dictating that the sexual harassment statute be revised so that the two statutes would be consistent.

Why lawmakers were more open to addressing coworker moral harassment in the first place, when they had not been willing to do so previously in the case of sexual harassment, is a question that warrants further study. I expect that it is because there are many people in France and elsewhere who still believe that (hetero)sexual desire is "always violent . . . often unilateral, and often harassing."[14] Moral harassment, however, was not about sex per se and therefore, I would speculate, lawmakers were more willing to ban it, even among coworkers. Perhaps they did not anticipate how the moral harassment law would lead to changes in the sexual harassment laws.

The newly revised sexual harassment statute in the French labor code states that "No employee can be penalized or dismissed for having submitted or refusing to submit to acts of harassment of any person whose goal is to obtain favors of a sexual nature for his own benefit or for the benefit of a third party." The revised penal code statute[15] would punish "the act of harassing another for the purpose of obtaining sexual favors" with a maximum fine of 15,000 euros and/or a maximum prison term of one year.

IVORY POWER

In January 2002, a group of graduate students launched a petition against sexual harassment in higher education, and a graduate student brought criminal charges of sexual harassment against her former dissertation advisor, a well-known Parisian intellectual. These events generated a flurry of articles in the leading French newspapers and newsmagazines. The extent of reporting revealed the centrality of Paris and of Parisian academics in French politics.

The details of the political formation of the group that launched the petition, CLASCHES (Collectif de Lutte Anti-Sexiste Contre le Harcèlement dans l'Education Supérieur [Collective for the anti-sexist fight against harassment in higher education]), showed that international feminist networks continued to facilitate mobilization but that actual political activity was still taking place on a very local level. It appears that CLASCHES has been so successful precisely because its members — students of sociology and gender *in France* — understood how to take advantage of French political opportunities and to adapt to political constraints.

In the petition, CLASCHES argued that the penal code was "indispensable" but "largely insufficient" and urged universities to "provide themselves with the means to fight against sexual harassment." Specifically, the petition demanded that universities: "(1) immediately clarify and disseminate information relative to sexual harassment and notably the law that punishes it; and (2) put in place disciplinary regulations and qualified commissions, including representation from students."[16]

According to a CLASCHES member who wishes to remain anonymous,[17] the group grew out of a friendship network among sociology graduate students who were in a reading group on theoretical approaches to gender. Over dinner, a few friends in this reading group began to discuss the sexism and sexual violence they had experienced. One spoke of sexist advertisements in the streets. Another told of how a "crazy guy" recently attacked her as she was leaving the subway. Others shared similar stories. It was in this context that they discussed cases they knew of where professors used their power to pressure their students into having sexual relations with them. The group, which studied issues of gender inequality and sexual violence, talked about how incredible it was that this sort of thing existed in their schools where they worked. "Are we going to let this go on without doing anything?" they asked. "If we don't address this, who will?" "Women's groups are rare in universities," one CLASCHES member explained, "and the student unions are not feminist."

As was the case in the 1990s, international feminist networks continued to be important in facilitating social mobilization in 2002. The morning after this discussion, several of the students in the gender studies reading group attended a colloquium. A panelist from Switzerland was part of a feminist group, Bad Girls Go Everywhere, which had supported a Swiss student in a sexual harassment lawsuit against her professor. The Swiss panelist described to some of the French students how Bad Girls Go Everywhere had proceeded and the obstacles they ran into, particularly around the legal case, which the plaintiff lost. The discussion further motivated the French students to act. It also served as a warning to them that they should not define their group around a legal case, because if the plaintiff were to lose, this could discredit the group itself. In general, the discussion with the Swiss panelist helped the French students reflect upon the social mechanisms that protect sexual harassers.

At the end of December, the students decided to form a collective and chose the name "CLASCHES." They chose to maintain their anonymity and to start a petition, which they wrote in January. They found the AVFT website particularly helpful as a legal guide, as none of the group members had legal training. "It was good to know that there was an existing association fighting this problem; otherwise, it would have been too discouraging," said one CLASCHES member.

With training in sociology and women's studies, the CLASCHES members had closely studied previous French women's movements, had seen the conditions under which they succeeded, and were aware of common political obstacles. They brought this knowledge to bear on their own mobilization. In mid-January, one CLASCHES member's professor was planning to speak about the status of doctoral students to professors at a meeting of the ASES (Association des Sociologues Enseignants du Supérieur [Association of teaching sociologists of higher education]). He encouraged her to present the CLASCHES petition there. CLASCHES chose a particular member of the group to present the petition along with a text the collective had prepared, as she was "calm" and "composed," far from the image of the "hysterical feminist."

After the presentation, the audience erupted in applause. The attending professors said that the group had spotlighted a major issue. Some said that they had encountered cases in the past but had felt powerless to act; others said they had been unaware of this problem. CLASCHES collected eighty signatures from ASES members that day. Soon afterwards, on 21 January 2002, with the help of a new member's boyfriend, they built a website to collect more signatures.

The site up and running, they made contact with a journalist at *Libération* and another at *Le Monde*. The CLASCHES members drew on their background in feminist history to carefully engineer the image they gave the journalists. They exaggerated both the numbers of total students in the group and the proportion that were male. They stressed that they had a critical perspective because they were sociology students but were less forthcoming about the fact that they worked in women's studies as well. They adopted this strategy so as not to be dismissed out of hand, but some were also concerned about the liabilities associated with not engaging in a feminist discourse. "I agreed at the beginning," said one, "but as time progressed, [this strategy] began to bother me. We had to choose our allies, and I wanted to be sure we were aligned with other feminist groups. We ran the risk of isolating ourselves. Now that we're accepted, it's important to get a feminist perspective across."

CLASCHES was pleased with the first article published in *Libération*,[18] the first of many in the leading newspapers and newsmagazines, but the group found it challenging to work with the media. According to one member:

> They wanted testimonies from sexually harassed students and told us that we weren't credible if we couldn't provide them. We worried that they would write "trash." There was pressure, even blackmail, in that we weren't sure they would communicate our message [unless we provided sensationalist copy]. It was as if they were saying, "We want to talk about [CLASCHES] but we want to talk about sex."

Those members of the group who were working most closely with the media thought that, without the media, they couldn't reach their goals and began to internalize the journalists' arguments, particularly that they were not credible without testimonies. Those who were in contact with unions and the Minister of Education did not see the media as so crucial. After a heated debate within the group, they finally decided not to accept any television invitations because they thought this format was too prone to sensationalism.

A SEXUAL HARASSMENT SCANDAL

The petition and the support it received [19] were in themselves newsworthy in a context where the existence of sexual harassment in France was minimized in general and in higher education in particular. The mass media interest, however, was heightened when it received an anonymous package containing a sexual harassment complaint filed in criminal court by doctoral student Sandrine Bertaux. In it she accused Professor Hervé Le Bras, a high-profile academic closely associated with the Socialist Party, of having retaliated when she refused to have a sexual relationship with him.[20]

Three factors explain why such a scandal erupted at this moment and not before. First and crucially, it had only been a year since the Cour de Cassation (French High Court) overturned a law forbidding the mass media from reporting on joint criminal and civil charges before prosecution.[21] Before this important decision, no respected news media would have reported on this case before prosecution began. Second, there would have been no charges to discuss if the plaintiff had not had the economic and cultural resources to fight back through the courts. The daughter of two academics, Sandrine Bertaux was unusually well placed, compared to most sexually harassed students, to bring charges against her professor. Finally, the fact that Bertaux's charges targeted a well-known and highly respected academic, politically active in antiracist politics, may have heightened the press's interest in the case. This made the story shocking and thus newsworthy. According to a member of CLASCHES:

> We tried absolutely everything to avoid the amalgam between us
> and Sandrine. It would be like in Switzerland. It would become for
> or against Le Bras, who had more power that he could use to prevail.
> We made an enormous rhetorical effort to say that the petition and
> her case were not linked.

The mass media, however, had different interests. For them, the personal drama was compelling and had high sales value.

In these respects, this media scandal was similar to American sexual harassment scandals of the 1990s, which also involved high-profile defendants, plaintiffs with the means to sue them (although contingency fees can aid American plaintiffs), and laws that allow reporting on criminal and civil charges. Yet, in many other ways, the manner in which the French media discussed both the petition and the legal charges revealed persistent national differences in how people — including journalists — view the issue of sexual harassment. First, some of the reporting suggested that the exchange of sexual relations for job advantages is still common and accepted in many French circles. Second, while French newspapers can now report on sexual harassment charges before the court renders a decision, many French people (no doubt unaware of this legal change) still consider this practice to be an unacceptable encroachment into the defendant's private life. Third, in France, abuse of professional hierarchical power is still seen as a central component of sexual harassment, despite legal reform. In fact, for many, sexual harassment is merely a smokescreen for underlying (gender-neutral) problems like the exorbitant power of professors over their students. Finally, the media coverage of the CLASCHES petition and the Bertaux charge reveal that those who wish to discredit sexual harassment victims and their advocates in France still use anti-American rhetoric to do so.

The discussion of the Bertaux case in the French media showed that many still view sexual harassment as a common and accepted practice. After writing what CLASCHES considered to be a fair and honest article about their petition, Blandine Grosjean, a journalist at *Libération*, wrote another that negatively portrayed Bertaux and CLASCHES and did precisely what CLASCHES had been trying so hard to avoid: it lumped the two separate events together as part of a coordinated movement.[22] One CLASCHES member remarked:

> When I saw the article by Grosjean, I thought that it was awful, total trash, loaded with clichés about how sexual harassment victims are "looking for what they get," and so on. I couldn't believe it. How could she seem like she understood us and write a good article and then write another one that was full of lies?

Though far from a social commentary on sexism in modern France, this article could be read as evidence that many French (including the journalist) still take for granted the fact that some professors exchange professional rewards for sexual relations:

> The [plaintiff's] laboratory colleagues demonstrated their cruelty to the young woman: "Sexual harassment in the university exists, and Sandrine is not a good victim for this battle," said one of them. "She

flirted with [Le Bras] for four years, moved up at an extraordinary pace thanks to him, while knowing full well what she was doing."

The implication of this statement and others that were recounted in the article is that the plaintiff "got what she had coming to her." She used her sexual attractiveness to advance professionally and should have expected to have to "foot the bill" at some point or another. This respondent, via the journalist and *Libération*, did not stress that it is unfair *and illegal* to create a system in which sexual relations or sex appeal is a criteria for distributing professional advantages, as have American university policies that prohibit relations between professors and the students they supervise. Rather, (s)he criticized women who try to benefit from such a system without paying the costs.

According to Robert Solé, an editor at *Le Monde*, it is difficult to define sexual harassment in higher education because normal relationships between professors and students are often quite intimate:

> Where does sexual harassment begin? The notion is complicated in a milieu as particular as higher education, where the relation between advisor [*maître*, literally "master"] and student is not limited to a hierarchical relationship between adults of different ages: it is also based on intellectual seduction and often emotional or sexual seduction [*séduction amoureuse*], in one direction or the other. By wanting to define the limits and by trying to control relations between the sexes, certain American campuses have gone to ridiculous extremes.[23]

Many American universities have prohibited sexual relations between professors and the students under their direct supervision because they considered the imbalance of power too ripe for abuse. In a system where sexual relations between professors and the students they supervise are accepted, as in France, it is more difficult to police the boundaries of consensual and coerced relations.

According to a student at the Ecole Normale Supérieure, one of the most prestigious universities in France, "When you choose your dissertation advisor, you also get information about his attitude towards women. At the university, you know which dissertation advisors are looking for 'privileged relations.'"[24] This student, who said she was herself pressured by her advisor to enter into such a "privileged relation" with him, continued, "Thanks to the petition, I can for the first time name that which had overwhelmed me and made me want to leave the university."[25]

The Bertaux–Le Bras event also revealed that, unlike in the United States, many in France even viewed reporting on the scandal as illegitimate. The leading French newspapers' reports on Bertaux's accusations against Le Bras provoked an outcry among many, who said the press reports encroached onto Le Bras's private life. Roland Etienne, former director of the French School in Athens, wrote that he felt "indignation to see the name of a friend dragged in the mud based on a legal complaint that has yet to be investigated; anger to see a newspaper like *Le Monde*, which was considered serious and a guarantor of a certain public morality, stoop to the level of an English tabloid." Claude Levi denounced "a lamentable article" and declared that he would "renounce buying this newspaper that I have read for years until the ruling on this case, which, I have no doubt, will be published in the same place and with the same prominence." In the opinion of Clément Weill-Raynal, journalist at France 3 television station, *Le Monde* tarnished the reputation of a university professor "without any consideration for the familial and personal consequences that would obviously ensue."[26]

In a *Le Monde* opinion piece, Le Bras's lawyer, Francis Terquem, referred to the press reports as the "new inquisition."[27] According to him, journalists were wrong to discuss "the private life of a man who, while an academic, is also a husband and a father" in "the columns of a respected daily paper" because they were incited to do so by "anonymous and evil-doing hands."[28] Le Bras himself referred to the accusations and reporting as a "manhunt" and said that "for five weeks I suffer like this with my family."[29] According to Le Bras: "Instead of discussing and criticizing my intellectual positions, one dissects a supposed private life, made up by an unhappy former student. Is this a way to contribute to the progress of justice and scientific research?"

One would expect Le Bras and his supporters to criticize Sandrine Bertaux's charge of sexual harassment. However, the fact that they challenged the press's discussion of the case at all reveals the extent to which such reporting is still unusual and not yet socially accepted in the French context. The particular content of these letters and editorials also demonstrates that arguments about the sanctity of the alleged harasser's "vie privée" are still persuasive in the French context.

In response to the letters cited above, *Le Monde* responded with an editorial by Robert Solé, mentioned above. Solé explained that, since February 2001 when the French High Court overturned the law that prevented the mass media from reporting on uninvestigated accusations, *Le Monde* had reported on several such charges, including one against a judge, another against Parisian police, and one involving Prime Minister Jospin. None of these were sexual harassment cases, however, which *Le Monde* is not in the habit of covering, according to Solé. "The subject of the reporting was especially unusual," he continued, "in that it involved a case against a politically involved academic in a prestigious university."[30] He admitted that reporting on such cases is tricky:

> It did not escape the editorial board that by making Sandrine
> Bertaux's complaint public, it was adventuring onto delicate ter-
> rain. In this type of affair, establishing the truth is not always easy.
> It's her word against his. Media coverage can seriously harm the
> accused, as it can harm the plaintiff.

Solé affirmed that *Le Monde* decided to publish this article because Bertaux's case, known in the small world of research, was a "first" and "had no reason to be hidden. After the investigation by the two authors, publication of the names seemed less hypocritical than an allusive article." Nonetheless, Solé added, apologetically, that the press "shouldn't have put the name of Hervé Le Bras in the title, knowing that rushed readers won't read any farther," and that "Sandrine Bertaux's charges were accompanied by and illustrated a collective process. They should have been published on the same day and on the same page as the petition." Associating the complaint with the petition, Solé thus affirmed the claims of Le Bras supporters: that the petition and the legal complaint were intentionally coordinated.

Media discussion of Bertaux's case also brought to the fore the centrality of professional hierarchical power, as opposed to gender inequality, in popular French understandings of sexual harassment. Bertaux's legal charges and subsequent media reports focused on the type of power dissertation advisors have over their students, and specifically on the extent of Le Bras's control over Bertaux. According to Bertaux's formal legal complaint, Le Bras's resignation as outside reviewer and member of her dissertation committee and his refusal to continue serving as an advisor, mentor, and reference was damaging retaliation because she refused his sexual advances. Bertaux's complaint cited other retaliatory measures, including Le Bras's demands that she return a laptop his laboratory had purchased for her research. In contrast, Le Bras claimed that he had no power over Bertaux because he was no longer her official dissertation advisor at the time she filed her complaint, so that he had "no hierarchical power over the doctoral candidate."[31]

In that the 2002 modernization law was not retroactive, Bertaux's lawyer had to prove that Le Bras abused his authority with the goal of obtaining sexual favors from his student. However, other commentators, who were not bound by law to stress the professional hierarchical dimension, also focused on this aspect of the problem, as opposed to, say, gender or sexual power. In an article published in *Libération* on 4 February 2002, Elisabeth Zucker-Rouvillois argued that "beyond sexual harassment, it's the exorbitant power of dissertation advisors that is condemnable."[32] Likewise, Pascal Degiovanni, president of the Dissertation Candidates Guild and Nicolas Legrand, president of the Student-Researchers Confederation argued in a *Libération* op-ed on 8 March 2002 that sexual harassment was part of larger problems in the advisor-advisee relationship.[33] The fundamental issues, for these authors, included ill-defined expectations, the advisee's extreme dependence on the advisor, insufficient guidance, and the lack of efficient mediation in cases of conflict.

They suggested that resolving these "universal," or non gender-specific, problems would get at the root of conflicts linked to abuse of authority, including sexual harassment. In other words, as French social commentators and policy makers have done in the past, the authors of this piece glossed over the specific problems of sexual inequality, sexism, and sexual violence. Yet a sexual harassment victim may receive a great deal of — too much — attention from her advisor and may be given enormous freedom to pursue exciting professional avenues, but only under the condition that she engage in flirtatious or sexual behavior with him.

Le Bras's lawyer also argued that the real problem in higher education was the "mandarin" structure and the arbitrary nature of power in the university, "of which women are not the only victims."[34] "Everyone knows that scientific and pedagogic competence is only one only criteria of recruitment among many others, such as manners, fortune, relations, and [social] origins," argued Le Bras's lawyer. He continued by noting that "if it's about leading this battle against the excesses of the mandarin system and for a democratic reform of the university, Hervé Le Bras has always been on the front lines." Though Terquem implied that if Le Bras was for class struggle he had to be also against sexual harassment, a competing analysis exists: that class struggle and the struggle for gender equality remain two quite distinct battles, and thus a person can be active in one but not the other.

Finally, reporting on the petition and the Bertaux–Le Bras case revealed that opponents still used anti-American rhetoric to discredit sexual harassment victims and their advocates. For instance, the second article by Blandine Grosjean published in *Libération*[35] and mentioned above affirmed:

> The petition started by the collective has been transformed into a reading of "for" or "against" Le Bras; and many intellectuals, not all friends of Le Bras, far from that, worry today about the procedural

excess *à l'américaine* of its creators. The latter pushed Sandrine
Bertaux to bring her case to court.

More than one respected news source propagated the myth that
CLASCHES manipulated Bertaux into pressing charges, despite ample
evidence to the contrary.[36] In fact, Bertaux addressed a formal complaint
to the university in September 2002.[37] The university, which had no
rules on the books concerning sexual harassment, transmitted her complaint to the Ministry of Education, which did nothing, prompting the
student to file criminal charges on 28 December.[38] The CLASCHES
petition was not made public until 28 January, a full month *after* Bertaux
filed her charges and several months after she complained to the president of her university.[39]

Yet an article in *Le Point* (falsely) reported that people with ulterior
motives — and under the sway of American "political correctness" —
manipulated Sandrine Bertaux:

> Eric Fassin, one of the importers in France of "politically correct"
> thinking, emailed her on 4 November. He said that he could not
> speak about the legal value of her problems with Le Bras, but that
> the justice system was not the only alternative, that she could, for
> example, solicit the media. Eric Fassin is not moved only by compas-
> sion. He had prepared a petition, Clashes [sic.], destined to warn
> about the poison of sexual harassment in the French universities.
> A petition without a concrete case, complaint, without testimony,
> that's thin. With the "Le Bras affaire," it's better.[40]

Eric Fassin is a sociologist of sex and gender and a French specialist on the
United States who has published articles and opinion pieces on sexual
harassment since 1991.[41] It was not Fassin, however, but the collective
CLASCHES that organized the sexual harassment petition, although
Fassin — like many others — signed it and officially supported it in an editorial published in *Le Monde*.[42] Moreover, in his 4 November email, mentioned but not cited in this article, Fassin actually advised Bertaux to think
for herself and to consider her own self-interest: "You can't renounce the

lawsuit to please certain people, but you can't begin one to please others. . . . I believe that a victim of harassment needs first to recover her freedom of decision." The article, however, did not cite this email or mention how the journalist obtained it. (A "friend" and colleague to whom Fassin sent a copy leaked it to the press.[43]) According to Fassin, the journalist did not try to contact him for an interview, in which she could have verified the independence of the petition and the correct acronym of the collective.[44] Instead, the article appears to have been politically motivated and to have labeled Fassin an "importer of politically correct thought" in order to discredit him and, by association, the petition.

Francis Terquem, Le Bras's lawyer, also resorted to anti-American rhetoric to discredit the plaintiff, referring to the "Anglo-Saxon [a euphemism for American] fashion" of making public "simple accusations that can contain a number of falsehoods." According to the members of CLASCHES, their opponents explained to them that "sexual harassment is a muddy concept, a fantasy based on the 'American example.'"[45] As mentioned above, *Le Monde*'s Robert Solé also spoke of how "certain American campuses have gone to ridiculous extremes" in their attempts to regulate sexual harassment.[46]

In response to these arguments, CLASCHES intentionally avoided invoking the American example, arguing instead that they wanted to enforce a *French* law. Likewise, the group made no mention of the fact that they were feminist or first began discussing this issue in a women's studies seminar. Similarly, Bertaux's lawyer argued in *Le Monde* that his client was involved in a classic "French story" of "*le droit de cuissage*," and that "sexual harassment did not surge into our French law as a clone thought up in Hollywood."[47] Similarly, Eric Fassin responded to accusations that he was an "importer of politically correct thinking" by pointing out that "demanding the application of the French law against sexual harassment, that's not 'importing.'"[48]

When one wishes to disqualify a point of view in the United States, one often labels it "communist," meaning "non-American," thus foreclosing further discussion.[49] The equivalent in France, as we have seen throughout this book, is to say one's opponents are trying to "Americanize" French society. Savvy political actors pushing for sexual harassment regulation in France have responded to such arguments for over a decade by stressing that their proposals are typically or quintessentially French, thus not American. Through this process, the nature of French culture evolves as its perceived "Frenchness" is preserved.

CONCLUSION

Studying legal and social definitions of sexual harassment is like shooting at a moving target. As this book was going to press, the French Parliament modified sexual harassment laws to apply to coworker harassment, and the first high-profile sexual harassment scandal erupted in the French press. At first glance, these events seem to suggest that France is beginning to resemble the United States in matters of harassment. However, as we have seen in this epilogue, important cross-national differences persist. Legal reform extended the French sexual harassment laws to coworker harassment but reinforced the French framing of sexual harassment as a form of interpersonal violence, rather than as an instance of group-based discrimination, and did little to strengthen employer liability. In 2002, the reporting and opinion columns revealed that anti-American rhetoric remained an important political strategy for discrediting those who tried to address the problem of sexual harassment in France. The media reporting further demonstrated that, for many French social commentators, there is nothing specific about sexism or sexual violence. Rather, for them, "universal" or gender-neutral questions of professors' power over students and class inequalities are the fundamental problems at stake.

Methodological Details

This book was based on multiple sources of data, collected using a range of quantitative and qualitative methods, which were only briefly discussed in the main text. These include: (1) content analysis of the major French and American sexual harassment legal texts, including statutes and jurisprudence; (2) a series of short telephone interviews with representatives of twenty-three French branches of large multinational corporations; (3) fifty-four in-depth interviews with French and American feminist activists, public figures, lawyers, human resource personnel, and union activists; and (4) an original data set of 681 articles on sexual harassment in six leading French and American newspapers and newsmagazines. The legal analysis and telephone interviews are described in sufficient detail in Chapters 1 and 2. In what follows, I provide greater detail about the in-depth interviews and media analysis. I conclude with a general discussion of how I tried to maximize both inside knowledge of American and French culture and the fresh perspective of an outsider.

The Interviews

I interviewed twenty lawyers, twelve activists, and six public figures, divided evenly between France and the United States. I also interviewed a total of sixteen human resource managers and representatives, general managers, and union activists from American and French branches of an American multinational

("AmeriCorp") and from American and French branches of a French multinational ("Frenchco").

I interviewed sixteen activists between 1995 and 1997. The activists, all women, were members of one of two national associations — the Association Européenne Contre les Violences Faites aux Femmes au Travail (AVFT [European Association Against Violence Toward Women at Work]) in France, and 9to5 National Association of Working Women in the United States.

The AVFT and 9to5 are the main nonprofit organizations that provide assistance to victims of sexual harassment in each country. The activities of both of these organizations include but are not limited to: lobbying, raising public awareness, providing legal advice and emotional support to victims, and research on sexual harassment, other forms of gender discrimination, or violence toward women. The AVFT is based in Paris, though its activists receive calls from and meet with people outside of Paris.[1] Four of the AVFT members interviewed were paid employees and two were volunteering at the time of the interview. Half of the 9to5 members were volunteers and half were paid employees based in cities across the United States.

It is worth mentioning that 9to5 and the AVFT are neither representative of American and French society at large nor of American and French women's movements. The active involvement of these associations in fighting for women's rights at work differentiates them from the general population. While they are actively engaged in improving women's lives, many 9to5 and AVFT members did not call themselves "feminists." The AVFT does identify itself as a feminist association, but 9to5 does not. The AVFT's official line is that both pornography and prostitution should be prohibited, a position that is not shared by many other French feminist groups.

I also interviewed six "public figures" between 1995 and 1996, who I expected would understand sexual harassment differently. Each was considered by the media to be an "expert" on issues of gender and sexuality in general or sexual harassment in particular, yet they had diverse approaches to these issues. Like the activists, these "public figures," many of whom are or have been activists, have also been engaged in a public contest over the meaning of sexual harassment. The arguments they deployed are therefore interesting, not because they are representative of the general population, which they are not, but because they are innovative and have an important societal impact through diffusion by the mass media and higher education.

The three American public figures include theorist, lawyer, and law professor Catharine MacKinnon; social critic and professor of humanities Camille Paglia; and lawyer, syndicated columnist, radio commentator, and national spokesperson for the conservative movement Phyllis Schlafly. The three French public figures include intellectual and activist Marie-Victoire Louis; writer, social critic, and professor of philosophy Elisabeth Badinter; and former Secretary of Women's Rights and author Françoise Giroud.[2]

Catharine MacKinnon is known worldwide for her pioneering and influential legal writings, especially on sexual harassment — the term she is most responsible for promoting — and pornography. Her 1979 book *Sexual Harassment of Working Women*, has greatly informed sexual harassment law in the United States. In the mass media, Camille Paglia and Phyllis Schlafly are among the most vocal critics of this legal interpretation, its political and social implications, and what they perceive to be "American feminism." Camille Paglia has received enormous media attention for her provocative theories of gender and sexuality and her virulent criticism of "mainstream American feminism."[3] Since the 1970s, Phyllis Schlafly has been a more traditional opponent of "American feminism." Speaking on behalf of the Christian Right, she has argued that the women's movement undermines "traditional values" of the family and female domesticity.

Elisabeth Badinter is a well-known intellectual, closely affiliated with the French Socialist Party (her husband, Robert Badinter, is a Socialist politician), who studies male-female social relations in France and is often interviewed by the mass media on subjects concerning gender.[4] In addition to having served as Secretary of Women's Rights in 1974–76 under President Giscard d'Estaing (U.D.F.), Françoise Giroud is a nationally renowned writer and editor, has published abundantly on the topic of gender and sexuality, and is often cited in the mass media.[5] Marie-Victoire Louis is a self-identified radical feminist, scholar, and activist who represents a vocal challenge to the French establishment. In 1985, she co-founded the AVFT, which led the campaign for a sexual harassment law, and was serving as president of this association in 1995, when the interview was conducted. In *Le droit de cuissage*, she explored the French history of sexual violence toward women.

Obviously, the women I interviewed do not come in perfectly comparable pairs. I consider Catharine MacKinnon and Marie-Victoire Louis to be most analogous in their analysis of sexual harassment, although they differ on several points. Moreover, both MacKinnon and Louis wrote pioneering books in their respective countries on this topic and fought for laws that would provide legal recourse for victims of sexual harassment. Both also lead a life of activism and scholarship, MacKinnon in law and Louis in social science. Finally, both women are self-defined feminists. MacKinnon's impact has, nonetheless, been greater than Louis's.

The violent criticisms Camille Paglia has launched at "American feminists" are the closest I found to the anti-American feminist discourse used by Elisabeth Badinter, Françoise Giroud, and others.[6] Both Badinter and Paglia identify themselves with feminism and the Left. Yet other American self-defined feminists call Paglia's politics "anti-feminist,"[7] and other French women who call themselves feminist have questioned Badinter's feminism in personal discussions or reactions to earlier versions of this book. I interviewed Phyllis Schlafly because of her prominent position within a movement that has had considerable sway over gender issues in the United States. I did not interview a similar figure from the French Right because I could find no one from a comparable movement who had made any public statement on sexual harassment, and my criteria of selection was participation in a public debate.

Between 1996 and 1997, I conducted in-depth interviews with ten French and ten American lawyers about their definitions of sexual harassment. I used two sources to build my sample of ten French lawyers. Four lawyers were referred by the AVFT. Two lawyers were referred by the Barreau des Avocats de Paris (the Parisian bar association), who in turn each referred me to two of their colleagues who had argued sexual harassment cases. Note that the respondents said that, because of the marginality of this issue in France, this relatively small sample of ten represented almost the whole universe of lawyers having argued sexual harassment cases in the greater Paris area at the time. Among the French lawyers, seven were men and three were women.

To maximize comparability, I mimicked in the United States the sampling method used in France, although there are a plethora of sexual harassment lawyers working here. Representatives of 9to5 from Philadelphia, Boston, and Atlanta referred me to one, two, and three local lawyers, respectively. I also asked the New Jersey Bar Association for referrals but was told that they only make referrals to potential clients, not researchers. The representative of the bar association told me to look in the phone book for names of lawyers working in this area. Using the Princeton–Suburban Trenton area and Manhattan phonebooks, I contacted an additional five lawyers. Six of the American lawyers were women and four were men.

I conducted sixteen interviews at AmeriCorp and Frenchco between 1997 and 1998. I selected respondents who were or would be held responsible for dealing with cases of sexual harassment, according to their own account and the account of others in their workplace. Among the sample of corporate respondents, eight were men and eight were women. The gender ratio was also roughly equal in each of the four work sites.

Due to national and corporate differences, there were some discrepancies in job titles across workplaces. In the American office of AmeriCorp, I interviewed three human resource managers. In the American branch of Frenchco, I interviewed the director of human resources for the entire country, another human resource manager, a human resource representative, and the manager of a large division. Likewise, I interviewed a personnel director in both the French office of AmeriCorp and the French office of Frenchco and two personnel representatives in the French office of AmeriCorp.

As is typical of larger national trends, while neither of these firms is unionized in the United States, they are both unionized in France, where unions play a central role in personnel disputes. Thus several people told me that if an incident of sexual harassment were to arise there, union representatives would be among those asked to intervene. I interviewed three union representatives in the French office of Frenchco and two in the French office of AmeriCorp.

In the French office of AmeriCorp, personnel representatives, who are employees elected yearly by their peers,[8] also play an advisory role in the firm. There is a higher proportion of women among the personnel representatives than in the more powerful unions. Because most sexual harassment victims, who are more likely to be female than male, prefer to discuss this issue with other women, I interviewed two female personnel representatives at the French branch of AmeriCorp.

I regard all of the respondents as cultural entrepreneurs. Unlike the general population, of which they are *not* representative, each of the people interviewed has been actively engaged in shaping the public meaning of sexual harassment.

The interviews lasted between thirty minutes and three hours, averaging about one hour and a half. I began each interview by asking: "How do you define sexual harassment?" I then asked the respondent whether or not she or he considered the legal definition appropriate. We explored any reservations the respondent had with national sexual harassment law, including prescribed remedies. In applicable cases, I asked respondents about their jobs and the types of cases they had encountered. I asked them to discuss their most difficult cases, especially those that seemed to defy the qualification "sexual harassment." This question revealed contradictions in legal and social definitions of this term.

I also presented respondents with a series of vignettes that described behavior that might be labeled sexual harassment.[9] The vignettes were used to see how the respondents reacted to specific situations, rather than abstract categories. After reading the story, I asked: "Is this sexual harassment? Why or why not?" The vignettes prompted respondents to offer a variety of arguments.

Feminist research, legal theory, and recorded cases provided the inspiration for my vignettes.[10] By systematically varying the hypothetical people's motives, gender, hierarchical position, sexual orientation, and relationships with each other, the vignettes were useful in revealing the respondents' criteria of evaluation. Using the vignettes, I also examined how closely the respondents followed the letter of their national law. At the phase of data analysis, using full interview transcripts, I systematically compared how each respondent evaluated the vignettes.

Media Analysis

Chapter 3, "Representation of Sexual Harassment in the Press: National Scandal, Pride, or Superiority?" draws chiefly on an original data set of 681 articles on sexual harassment in six leading French and American newspapers and newsmagazines. Below I describe how the media sample was collected and analyzed.

The media sample was drawn from the newspapers *The New York Times* and *Le Monde*,[11] and the newsmagazines, *Time, Newsweek, L'Express* and *Le Nouvel Observateur*.[12] The sample begins with the first articles to use this term, coined only in 1975, and stops on 31 December 2000. The *New York Times* and *Newsweek* are available on Nexus after 1975. Nexus includes all issues from *Time* and *Le Monde* beginning in 1981 and 1990, respectively. For these publications, I used the "hlead" function in Nexus to select those articles published during the available years that included the term "sexual harassment" or its French equivalent, "*harcèlement sexuel*," in any of the headings or leading paragraphs. A research assistant did a manual search for *Time* for the years 1975–81. I searched the comprehensive archive on sexual harassment at AVFT for articles published prior to 1990 in *Le Monde* and found none, which is confirmed by previous research.[13]

Through a serendipitous contact with a journalist at *L'Express*, I was able to use the in-house electronic archives to select all articles containing the words "*harcèlement*" and "*sexuel*" from January 1992 until December 1998. For the years 1999 and 2000, which I collected in January 2001, I used *L'Express* archives, which were by then publicly available on the Internet. For all years, I retained only those articles that, like the Nexus sample, included the term "*harcèlement sexuel*" in the heading or lead paragraphs. The *Express* journalist used another in-house database and paper archives to search for articles on the subject from 1987–92. Although she did find two articles published in this time period, I did not retain them in the sample because the term "*harcèlement sexuel*" did not appear in the heading or lead paragraphs in either instance. I did not search articles published in *L'Express* before 1987. However, previous research suggests that *L'Express* did not publish anything before this time.[14]

When I did the first round of data collection, electronic archives of the *Nouvel Observateur* were only available over the Internet for issues after January 1996. For these years, I used a key-word search to select all articles in which the term "*harcèlement sexuel*" appears. I then retained only those articles where this term appeared in the headings or lead paragraphs. I did a manual search using microfilm for *Nouvel Observateur* articles published from 1990–96 and included in my sample only those articles in which the term "*harcèlement sexuel*" appeared in the headings and leading paragraphs. I used the same search criteria in January 2001 to search the public archives (by then available on the Internet) for the years 1999 and 2000. For the years before 1990, I relied on the AVFT archives.

Such a key-word search method misses some articles that discuss sexual harassment without using the exact term "sexual harassment." This method is nonetheless preferable to others because the purpose of this study is precisely to trace the evolving meaning of the term "sexual harassment." The "hlead" method is a useful mechanism for narrowing the sample to articles in which sexual harassment is the main theme. Nevertheless, this method inevitably misses some articles in which sexual harassment is the main topic but where the term appears later in the article. However, this should be equally true for all of the publications and should therefore not bias the sample. By using the "hlead" search method, one inevitably also selects some articles that are not about sexual harassment but employ the term in passing. I coded for whether a given article focused on sexual harassment, mentioned it in passing, or said nothing substantive about it at all, which allowed me to analyze these subsamples separately.

I conducted a stratified random sample by year of 25 percent of the *New York Times* articles and randomly sampled one half of the articles for all years for *Time* and *Newsweek*. For both magazines, the number of articles in the 50 percent sample is more than half that of the full universe. This is because in a few cases

Nexus grouped together several articles, such as letters to the editor, but I, in the coding process, considered each of these articles separately.

I chose to include a smaller proportion of *New York Times* articles than *Time* or *Newsweek* articles so that the number of *New York Times* articles would not entirely dwarf the number of magazine articles. However, this raises the question of whether, among the American publications, there is a significant effect of publication on the variables examined. I tested this for all of the variables discussed in Chapter 3. Articles in *Newsweek* and *Time* were significantly more likely than *The New York Times* to employ the following frames: politics, scandal, and women's issue. Therefore, by including proportionately more articles from the newsmagazines than from the newspaper, I have *overestimated* the prevalence of these frames in the American press. However, the same cross-national analyses of frames conducted on a random 25 percent sample of all of the American publications provided identical results. Because of their relatively small number, I retained all of the sampled articles from the French publications.

I coded each of the 681 articles for 144 variables. I describe below only those substantive variables that are examined in this book.[15] Articles that said nothing substantive about sexual harassment were coded 0 for the variable "aboutsh." Articles that mentioned sexual harassment but then proceeded to focus on another topic (such as Bill Clinton's consensual relationship with Monica Lewinsky) were coded 1 for "aboutsh." Finally, the majority of articles that focused on the topic of sexual harassment (at least half of the article is about sexual harassment) were coded 2 for this variable.

The variable "foreign" was coded as 0 if the article focused on the home nation and did not mention any other countries, 1 if it focused on the home nation but also discussed another nation or nations, and 2 if it focused on another country or countries. The "mirror" variable was coded as 0 in American articles that made no mention of France and French articles that made no mention of the United States; articles that did discuss the other country case were coded as 1 for the "mirror" variable.

I coded for whether the article focused on, mentioned, or did not discuss sexual harassment occurring in a particular place, such as the workplace, elementary school, college, the military, military school, prisons, housing, transportation, or the streets. I included dichotomous variables for four high-profile "scandals," including the Anita Hill–Clarence Thomas debates, the Packwood scandal, the Tailhook scandal, and Paula Jones's lawsuit against Bill Clinton.[16] I coded as 1 articles that mentioned the particular scandal, as 2 articles that focused on that particular high-profile case, or as 0 articles that made no mention of the given case.

I coded for the presence of different elements of sexual harassment frames, including women's issue, social problem, scandal, politics, power, sex discrimination, violence, morality, and making money on lawsuits. Each variable was coded 0 when neither the journalist nor anyone cited in the article presented sexual harassment, in general, or the particular incident of sexual harassment discussed in the article, as a problem of, say, sex discrimination. Each variable was coded as 1 when the journalist or someone cited did frame sexual harassment or the particular incident that way.

I used strict criteria to judge whether or not a given element was being used. For instance, in order to code the sex discrimination variable 1, it had to be *explicitly* stated somewhere in the article that sexual harassment was a form of sex discrimination. Likewise, in all articles that were coded 1 for power, or violence, there was explicit reference *by name* to these concepts in explaining the phenomenon of sexual harassment. Articles in which the morality variable was 1 used words like "puritanism" or stressed the marital status of those involved. The making-money-on-lawsuits frame was coded as 1 when the attitude was expressed in the article that sexual harassment plaintiffs in general, or a particular plaintiff, filed suit for the money.

The politics frame variable was coded as 1 when the article discussed sexual harassment in the light of struggles between political parties or on the fate of a politician or party (such as President Clinton's popularity in the wake of the Jones lawsuit). The scandal frame was coded as 1 when the article or someone quoted in the article framed sexual harassment in the context of a political scandal. For instance, many articles about the Paula Jones lawsuit against Bill Clinton said almost nothing about the phenomenon of sexual harassment, but instead reported on the effect of this scandal on Clinton's popularity. These were coded 1 on the scandal and politics frames. On the other hand, if an article used the Jones lawsuit to open a more general discussion on the prevalence of sexual harassment, this article was coded 0 on the scandal frame but 1 on the social problem frame. Finally, if the article discussed the Jones lawsuit as a political scandal for Clinton *and* continued by explaining that sexual harassment is a form of sex discrimination that affects many women, it would be coded as 1 on the scandal, social problem, *and* sex discrimination variables. A given article could thus be coded 1 for several frames.

For most categories, I included "other" variables to record information that I did not initially anticipate. When certain information recurred in the "other" box, I used this information to create new variables. After I coded about fifty articles, I systematically recoded five of the fifty, or 5 percent of the sample, and compared results. For any given article, I coded 0 to 5 variables differently, averaging 98 percent internal reliability. A research assistant coded 48 articles, 6 percent of which I also coded to test for intercoder reliability, which was 91 percent.

Working From Multiple Standpoints

In doing comparative cultural sociology, I have tried to strike a balance between the contextual knowledge of a social insider and the fresh perspective of an outsider. On the one hand, a certain amount of familiarity is necessary in order to be able to accurately portray the culture being studied. Otherwise the researcher is likely to misinterpret cultural cues. There is a great temptation to impose one's own worldview onto a foreign culture, completely losing sight of the latter's own coherent logic. This is a problem that anthropologists, who typically study "primitive" societies, have faced for years. In attempting to overcome this problem, some anthropologists have "gone native," or completely assimilated the values and customs of the society under study and, at the extreme, have become unable or unwilling to communicate with their culture of origin. The trick is to strike a balance between these two poles, so that one has enough knowledge to be able to make sense of social behavior but enough distance that the particular social rules need explaining.

Researchers studying their own culture encounter an obstacle similar to that faced by the anthropologist gone native. Because they subscribe to many of the same arbitrary cultural assumptions that govern the lives of the people they study, they are often unable to see these clearly. This is a problem typically faced by sociologists, who tend to study their country of residence. These researchers must learn to "make the familiar strange," in order to bring to the fore the taken-for-granted assumptions that need explaining. Many sociologists use comparative work in order to accomplish this task. By contrasting different historical periods, specific subcultures within a nation, or distinct countries, researchers can gain some leverage on cultural assumptions. Invariably, cultural perspectives differ in some way across the two cases, so that the comparison reveals the "strangeness," or arbitrary quality, of each.

Comparing one's own culture against another is analytically powerful and empirically useful. However, the trap inherent in this approach is that the researcher will consider the "other" society stranger than her own. She may inappropriately impose her social criteria on the other culture, while failing to see the ways in which her social expectations are themselves strange, thereby reifying rather than analyzing her own taken-for-granted assumptions.

Because cultural repertoires are social products, an indispensable part of doing comparative cultural sociology research involves interacting — actually living — in each society under study. I have spent much of my life in the United States, where I attended American K–12, college, and graduate school. I learned French in high school and college, spent three weeks in the southern city of Toulon as part of a high school French exchange program, participated in a "semester abroad" in Paris, and spent a summer doing research on the French women's movement during college. I lived in France for an additional two years in 1992–94, during which time I completed a French masters degree in social science, jointly at the Ecole des Hautes Études en Sciences Sociales and at the Ecole Normale Supérieure.

After beginning the research for this book in 1995, I spent several months of each year in France. Some of that time was used to gather data, but an equal amount was spent discussing with French colleagues and friends how I was analyzing the data I had already collected. I had similar discussions with American colleagues, which were extremely valuable. However, it was often the discussions with my French colleagues and friends that forced my own taken-for-granted assumptions as an American to the fore, adding balance to my analysis. Daily discussions with my (French) husband have further enhanced my sensitivity to differences in American and French culture.

NOTES

INTRODUCTION

1. These events are recounted in *Harris v Forklift Systems*, 510 US 17 (1993).

2. *Harris v Forklift Systems*, 510 US 17 (1993).

3. *Harris v Forklift Systems*, 510 US 17, 17 (1993). See also Catharine Mac-Kinnon, *Sexual Harassment of Working Women* (New Haven, Conn.: Yale University Press, 1979).

4. *Barnes v Costle*, 561 F2d 983 (DC Cir 1977).

5. For a discussion of how sexual harassment has been defined in Austria, see Mia Cahill, *The Social Construction of Sexual Harassment Law* (Aldershot: Ashgate, 2001). For a discussion of sexual harassment in Sweden, see R. Amy Elman, *Sexual Subordination and State Intervention: Comparing Sweden and the United States* (Providence, R. I.: Berghahn Books, 1996). On Spain, see Celia Valiente, "Sexual Harassment in the Workplace: Equality Policies in Post-Authoritarian Spain," in *Politics of Sexuality: Identity, Gender, Citizenship*, ed. Terrell Carver and Veronique Mottier (London: Routledge, 1998), 169–79. On Germany, see Kathrina Zippel, "Comparative Perspectives of Sex Equality Policies in Germany, the European Union, and the United States: The Example of Sexual Harassment," Ph.D. diss., Department of Sociology, University of Wisconsin, Madison, 2000. On India, see Martha Nussbaum, "The Modesty of Mrs. Bajaj: India's Problematic Route to

Sexual Harassment Law," *New Directions in Sexual Harassment Law*, ed. Reva Siegel and Catharine MacKinnon (New Haven: Yale University Press, in press).

6. Code pénal [C. Pén.] art. 222–33 (Fr.). As this book was going to press, the French Parliament extended the French legal definition of sexual harassment to coworkers, suggesting that a threat of economic retaliation is no longer necessary for there to be sexual harassment. However, the sexual harassment labor statute *only* prohibits retaliation and not the sexual harassing behavior itself, and both the labor and penal statutes still define sexual harassment as "the act of harassing another for the purpose of obtaining sexual favors." It is unclear whether a judge would see Charles Hardy's behavior, as offensive as it was, as a plot to obtain "sexual favors" from Teresa Harris. As the French legal reform is not retroactive, it will be some time before we see the concrete impact of this reform. For a discussion of these legislative changes, see the Epilogue.

7. John Boli and George M. Thomas, "World Culture in the World Polity: A Century of International Non-Governmental Organization," *American Sociological Review* 62, no. 2 (1997): 171–90; See also John W. Meyer, John Boli, and George M. Thomas, "Ontology and Rationalization in the Western Cultural Account," in *Institutional Environments and Organizations: Structural Complexity and Individualism*, ed. Richard Scott and John Meyer (Thousand Oaks, Calif.: Sage, 1994); John W. Meyer, David Kamens, Aaron Benavot, Yun Kyoung Cha, and Suk-Ying Wong, "Knowledge for the Masses: World Models and National Curricula, 1920–1986," *American Sociological Review* 56, no. 1 (1991): 85–100; David Strang and John Meyer, "Institutional Conditions for Diffusion," *Theory and Society* 22 (1993): 487–511.

8. See Christine Cousins, "Women and Employment," in *Society, Work and Welfare in Europe* (London: Macmillan Press, 1999), pp. 72–96.

9. According to MacKinnon, *Sexual Harassment of Working Women*, p. 250, "Working Women United Institute . . . seems to have been the first to use these words as anything approaching a term of art . . . [in] 1975."

10. Both American and French sexual harassment law is gender neutral, meaning that men and women can harass someone of either sex. However, it is widely recognized that most of the time it is men who harass women. For the sake of simplicity, I often refer to the sexual harasser as "he" or "him" and the victim as "she" or "her."

11. Vivienne Walt, "Regarding Sexism on the Job: Plus Ça Change . . . ," *New York Times*, 24 May 2000, sec. G, col. 1–3, p. 1.

12. See Abigail C. Saguy, "Puritanism and Promiscuity? Sexual Attitudes in France and the United States," *Comparative Social Research* 18 (1999): 227–47.

13. Peter L. Berger, *The Sacred Canopy: Elements of a Sociological Theory of Religion* (New York: Anchor Books, 1969), p. 6; cited in Wendy Griswold, *Cultures and Societies in a Changing World* (Thousand Oaks, Calif.: Pine Forge Press, 1994), p. 8.

14. There are more than 160 meanings of culture in the social scientific literature. See Alfred L. Kroeber and Clyde Kluckhohn, *Culture: A Critical Review of Concepts and Definitions* (Cambridge, Mass.: Harvard University Peabody Museum of American Archaeology and Ethnology, 1952); cited in Griswold, *Cultures and Societies in a Changing World*, p. 8. This study focuses on cultural or social assumptions about how the world works, which I regard as historically embedded, socially changing, and contested. I employ the concept of cultural repertoire to capture how individuals choose from among a varied but limited set of cultural "tools," based on their social situation, especially their national and institutional context.

15. See Françoise Dekeuwer-Defossez, "Le harcèlement sexuel en droit français: Discrimination ou atteinte à la liberté?" *La Semaine juridique* 3662, no. 13 (1993): 137–41.

16. See Chapter 4; Jacqueline Remy, "Les françaises accusent," *L'Express*, 13 March 1999. In 2002, the French Parliament expanded sexual harassment laws to cover coworker harassment, but the violence frame was preserved. See the Epilogue.

17. I borrow the concept of frame from social movement research (William Gamson, *Talking Politics* [Cambridge: Cambridge University Press, 1992]; David Snow and Robert D. Benford, "Ideology, Frame Resonance and Participant Mobilization," *International Social Movement Research* 1 [1988]: 197–217; Sidney Tarrow, "Mentalities, Political Cultures, and Collective Action Frames: Constructing Meanings Through Action," in *Frontiers in Social Movement Theory*, Aldon D. Morris and Carol McClurg Mueller, eds. [New Haven, Conn.: Yale University Press, 1992], pp. 174–202.). According to Snow and Benford ("Ideology, Frame Resonance and Participant Mobilization," p. 198), social movements "frame, or assign meaning to and interpret, relevant events and conditions in ways that are intended to mobilize potential adherents and constituents, to garner bystander support, and demobilize antagonists." The way social movement theorists use the term is quite different from Goffman's original concept of "frame" (Erving Goffman, *Frame Analysis: An Essay on the Organization of Experience* [New York: Harper Colophon, 1974]; see Nathalie Heinich, "Pour introduire la cadre-analyse," *Critique* 535 [1991]: 936–53.).

18. In February 2002, a small (by American standards) media scandal

erupted in France over a sexual harassment charge by a doctoral candidate against her dissertation advisor, a well-known Parisian intellectual. See the Epilogue for a discussion of what facilitated the media's treatment of this event and how the press represented these charges.

19. See Joseph R. Gusfield, *The Culture of Public Problems: Drinking-Driving and the Symbolic Order* (Chicago: University of Chicago Press, 1981).

20. See Lauren B. Edelman, Christopher Uggen, and Howard S. Erlanger, "The Endogeneity of Legal Regulation: Grievance Procedures as Rational Myth," *American Journal of Sociology* 105, no. 2 (1999): 406–54.

21. *Burlington Industries v Ellerth*, 524 US 742 (1998); *Faragher v City of Boca Raton*, 524 US 775 (1998).

22. Lauren Edelman, Steven E. Abraham, and Howard S. Erlanger, "Professional Construction of Law: The Inflated Threat of Wrongful Discharge," *Law and Society Review* 26, no. 1 (1992): 47–83; Erin Kelly and Frank Dobbin, "Civil Rights Law at Work: Sex Discrimination and the Rise of Maternity Leave Policies," *American Journal of Sociology* 105, no. 2 (1999): 455–92.

23. Terry Morehead Dworkin, "Harassment in the 1990s: Sexual Harassment in the Workplace: Women in Business," *Business Horizons* 36, no. 2 (1993): 52; "Thank You, Anita Hill, for the Civil Rights Act of 1991," *Christian Science Monitor*, 29 October 1991, sec. Editorial; for a discussion of the merits of these claims, see Roger Clegg, "A Brief Legislative History of the Civil Rights Act of 1991," *La. L. Rev.* 54 (1994): 1459–71.

24. See Robin Stryker, "Rules, Resources, and Legitimacy Processes: Some Implications for Social Conflict, Order and Change," *American Journal of Sociology* 99, no. 4 (January 1994): 847–911.

25. For an excellent history of affirmative action, see John David Skrentny, *The Ironies of Affirmative Action: Politics, Culture and Justice in America* (Chicago: University of Chicago Press, 1996).

26. See Erik Bleich, *Race Politics in Britain and France: Ideas and Policy-Making since the 1960s* (New York: Cambridge University Press, in press).

27. See Gosta Esping-Andersen, *The Three Worlds of Welfare Capitalism* (Princeton, N. J.: Princeton University Press, 1990); Michèle Lamont and Laurent Thévenot, eds., *Rethinking Comparative Cultural Sociology: Polities and Repertoires of Evaluation in France and the U.S.* (Cambridge/ Paris: Cambridge University Press and the Presses de la Maison des Sciences de l'Homme, 2000); Erik Olin Wright, Janeen Baxter, and Gunn Elizabeth Birkelund, "The Gender Gap in Workplace Authority: A Cross-National Study," *American Sociological Review* 60, no. 3 (1995): 407–35.

28. See Deborah A. Prentice and Dale T. Miller, "Pluralistic Ignorance and the Perpetuation of Social Norms by Unwitting Actors," *Advances in Experimental Social Psychology* 28 (1996): 161–209.

29. I borrow the concept of boundary work from sociologist Michèle Lamont (*Money, Morals and Manners: The Culture of the French and American Upper-Middle Class* [Chicago: University of Chicago Press, 1992]) who, in her cross-national work on the culture of upper-middle-class men in France and the United States, points to the way in which people often emphasize, through boundary work, their identity in relation to others. By drawing inclusive boundaries, individuals affirm similarities between themselves and specific others, thereby affirming some group identity. In contrast, by drawing exclusive boundaries, individuals define their own identity in opposition to others. Though Lamont uses the concept of symbolic boundaries to explain interpersonal behavior, I show that it is also useful for understanding more macro political and cultural processes. From this perspective, the kind of macro cultural convergence noted by students of globalization can occur when political elites affirm international similarities, often as a way of gaining political legitimacy. However, political elites can alternatively reject international cultural models by drawing exclusive boundaries.

30. Frank M. Serusclat, "Rapport du sénat," *Seconde session ordinaire de 1991–1992* 350 (1992), pp. 16–17.

31. For an excellent overview of elite French writings about America, both negative and positive, see Jean-Philippe Mathy, *Extrême-Occident: French Intellectuals and America* (Chicago: University of Chicago Press, 1993). See also Stanley Hoffmann, "Deux universalismes en conflit," *Tocqueville Review* 21, no. 1 (2000): 65–71, which attributes such conflict to centuries-old competition over visions of universalism.

32. See Diana Crane, ed., *The Sociology of Culture: Emerging Theoretical Perspectives* (Oxford: Basil Blackwell, 1994); Joshua Gamson, *Freaks Talk Back: Tabloid Talk Shows and Sexual Nonconformity* (Chicago: University of Chicago Press, 1998).

33. For further details about the methodology, see the Appendix.

34. This chapter thus follows in a tradition of work that examines the meaning of law in people's everyday lives, e.g., Patricia Ewick and Susan S. Silbey, *The Common Place of Law: Stories From Everyday Life* (Chicago: University of Chicago Press, 1998). However, it also pays particular attention to the effect of national and institutional context on personal perceptions of the law.

35. See W. Lance Bennett, *News: The Politics of Illusion* (New York: Long-

man, 2001); Steven Brill, "War Gets the Monica Treatment," *Brill's Content*, 99–137 (July/August 1999); Robert Entman, *Democracy Without Citizens: Media and the Decay of American Politics* (Oxford: Oxford University Press, 1989); Herbert Gans, *Deciding What's News* (New York: Pantheon, 1979), 78–80; Todd Gitlin, *The Whole World Is Watching: Mass Media in the Making and Unmaking of the New Left* (Berkeley: University of California Press, 1980).

36. Ann Swidler, "Culture in Action: Symbols and Strategies," *American Sociological Review* 51, no. 2 (1986): 273–86.

CHAPTER 1: SEXUAL HARASSMENT LAW
ON THE BOOKS

This chapter draws from Abigail C. Saguy, "Employment Discrimination or Sexual Violence? Defining Sexual Harassment in American and French Law," *Law and Society Review* 34, no. 4 (2000).

1. See *Harris v Forklift Systems*, 510 US 17, 19–20 (1993).
2. See *Harris v Forklift Systems*, 510 US 17, 21–22 (1993).
3. See *Harris v Forklift Systems*, 510 US 17, 21–22 (1993).
4. Article 222–33 of the penal code (Fr.). "Serious pressure" was added when the law was amended in 1997 (Charles Jolibois, "Rapport," *Sénat: Session ordinaire de 1997–1998*, 265 [1998]). In actuality, to date no one has yet been sentenced to jail for sexual harassment alone under this law. Several convicted harassers have received suspended sentences. When harassers have been sentenced to jail, they have been convicted not only of sexual harassment but also of *agression sexuelle*, which involves physical sexual attacks. In many of these cases, the judge was aware that the victim had been raped but could not prove that charge, according to AVFT activists who were involved in such cases. In 2002, Parliament extended this statute to colleagues by revising it to condemn simply "the act of harassing another with the purpose of obtaining sexual favors." See the Epilogue.
5. Article L. 122–46 of the labor code (Fr.).
6. Assemblée Nationale, "Projet de loi relatif à la prévention et à la répression des infractions sexuelles ainsi qu'à la protection des mineurs" (1998).
7. Jolibois, "Rapport"; Journal Officiel de la République Française, "Compte rendu intégral: Séance du mardi 31 mars 1998," *Sénat débats parlementaires journal officiel de la République Française*, no. 25 (April 1 1998): 1369–70.

8. Jolibois, "Rapport."

9. As is discussed below, while a separate labor statute does address employment retaliation following workplace sexual harassment, it does not conceptualize such retaliation as a form of gender discrimination.

10. In January 2002, the French Parliament would effectively eliminate the requirement that sexual harassment involve such constraint, while still framing sexual harassment as a form of sexual violence. For a discussion of this legal reform and its significance, see the Epilogue.

11. In actuality, to date no one has been sentenced to jail for sexual harassment alone, which, according to French law, does not involve physical touching. See note 4. Unlike in American criminal proceedings, it is possible in French penal courts to request civil awards.

12. Title VII also exempts Congress, Native American tribes, private membership clubs, and religious groups. Plaintiffs bringing claims of racial or national origin but not sex discrimination can circumvent the fifteen or more employees limitation by bringing their case under 42 U.S.C. Sec. 1981 instead of Title VII. Some sexual harassment plaintiffs can, however, appeal to state statutes that extend protection from sexual harassment to smaller businesses.

13. Katherine Franke, "What's Wrong with Sexual Harassment?" *Stanford Law Review* 49, no. 4 (1997): 691–772.

14. See Stephen J. Schulhofer, *Unwanted Sex: The Culture of Intimidation and the Failure of Law* (Cambridge, Mass.: Harvard University Press, 1998).

15. American students can seek redress for sexual harassment in education under Title IX of the Education Amendment Acts of 1972, which outlaws sexual harassment in schools (receiving federal funds) as illegal sex discrimination. There have also been a few lower court rulings and two circuit court rulings that have recognized a cause for action for hostile housing environment under Title VIII of the Fair Housing Act ("Fair Housing Law Is Applied in a Sexual Harassment Case," *New York Times*, 11 December 1983, sec. 1, p. 44; Deborah Zalesne, "The Intersection of Socioeconomic Class and Gender in Hostile Housing Environment Claims under Title VIII: Who Is the Reasonable Person?" *Boston College Law Review* 38, no. 4 [1997]: 868–69; *Honce v Vigil*, 1 F3d 1085 [10th Cir 1993]; *DiCenso v Cisneros*, 96 F3d 1004 [7th Cir 1996]). However, the most developed sexual harassment jurisprudence is under Title VII, which is also my focus.

16. Vicki Schultz, "Reconceptualizing Sexual Harassment," *Yale Law Journal* 107, no. 1683 (1998): 1732–805. Catharine MacKinnon, however, states that gender harassment is clearly covered under Title VII, largely as a result of the

development of sexual harassment law (personal correspondence, February 20, 2001), citing as a few examples *McKinney v Dole*, 765 F2d 1129, 1138–39 (DC Cir 1985) (ruling that a physically aggressive but not explicitly sexual act by a male supervisor against a female employee may constitute part of a prohibited pattern of sexual discrimination); *Cline v General Electric*, 757 FSupp 923, 931–33 (ND Ill 1991) (same); and *Accardi v Superior Court*, 21 CalRptr2d 292 (1993) (ruling that "sexual harassment does not necessarily involve sexual conduct. It need not have anything to do with lewd acts, double entendres or sexual advances. Sexual harassment may involve conduct, whether blatant or subtle, that discriminates against a person solely because of that person's sex."); *Harris v Forklift Systems*, 510 US 17, 25 (ruling, on facts most of which are not sexual but gender-based, that "the critical issue, Title VII's text indicates, is whether members of one sex are exposed to disadvantageous terms or conditions of employment to which members of the other sex are not exposed."); *Oncale v Sundowner Offshore Services, Inc.*, 523 US 75, 80 (1998) (same quotation reaffirmed). The fact that courts apply varying standards of "severity" in hostile environment gender harassment cases that involve both sexual and nonsexual behaviors, as most do, complicates the question.

17. In order to bring a Title VII claim for sexual harassment, the plaintiff must file a complaint with the EEOC, which is supposed to conduct an investigation. Because of budget constraints, however, the EEOC is not able to investigate most of the complaints it receives. One hundred and eighty days after the formal complaint of discrimination has been filed, the plaintiff can request a "right to sue letter," which is required to bring a private lawsuit and is issued automatically after the time requirements have been met. The plaintiff may not wish to bring a private lawsuit, say for financial reasons, or may have difficulty finding a lawyer to take the case, at which point the plaintiff can pressure the EEOC to investigate. After the EEOC concludes an investigation, which can take several years, it issues a "determination letter," ruling in favor of either the employer or the employee. The EEOC can also become a plaintiff in a civil suit. A ruling in favor of the employee is rare, according to a 9to5 National Association of Working Women activist who received such a letter in her own case in 1998, and strengthens the plaintiff's case considerably. After she received such a ruling, for example, this 9to5 activist found that several of the top law firms were interested in representing her. Despite the help that this activist received from the EEOC, she agrees with all of the six 9to5 activists and ten American lawyers that I interviewed, that the EEOC is an ineffective organization that is more a hindrance than an aid to victims of sex discrimination.

18. *Meritor v Vinson*, 477 US 57 (1986). The plaintiff in this first Supreme Court ruling, Mechelle Vinson, alleged that her boss not only made offensive sexual comments to her but that he raped her on several occasions in the workplace. Rape victims and victims of sexual assault can, of course, press criminal charges instead of or in addition to civil ones. My argument is that sexual harassment under Title VII includes anything from (severe and pervasive) sexual or sexist comments to rape, as long as such behavior occurs at work and has a detrimental effect on the victim's employment.

19. The statute, as it was revised in January 2002, still defined sexual harassment as behavior that had as its purpose "obtaining sexual favors." However, whether "sexual favors" constitutes engaging in sexual intercourse, putting up with sexual commentary, or something in between is a matter of some disagreement among French courts. See Catherine Le Magueresse, "Harcèlement sexuel au travail," in *Dictionnaire des sciences criminelles* (Paris: Éditions Dalloz, 2003).

20. As a general rule, it is possible to sue for civil damages during a French penal trial, unlike in the United States, where a separate civil trial is necessary.

21. Code de travail [C. Trav.] art. L. 122–46 (Fr.). In January 2002, this statute was revised to state that "no employee can be penalized nor dismissed for having submitted or refusing to submit to acts of harassment of any person whose purpose is to obtain favors of a sexual nature for his own benefit or for the benefit of a third party." See the Epilogue.

22. Code de travail [C. Trav.] art. L. 122–47 (Fr.).

23. Code de travail [C. Trav.] art. L. 122–34, L. 123–7, L. 122–12 (Fr.).

24. Code de travail [C. Trav.] art. L. 122–48 (Fr.); Mirielle Benneytout, Sylvie Cromer, and Marie-Victoire Louis, "Harcèlement sexuel: Une réforme restrictive qui n'est pas sans danger," *Semaine sociale Lamy* 599 (1992): 3–4; Margot Felgentrager, "Droit et harcèlement sexuel," *Pratiques psychologiques*, no. 3 (1996): 45–48.

25. Jane Aeberhard-Hodges. "Sexual Harassment in Employment: Recent Judicial and Arbitral Trends." *International Labour Review*, no. 135 (1996): 499–533.

26. Schultz, "Reconceptualizing Sexual Harassment," but see note 16.

27. Lin Farley, *Sexual Shakedown: The Sexual Harassment of Women on the Job* (New York: McGraw-Hill, 1978), p. xi.

28. Farley, *Sexual Shakedown*, p. xi.

29. Elman, *Sexual Subordination and State Intervention*, p. 98.

30. Farley, *Sexual Shakedown*; MacKinnon, *Sexual Harassment of Working Women*; Martha J. Langelan, *Back Off! How to Confront Sexual Harassment and*

Harassers (New York: Fireside, 1993); Zippel, "Comparative Perspectives of Sex Equality Policies in Germany, the European Union, and the United States."

31. Elman, *Sexual Subordination and State Intervention*, p. 98; Farley, *Sexual Shakedown*, p. 70.

32. Ralph Craib, "Sex and Women at UC Berkeley — 2 Surveys," *San Francisco Chronicle*, 22 July 1977; "How Do You Handle Sex on the Job: A Redbook Questionnaire" (January 1976): 74–75; U.S. Merit Systems Protection Board, *Sexual Harassment in the Federal Workforce: Is It a Problem?* (Washington, D. C.: U.S. Government Printing Office, 1981); Working Women United Institute, *Sexual Harassment on the Job: Results of a Preliminary Survey* (New York: Working Women United Institute, 1975). Results from these early surveys vary widely. For instance, according to Craib, 20 percent of women have been sexually harassed, while *Redbook* estimated 88 percent. The differences depend on sample bias and on question wording, particularly how sexual harassment is defined. The U.S. Merit Systems Protection Board, the most comprehensive and systematic study, found that 40 percent of female federal employees surveyed had been sexually harassed.

33. Rosemarie Tong, *Women, Sex and the Law* (Totowa, N. J.: Rowman & Allanheld, 1984), p. 65.

34. Elman, *Sexual Subordination and State Intervention*, p. 97, n. 10.

35. Elman, *Sexual Subordination and State Intervention*; Farley, *Sexual Shakedown*; MacKinnon, *Sexual Harassment of Working Women*.

36. Tong, *Women, Sex and the Law*, p. 71. See also Elizabeth Schneider, *Battered Women and Feminist Lawmaking* (New Haven, Conn.: Yale University Press, 2000) for an excellent discussion of the promises and limitations of American criminal law in dealing with men who batter their wives or partners. Schneider's work further demonstrates how the choice of law (criminal or civil) is both dictated by and reinforces the particular framing of a given legal harm. Unlike sexual harassment, which was ultimately framed as a civil harm of employment discrimination in the United States, battering was conceptualized as (gendered) violence, dictating penal remedies. These remedies, in turn, have reinforced the violence frame in this case.

37. In France, where sexual harassment is addressed under penal law, insensitivity on the part of the police and state prosecutors is also an important problem, according to the lawyers, activists, and the one prosecutor I interviewed. However, in France the burden of proof in penal court is lighter.

38. MacKinnon, *Sexual Harassment of Working Women*, p. 172; Tong, *Women, Sex and the Law*, p. 73.

39. *Rabidue v Osceola Refining Co.*, 584 FSupp 419, 428 n36 (ED Mich 1984).

40. Robert C. Bird, "More Than a Congressional Joke: A Fresh Look at the Legislative History of Sex Discrimination of the 1964 Civil Rights Act," *William and Mary Journal of Women and the Law* 3 (Spring 1997): 137–61; Carl M. Brauer, "Women Activists, Southern Conservatives, and the Prohibition of Sex Discrimination in Title VII of the 1964 Civil Rights Act," *Journal of Southern History* 49–56 (1983), p. 37; Sara Evans, *Born for Liberty* (New York: Free Press, 1989); Michael Evan Gold, "A Tale of Two Amendments: The Reasons Congress Added Sex to Title VII and Their Implication for the Issue of Comparable Worth," *Duquesne Law Review* 19 (Spring 1981): 453; Leila Rupp and Verta Taylor, *Survival in the Doldrums* (New York: Oxford University Press, 1987).

41. Bird, "More Than a Congressional Joke," p. 155.

42. Bird, "More Than a Congressional Joke," p. 158.

43. For a compelling account of how activists used "legal mobilization" as a means to achieve pay equity on the basis of gender, as well as a general discussion of the limits and promises of legal mobilization, see Michael McCann, *Rights at Work: Pay Equity Reform and the Politics of Legal Mobilization* (Chicago: University of Chicago Press, 1994).

44. See Anna-Marie Marshall, "Closing the Gaps: Plaintiffs in Pivotal Sexual Harassment Cases," *Law & Social Inquiry* 23, no. 4 (1998): 784.

45. Marshall, "Closing the Gaps," p. 786.

46. Farley, *Sexual Shakedown*; Gilbert J. Ginsburg and Jean Galloway Koreski, "Sexual Advances by an Employee's Supervisor: A Sex-Discrimination Violation of Title VII?" *Employee Relations Law Journal* 3 (1977): 83; MacKinnon, *Sexual Harassment of Working Women*; Jack J. McGee, Jr., "Note, Sexual Advances by Male Supervisory Personnel as Actionable under Title VII of the Civil Rights Act of 1964: *Corne v. Bausch & Lomb, Inc., Williams v. Saxbe*," *S. Texas Law Journal* 17 (1976): 409; Mich. L. Rev., "Note, Sexual Harassment and Title VII: The Foundation for the Elimination of Sexual Cooperation As an Employment Condition," *Michigan Law Review* 76 (1978): 1007; Minn. L. Rev., "Note, Legal Remedies for Employment Related Sexual Harassment," *Minnesota Law Review* 64 (1979): 151; NYU Law Review, "Comment," *New York University Law Review* 51 (1976): 148; William C. Seymour, "Sexual Harassment: Finding a Cause for Action under Title VII," *Labor Law Journal* 30 (1979): 139; Nadine Taub, "Keeping Women in Their Place: Stereotyping Per Se as a Form of Employment Discrimination," *Boston College Law Rev.* 21 (1980): 345–418.

47. Marshall, "Closing the Gaps," p. 787.

48. MacKinnon, *Sexual Harassment of Working Women*, pp. xi, 172.

49. MacKinnon, *Sexual Harassment of Working Women*, p.172.

50. *Craker v The Chicago and Northwestern Railway Co.*, 36 Wis. 657, 674, 17 Am. Rep. 504 (1895); cited in MacKinnon, *Sexual Harassment of Working Women*, p. 172.

51. MacKinnon, *Sexual Harassment of Working Women*, p. 172.

52. Snow and Benford, "Ideology, Frame Resonance and Participant Mobilization"; David A. Snow, E. Burke Rochford, Jr., Steven K. Worden, and Robert D. Benford, "Frame Alignment Processes, Micromobilization, and Movement Participation," *American Sociological Review* 51, no. 4 (1986): 464–81.

53. See Esping-Andersen, *The Three Worlds of Welfare Capitalism*; Lamont and Thévenot, eds., *Rethinking Comparative Cultural Sociology*; Wright, Baxter, and Birkelund, "The Gender Gap in Workplace Authority." "Decommodification" means freedom from the labor market. People who have sufficient income, often through governmental support that is not contingent on employment, have a high degree of decommodification. Those who need to be engaged in paid employment to support themselves have a low degree of decommodification.

54. MacKinnon, *Sexual Harassment of Working Women*, p. 7.

55. See Wright, Baxter, and Birkelund, "The Gender Gap in Workplace Authority."

56. See Lamont and Thévenot, eds., *Rethinking Comparative Cultural Sociology*; see also Chapters 2 and 4.

57. *Barnes v Train*, 13 Fair Empl Prac Cas (BNA) 123 (DDC 1974); *Corne v Bausch & Lomb Inc.*, 390 FSupp 161 (DAriz 1975); *Miller v Bank of America*, 418 FSupp 233 (NDCal 1976); *Tomkins v Public Service Electric and Gas Co.*, 422 FSupp 533 (DNJ 1977).

58. For instance, some legal critics argue that employers should not be held liable for sexual harassment in general or for sexual harassment among coworkers specifically. Instead, they contend that all or some forms of sexual harassment should be conceptualized as personal torts in state court (Anita Bernstein, "Law, Culture, and Harassment," *University of Pennsylvania Law Review* 142, no. 4 [1994]: 1227–311; Mark McLaughlin Hager, "Harassment as a Tort: Why Title VII Hostile Environment Liability Should Be Curtailed," *Connecticut Law Review* 30 [1998]: 375–437; Michael D. Vhay, "The Harms of Asking: Towards a Comprehensive Treatment of Sexual Harassment." *University of Chicago Law Review* 55, no. 1 [1988]: 328–62.). Such authors have argued that, since sexual harassment reduces workers' productivity, holding employers liable constitutes

a double punishment and makes employers "overzealous" in their efforts to curb sexual harassment (Kingsley Browne, "Free Speech," in *Directions in Sexual Harassment Law*, ed. Reva Siegel and Catharine MacKinnon [New Haven, Conn.: Yale University Press, in press]; Lloyd R. Cohen, "Sexual Harassment and the Law," *Society* [May/June 1991]: 8–13; Hager, "Harassment as a Tort.").

59. *Barnes v Costle*, 561 F2d 983 (DC Cir 1977). The late George MacKinnon, Catharine MacKinnon's father and a conservative Republican, was one of the judges on the panel.

60. Jeffrey Toobin, "The Trouble With Sex: Why the Law of Sexual Harassment Has Never Worked," *New Yorker*, 9 February 1998, sec. Annals of Law, p. 50.

61. *Barnes v Costle*, 561 F2d at 990.

62. *Barnes v Costle*, 561 F2d at 990 n55. In the years following *Barnes*, there was some uncertainty among the courts about whether or not same-sex harassment was indeed covered by Title VII. In 1998, however, the High Court clarified that same-sex harassment is covered under Title VII, as long as the plaintiff can show that there was discrimination on the basis of sex (*Oncale v Sundowner Offshore Services, Inc.*, 523 US 75 [1998]).

63. *Garber v Saxon Business Products*, 552 F2d 1032 (4th Cir 1977); *Tomkins v Public Service Electric and Gas Co.*, 568 F2d 1044 (3rd Cir 1977).

64. 454 F2d 234 (5th Cir 1971).

65. *Rogers v EEOC*, 454 F2d at 238.

66. *Bundy v Jackson*, 641 F2d 934, 945 (DC Cir 1981).

67. *Henson v City of Dundee*, 682 F2d 897 (11th Cir 1982).

68. *Henson*, 682 F2d at 33, n18.

69. *Henson*, 682 F2d at 902.

70. *Meritor v Vinson*, 477 US 57 (1986).

71. Civil Rights Act of 1991, 42 U.S.C. § 2000e-5(k)(1996).

72. Dworkin, "Harassment in the 1990s"; "Thank You, Anita Hill." For a discussion of the merits of these claims, see Clegg, "A Brief Legislative History of the Civil Rights Act of 1991."

73. *Harris v Forklift Systems*, 510 US at 22.

74. Edelman, Uggen, and Erlanger, "The Endogeneity of Legal Regulation."

75. See David Benjamin Oppenheimer, "Exacerbating the Exasperating: Title VII Liability of Employers for Sexual Harassment Committed by Their Supervisors," *Cornell Law Review* 81, no. 1 (1995): 66–153.

76. *Burlington Industries v Ellerth*, 524 US at 770.

77. See, e.g., Peter L. Berger and Thomas Luckman, *The Social Construction of Reality* (Garden City, N. Y.: Doubleday Anchor, 1967); Luc Boltanski and Laurent Thévenot, *De la justification: Les économies de la grandeur* (Paris: Gallimard, 1991); Mary Douglas, *How Institutions Think* (Ithaca, N. Y.: Cornell University Press, 1986); Emile Durkheim, *Les formes élémentaires de la vie religieuse: Le système totémique en Australie* (Paris: Quadrige/Presses Universitaires de France, 1960); Susan T. Fiske and Patricia W. Linville, "What Does the Schema Concept Buy Us?" *Personality and Social Psychology Bulletin* 6 (1980): 543–57; Roger Friedland and Robert Alford, "Bringing the State Back In: Symbols, Practices, and Institutional Contradictions," in *The New Institutionalism in Organizational Analysis*, ed. Walter W. Powell and Paul J. DiMaggio (Chicago: University of Chicago Press, 1991), pp. 232–63; Anthony Giddens, *The Constitution of Society: Outline of the Theory of Structuration* (Cambridge: Polity Press, 1984); Michele Lamont and Robert Wuthnow, "Betwixt and Between: Recent Cultural Sociology in Europe and the United States," in *Frontiers of Social Theory: The New Synthesis*, ed. George Ritzer (New York: Columbia University Press, 1990), pp. 287–315; Karl Mannheim, *Essays on the Sociology of Culture* (London: Routledge and Kegan Paul, 1956); Serge Moscovici, "The Phenomenon of Social Representations," in *Social Representations*, ed. R. M. Farr and Serge Moscovici (New York: Cambridge University Press, 1984); Swidler, "Culture in Action"; Robert Wuthnow, *Meaning and the Moral Order: Explorations in Cultural Analysis* (Berkeley: University of California Press, 1987).

78. See Lynn Chancer, *Sadomasochism in Everyday Life: The Dynamics of Power and Powerlessness* (New Brunswick, N. J.: Rutgers University Press, 1992).

79. Franke, "What's Wrong with Sexual Harassment?"

80. See, e.g., *Barnes v Costle*, 561 F2d; MacKinnon, *Sexual Harassment of Working Women*.

81. See, e.g., Kathryn Abrams, "Symposium: The State of the Union: Civil Rights: Gender Discrimination and the Transformation of Workplace Norms," *Vand. L. Rev.* 42 (May 1989): 1209; Susan Estrich, "Sex at Work," *Stanford Law Review* 43 (1991): 830; Catharine MacKinnon, "Feminism, Marxism, Method and the State: An Agenda for Theory," *Signs* 7 (1982): 533.

82. See, e.g., MacKinnon, *Sexual Harassment of Working Women*, p.116.

83. But see *Doe v Belleville*, 119 F3d 563, 581 (7th Cir 1997, holding that "[a] man who is harassed because his voice is soft, his physique is slight, his hair is long, or because in some other respect he exhibits his masculinity in a way that does not meet his coworkers' idea of how men are to appear and behave, is harassed 'because of' his sex"). For a discussion of same-sex sexual harassment

jurisprudence, see Hilary S. Axam and Deborah Zalesne, "Simulated Sodomy and Other Forms of Heterosexual 'Horseplay': Same Sex Sexual Harassment, Workplace Gender Hierarchies and the Myth of the Gender Monolith Before and After *Oncale*," *Yale Journal of Law and Feminism* 11 (1999): 155–243.

84. *Oncale v Sundowner Offshore Services, Inc.*, 523 US 75 (1998).

85. Schultz, "Reconceptualizing Sexual Harassment," but see note 16.

86. While contested as a trend in jurisprudence, this seems to be the trend in American workplaces, where managers express more concern over consensual office romance than sexist behavior. See Chapters 2 and 4.

87. See Judith Ezekiel, "Anti-féminisme et anti-américanisme: Un mariage politiquement réussi," *Nouvelles questions féministes* 17, no. 1 (1995): 59–76; Marie-Victoire Louis, "Harcèlement sexuel et domination masculine," *Un siècle d'anti-féminisme*, ed. Christine Bard (Paris: Fayard, 1999); Joan W. Scott, "Vive la différence!" *Le Débat* 87 (November–December 1995): 134–39.

88. E.g., Benneytout, Cromer, and Louis, "Harcèlement sexuel"; Sylvie Cromer, "France: AVFT," in *De l'abus de pouvoir sexuel: Le harcèlement sexuel au travail*, ed. AVFT (Paris and Montreal: La Découverte/Le Boréal, 1990), pp. 223–30; Sylvie Cromer, "Histoire d'une loi: La pénalisation du harcèlement sexuel dans le nouveau code pénal," *Projets féministes* 1 (March 1992): 108–17; Sylvie Cromer, *Le harcèlement sexuel en France: La levée d'un tabou 1985–1990* (Paris: Documentation Française, 1995); Sylvie Cromer and Marie-Victoire Louis, "Existe-t-il un harcèlement sexuel "à la française"?" *French Politics and Society* 10, no. 3 (1992): 37–43; Marie-Victoire Louis, *Le droit de cuissage* (Paris: Les Editions de l'Atelier, 1994).

89. Cromer, "Histoire d'une loi," p. 224.

90. AVFT, ed., *De l'abus de pouvoir sexuel: Le harcèlement sexuel au travail* (Paris and Montreal: La Découverte/Le Boréal, 1990).

91. Interview with Anne Zelensky, 23 June 1995; Françoise Picq, *Libération des femmes: Les années-mouvement* (Paris: Seuil, 1993), p. 203.

92. AVFT, "Proposition d'amendement de l'AVFT," *Cette violence dont nous ne voulons plus* 10 (June 1990): 59–63.

93. UFF, "Propositions de loi pénale de l'UFF," *Clara* 19 (summer 1991): 23–27.

94. 76/207/CEE.

95. Michael Rubinstein, "La dignité des femmes dans le monde du travail: Rapport sur le problème du harcèlement sexuel dans les états membres des communautés européennes" (Bruxelles, 1987).

96. Louis Harris, "Le harcèlement sexuel: Enquête des français: Perceptions, opinions et évaluation du phénomène" (1991).

97. See, e.g., Elisabeth Badinter, "La chasse aux sorcières," *Le Nouvel Observateur*, 17–23 October 1991, p. 82; see Chapter 3.

98. *Le Point*, 25 January 1992.

99. *Libération*, 30 April 1992.

100. Swidler, "Culture in Action."

101. To say that French men rejected arguments about sexism because it was in their interest to do so is to miss the point. First of all, as members of the ruling elite, it was no more in their interest to embrace analyses of class inequality or abuse of power than those of gender inequality. Second, while men, as employers and bosses, may wish to sustain male privilege, as fathers they may want to protect their daughters from sexual abuse and employment discrimination. Moreover, American men, as lawyers, legal scholars, and judges, did connect sexism to racism, although they share the same stakes in patriarchy as French men. Rather, it seems that one's interests are themselves largely a product of one's cultural categories and narratives.

The Communist group also proposed two amendments, inspired by the UFF proposal. The bills presented sexual harassment as an affront to "dignity." Unlike Roudy's proposals, which made abuse of authority a necessary component of sexual harassment, the communist bills, consistent with the UFF proposal, considered them to be aggravating circumstances that raise the maximum penalties (Journal Officiel, "2e séance du 2 décembre 1991," *Journal Officiel: Assemblée Nationale* [1991], 3567). Rather than the communist version, Roudy's more modest bill passed, suggesting that Roudy's calculations about how far her colleagues were likely to go were accurate.

102. Sylvie Cromer, "Histoire d'une loi."

103. Sylvie Cromer, "Histoire d'une loi."

104. Sylvie Cromer, "Histoire d'une loi."

105. Dekeuwer-Defossez, "Le harcèlement sexuel en droit français."

106. The only surviving link in French law between sexual harassment and discrimination is found in Article L. 123–1 of the labor code (Fr.). This statute, which is included in the chapter on professional equality, states that employment decisions should not account for whether the employee submitted to or refused to submit to demands for sexual relations from someone with "official authority" over her or him. The inclusion of sexual harassment under sex discrimination in this statute has been analyzed as an "opportunistic text" because, in conjunction with another labor statute (Article L. 152-1-1), it gives the inspector of work the

right to investigate infractions and impose penalties. Because the inspector usually forgoes the penalties for employers who demonstrate goodwill by trying to rectify the problem, this law serves primarily as an arm of dissuasion (Claude Roy-Loustaunau, "Le droit du harcèlement sexuel: Un puzzle législatif et des choix novateurs," *Droit Social* 6 [June 1995]: 545–50.).

107. *Le Monde*, 28 June 1991.

108. Jane Jenson and Mariette Sineau, *Mitterand et les françaises: Un rendez-vous manqué* (Paris: Presses de la Fondation Nationale des Sciences Politiques, 1995), p. 287.

109. *Le Monde*, 23 May 1992.

110. *Le Monde*, 2 June 1992.

111. Assemblée Nationale, "Projet de loi relatif à la prévention et à la répression des infractions sexuelles ainsi qu'à la protection des mineurs."

112. Jolibois, "Rapport"; *Journal officiel de la République Française*, "Compte rendu intégral."

113. Jolibois, "Rapport."

114. Gerard Noiriel, *Population, immigration et identité nationale en France XIXe-XXe siècle* (Paris: Hachette, 1992), p. 109. Joan Scott (*Only Paradoxes to Offer* [Cambridge, Mass: Harvard University Press, 1996]) argues that this political model presents a paradox for feminists, who simultaneously argue that women should be permitted to participate in government because they are like men and yet, by demanding rights for women, affirm the specificity of women as a group.

115. The association of race statistics with the Vichy regime further justifies this principle. See Henry Rousso, *The Vichy Syndrome: History and Memory in France Since 1944*, trans. Arthur Goldhammer (Cambridge, Mass.: Harvard University Press, 1994).

116. The opposite side of the coin is that racial categorization in the United States can serve to reify "races" and reinforce racism. In other words, as Martha Minow (*Making All the Difference* [Ithaca, N. Y.: Cornell University Press, 1990]) has argued, inequality is reproduced whether it is noticed or ignored.

117. Rogers Brubaker, *Citizenship and Nationhood in France and Germany* (Cambridge, Mass.: Harvard University Press, 1992); Eric Fassin, "PaCS socialista : La gauche et le 'juste milieu,' " *Le Banquet*, nos. 12–13 (1998): 147–59; Joan W. Scott, "'La Querelle des Femmes' in the Late Twentieth Century," *New Left Review*, no. 226 (1997): 3–19.

118. Luc Boltanski, *The Making of a Class: Cadres in French Society* (Cambridge/Paris: Cambridge University Press and Maison de la Science de l'Homme,

1987); Alain Desrosières and Laurent Thévenot, *Les catégories socio-professionelles* (Paris: La Découverte, 1988).

119. Michel Crozier, *The Bureaucratic Phenomenon* (Chicago: University of Chicago Press, 1964), p. 220.

120. Lamont, *Money, Morals, and Manners,* p. 49.

121. Whether *le droit de cuissage* actually existed or was a "myth" is contested. See Alain Boureau, *Le droit de cuissage: La fabrication d'un mythe XIIe-XXe siècle* (Paris: Albin Michel, 1995); Louis, *Le droit de cuissage.* However, records of the *droit de cuissage* tax do exist.

122. Louis, *Le droit de cuissage.*

123. Schultz, "Reconceptualizing Sexual Harassment," but see note 16.

124. Legal reform in January 2002 extended the scope of the French sexual harassment laws to coworker harassment. See the Epilogue.

CHAPTER 2: SEXUAL HARASSMENT LAW IN ACTION

1. See Lauren B. Edelman and Mark C. Suchman, "When the 'Haves' Hold Court: Speculations on the Organizational Internalization of Law," *Law & Society Review* 33, no. 4 (1999): 941–91, for a sophisticated discussion of how large bureaucratic organizations are "internalizing" legal rules, structures, personnel, and activities, and the effect this has on the balance of power between employees and employers. Although I am focusing on the ways in which corporate policies on sexual harassment assist sexual harassment victims, it is important to keep in mind that, as corporations "hold court," they also reinforce their authority over their employees.

2. See Cass Sunstein, "Damages in Sexual Harassment Cases," in *Directions in Sexual Harassment Law,* ed. Reva Siegel and Catharine MacKinnon (New Haven, Conn.: Yale University Press, in press).

3. See Edelman, Abraham, and Erlanger, "Professional Construction of Law"; Kelly and Dobbin, "Civil Rights Law at Work."

4. Christine Coyne, "*Anjelino v New York Times Co.*: Granting Men Standing to Fight Injuries Received as a Result of Sexual Discrimination Towards Female Co-Workers," *Villanova Law Review* 45 (2000): 651–88; Anne Lawton, "The Emperor's New Clothes: How the Academy Deals with Sexual Harassment," *Yale Journal of Law & Feminism* 11 (1999): 75–145; John Whitehead, "Eleventh Hour Amendment or Serious Business: Sexual Harassment and the United

States Supreme Court's 1997–1998 Term," *Temple Law Review* 71 (1998): 773–837; Deborah Zalesne, "Sexual Harassment Law in the United States and South Africa: Facilitating the Transition from Legal Standards to Social Norms," *Harvard Women's Law Review* 25 (2002): 143–220.

5. Steven Greenhouse, "Companies Set to Get Tougher on Harassment: Policies Under Review After Court Decision," *New York Times*, 28 June 1998, sec. National, pp. A1, A14.

6. Cal. Gov't Code 12940 (West 1992 & Supp. 1998).

7. *Burlington Industries v Ellerth*, 524 US 742 (1998); *Faragher v City of Boca Raton*, 524 US 775 (1998).

8. See, for example, Edelman, Uggen, and Erlanger, "Endogeneity of Legal Regulation"; Kelly and Dobbin, "Civil Rights Law at Work."

9. On the limited stance unions have taken in regard to sexual harassment, see AVFT, ed., *De l'abus de pouvoir sexuel*. In interviews with members of the AVFT, I was told of several cases in which the alleged harasser was supported by his union. For discussions of the historically difficult relationship between feminists and leftist male activists, see Annie de Pisan and Anne Tristan, *Histoires du MLF*, preface by Simone de Beauvoir (Paris: Calmann-Lévy, 1977); Claire Duchen, *Feminism in France: From May '68 to Mitterrand* (London: Routledge & Kegan Paul, 1986); Picq, *Libération des femmes*.

10. CA Paris, 18 September 1996. SA Frans Maas c./Mme. Ch. L'H, cited in Catherine Le Magueresse, "Sur la nullité des mesures prises à l'encontre d'une salariée victime de harcèlement sexuel," *Droit Social* 5, (May 1998): 437–41.

11. Among the people I spoke to, five were directors of human resources, nine were secretaries or assistants to directors of human resources, one was the Director of Social Issues *(Directeur des Affaires Sociales)*, one was the Director of Communications, one was a secretary for the Director of Communications, and six were unidentified by job title.

12. See note 9.

13. See Lamont and Thévenot, *Rethinking Comparative Cultural Sociology*; Marie-France Toinet, Hubert Kempf, and Denis Lacorne, *Le libéralisme à l'américaine: L'état et le marché* (Paris: Economica, 1989).

14. N = 1000. Sophie Coignard, "Médiations," *Le Point*, 25 January 1992, sec. Société, pp. 63–69.

15. Mona Ozouf has gone furthest in developing this argument. See Mona Ozouf, *Les mots des femmes: Essai sur la singularité française* (Paris: Fayard, 1995). For a critique, see Ezekiel, "Anti-féminisme et anti-américanisme"; Scott, "Vive la différence!"

16. E.g., Badinter, "La chasse aux sorcières."

17. Jenson and Sineau, *Mitterand et les françaises*, p. 334.

18. Janine Mossuz-Lavau, *Les lois de l'amour: Les politiques de la sexualité en France (1950–1990)* (Paris: Editions Payot, 1991). It was only recently prohibited for defendants in rape (and by extension sexual harassment) cases to use as evidence the sexual past of the plaintiff to demonstrate that she welcomed the assault (Violence Against Women Act of 1994, 42 U.S.C. § 302 (1994)).

19. Viviana Zelizer, "The Purchase of Intimacy," *Law & Social Inquiry* 25, no. 3 (2000): 817–48; Steven P. Crowley and Jon D. Hanson, "The Nonpecuniary Costs of Accidents: Pain-and-Suffering Damages in Tort Law," *Harvard Law Review*, no. 108 (June 1995): 1785–917.

20. See Ezekiel, "Anti-féminisme et anti-américanisme"; Louis, "Harcèlement sexuel et domination masculine"; Scott, "Vive la différence!"

21. Louis, "Harcèlement sexuel et domination masculine"; see also Ezekiel, "Anti-féminisme et anti-américanisme."

CHAPTER 3: SEXUAL HARASSMENT IN THE PRESS

This chapter draws on Abigail C. Saguy, "Sexual Harassment in the News: The United States and France," *Communication Review* 5, no. 2 (2002): 109–41. Reproduced by permission of Taylor & Francis, Inc., http://www.routledge-ny.com.

1. 42 U.S.C. §§ 2000e to 2000e-17 (1994).

2. See, e.g., Badinter, "La chasse aux sorcières."

3. French lawmakers extended the legal definition of sexual harassment to coworkers eleven years later, however. See the Epilogue.

4. See James Lull and Stephen Hinerman, "The Search for Scandal," in *Media Scandals*, ed. James Lull and Stephen Hinerman (Oxford: Polity Press, 1997), 19–20, for a discussion of media scandals implicating institutions.

5. Jill Smolowe, "The Feminist Machine: Women Candidates Hope to Make 1992 a Banner Year, but Will Enough Voters Share Their Rage About Abortion Rights and Anita Hill to Make a Difference at the Polls?" *Time*, 4 May 1992, sec. Cover Stories, p. 34 (emphasis added).

6. Eric Schmitt, "Aftermath of Tailhook: The Pentagon's Accountant Takes over a Troubled Navy," *New York Times*, 12 July 1992, sec. 4, Week in Review Desk, col. 4 p. 2 (emphasis added).

7. Specifically, the Pearson correlation between the politics and scandal frame was .528, statistically significant at a p< .001 level.

8. R. W. Apple Jr., "Harassment Case Against Clinton Now at Highest Level," *New York Times*, 12 January 1997, sec. National Desk, col. 1 p. 16, emphasis added.

9. The Pearson's coefficient was .438 and statistically significant at a p< .001 level.

10. Aric Press, "Abusing Sex at the Office," *Newsweek*, 10 March 1980, sec. Justice, p. 81, emphasis added.

11. See Ryken Grattet and Scott Phillips, "Judicial Rhetoric, Meaning-Making, and the Institutionalization of Hate Crime Law," *Law & Society Review* 34, no. 3 (2000): 567–606.

12. Based on a Chi-Square test, p< .05.

13. Based on a Chi-Square test, p< .001.

14. The prevalence of the social problem frame in the Hill, Packwood, Tailhook, and Jones stories, respectively, was: 41 percent, 32 percent, 82 percent, and 8 percent.

15. See Deborah Zalesne, "Sexual Harassment Law: Has It Gone Too Far, or Has the Media?" *Temple Political & Civil Rights Law Review* 8, no. 2 (1999): 351–76.

16. See Zalesne, "Sexual Harassment Law."

17. *Meritor v Vinson*, 477 US 57 (1986).

18. Seth Faison, "Sexual Harassment New as Legal Issue," *New York Times*, 7 October 1991, sec. A, National Desk, col. 1, p. 14, emphasis added.

19. Nancy Gibbs, "Office Crimes: In a Matter of Hours, a New Vocabulary of Laws and Risks and Expectations Entered the Language of the Factory Floor and the Tower Suite," *Time*, 21 October 1991, sec. Nation, p. 52 (emphasis added).

20. Janice Castro, "Sexual Harassment: A Guide: An Instant 'How-Not-to' Book Prompted by the Thomas Hearings Spells It out with Classroom Clarity," *Time*, 20 January 1992, sec. Business, p. 37 (emphasis added).

21. See, e.g., MacKinnon, *Sexual Harassment of Working Women*.

22. Based on Chi-Square tests, p<.001 for power and violence, p<.05 for morality and women's issue, and p<.10 for scandal and making money on lawsuits.

23. For politics, p<.001; for scandal, p<.01; for morality, p<.10; and for plaintiffs' desires to make money in lawsuits, p<.01, based on Chi-Square tests.

24. Based on Chi-Square tests, p<.01 for scandal and p<.001 for politics.

25. The difference between these two ratios was statistically significant at p<.01, based on a Chi-Square test.

26. Based on a Chi-Square test, p<.01.

27. Based on a Chi-Square test, p <.10.

28. The comparable figure for French articles reporting on the United States is 11 percent, but this difference is not statistically significant.

29. Laurent Zecchini, "Accusé de harcèlement sexuel, un tenor du sénat américain démissionne," *Le Monde*, 9 September 1995, sec. International (emphasis added).

30. Elisabeth Badinter, "Ici, en droit, nous avons tout obtenu," *Le Nouvel Observateur*, 19 May 1994, pp. 102–5.

31. The difference is statistically significant at p<.01, based on a Chi-Square test.

32. The difference is statistically significant at p<.001, based on a Chi-Square test.

33. Based on a Chi-Square test, p<.26. Consistent with American and French reporting on sexual harassment more generally, when reporting on the Hill-Thomas debate, French reporters were significantly more likely to frame sexual harassment as a form of violence (p<.01) while American reporters were significantly more likely to frame it as an instance of discrimination (p<.01).

34. Based on a Chi-Square test, p<.001. The French press was also significantly more likely to frame the Jones case as a scandal (p<.10) and as political (p<.05).

35. Though penal law is not limited to the workplace, labor law is.

36. Based on a Chi-Square test, p<.001.

37. Ursula Gauthier, "Suède: La fin des filles publiques," *Le Nouvel Observateur*, 14 January 1999, sec. Notre époque, p. 86 (emphasis added).

38. Marie Huret, "Au tribunal, parole contre parole," *L'Express*, 13 March 1999 (emphasis added).

39. Based on a Chi-Square test, p<.05. Moreover, the size and statistical significance of the national difference in the prevalence of the violence frame is also greater in this sample.

40. Rafaele Rivais, "La commission européenne s'attaque au harcèlement sexuel au travail," *Le Monde*, 9 June 2000, sec. Dernière page.

41. Badinter, "La chasse aux sorcières."

42. Rapport officiel du Sénat, n° 350, Seconde Session Ordinaire de 1991–1992, pp.16–17.

43. The French Parliament extended the sexual harassment statutes to coworkers, however, in January 2002. See the Epilogue.

44. This law was overturned by the Cour de Cassation on 20 February 2001 (Arrêt n° 810 du 20 février 2001, Cour de Cassation — Chambre criminelle). See the Epilogue for a discussion of how this High Court decision enabled media reporting on sexual harassment cases.

45. See Bennett, *News*; Brill, "War Gets the Monica Treatment"; Entman, *Democracy Without Citizens*; Gans, *Deciding What's News*; Gitlin, *The Whole World Is Watching*.

46. See Bennett, *News*; Entman, *Democracy Without Citizens*.

47. Pierre Albert, *La presse française* (Paris: La Documentation Française, 1998); Mark Hunter, *Le journalisme d'investigation* (Paris: Presses Universitaires de France, 1997); Raymond Kuhn, *The Media in France* (London: Routledge, 1995).

48. Rodney Benson, "La logique du profit dans les médias americains," *Actes de la Recherche en Sciences Sociales* 131–32 (2000): 107–15; Rodney Benson, "The Mediated Public Sphere: A Model for Cross-National Research," Working Paper 2001 series, Center for the Study of Culture, Organizations and Politics, University of California, Berkeley. Benson notes, however, that the Paris national newspapers' reliance on daily newsstand sales for most of their revenues (with the exception of *Le Figaro*) may also sensationalize press treatment of politics, though within the legal and normative limits of information typically covered by French journalists.

49. See Rodney Benson, "Shaping the Public Sphere: Journalistic Fields and Immigration Debates in the United States and France, 1973–1994," Ph.D. diss., Department of Sociology, University of California, Berkeley, 2000.

50. See, e.g., U.S. Merit Systems Protection Board, *Sexual Harassment in the Federal Workforce*; Harris, "Le harcèlement sexuel."

CHAPTER 4: DISCRIMINATION, VIOLENCE, PROFESSIONALISM, AND THE BOTTOM LINE

1. These statistics should be interpreted with caution due to the nonrepresentative nature of this small sample.

2. I expect that if I had a larger sample of respondents, more of the national differences would have been statistically significant.

3. *Burlington Industries v Ellerth*, 524 US 742 (1998); *Faragher v City of Boca Raton*, 524 US 775 (1998).

4. See Chapter 1; Franke, "What's Wrong with Sexual Harassment?"; Axam and Zalesne, "Simulated Sodomy and Other Forms of Heterosexual 'Horseplay.'"

5. *McKinney v Dole*, 765 F2d 1129, 1138–39 (DC Cir 1985); *Cline v General Electric*, 757 FSupp 923, 931–33 (ND Ill 1991); *Accardi v Superior Court*, 21 Cal-Rptr2d 292 (1993).

6. *Lehman v Toys 'R' Us*, 626 A2d 445 (NJ 1993).

7. *Oncale v Sundowner Offshore Services, Inc.*, 523 US 75, 80 (1998).

8. For a thoughtful discussion of how Title VII could be recast to better accommodate the phenomenon of same-sex harassment, see Franke, "What's Wrong with Sexual Harassment?"

9. If we were to interpret these findings in light of Vicki Schultz's argument ("Reconceptualizing Sexual Harassment"), we would arrive at the more pessimistic conclusion that the discrimination component of sexual harassment has been replaced by an exclusive focus on sexuality. Yet, when presented with Vignette 10, in which a (male) boss calls his female but not male employees "stupid, slow, and incompetent" without using any sexual innuendo, 35 percent of the American respondents said this was sexual harassment and another 43 percent said it fell under Title VII as "gender harassment."

10. Discrimination on the basis of sexual orientation is prohibited by several state laws and institutional guidelines, although not under sexual harassment regulation.

11. See Michel Minet and Francis Saramito, "Le harcèlement sexuel," *Droit Ouvrier* (February 1997): 48–91, for a review of this jurisprudence.

12. Her description of the "petits chefs" echoes the *droit de cuissage* of the nineteenth century (Louis, *Le droit de cuissage*). Political scientists Jane Jenson and Mariette Sineau find that this type of analysis dominated French press coverage of sexual harassment (*Mitterand et les françaises*, p. 288). Likewise, as discussed in Chapter 3, the French articles I analyzed were more likely to frame sexual harassment as an abuse of (hierarchical) power than to employ any other frame.

13. The AVFT has supported the passage of an "antisexist" bill — like the one proposed by Yvette Roudy in 1983 but squashed in Parliament — that would condemn sexist statements like the antiracist law condemns racist ones (see Jenson and Sineau, *Mitterand et les françaises*, pp. 272–79).

14. See, e.g., AVFT, ed. *De l'abus de pouvoir sexuel*; Cynthia Cockburn, *In the Way of Women: Men's Resistance to Sex Equality in Organizations* (Ithaca, N. Y.: ILR

Press, 1991); Cromer, *Le harcèlement sexuel en France*; Cynthia Fuchs Epstein, "Tinkerbells and Pinups," in *Cultivating Differences: Symbolic Boundaries and the Making of Inequality*, ed. Michèle Lamont and Marcel Fournier (Chicago: University of Chicago Press, 1992); Rosabeth M. Kanter, *Men and Women of the Corporation* (New York: Basic Books, 1977); Schultz, "Reconceptualizing Sexual Harassment"; Christine Williams, *Still a Man's World: Men Who Do Women's Work* (Berkeley: University of California Press, 1995).

15. See Frank Dobbin and John R. Sutton, "The Strength of a Weak State: The Rights Revolution and the Rise of Human Resources Management Divisions," *American Journal of Sociology* 104, no. 2 (1998): 441–76.

16. See Toinet, Kempf, and Lacorne, *Le libéralisme à l'américaine*.

17. This said, free-market or *libéralisme du marché* arguments are gaining influence in France. See Pierre Bourdieu, *Acts of Resistance: Against the Tyranny of the Market*, trans. Richard Nice (New York: New Press, 1998).

18. Camille Paglia, *Vamps and Tramps* (New York: Vintage, 1994), p. 49.

19. Paglia, *Vamps and Tramps*, p. 48.

20. Paglia, *Vamps and Tramps*, p. 27.

21. *Meritor v Vinson*, 477 US at 67.

22. *Meritor v Vinson*, 477 US 57 (1986).

23. France also has laws that only apply to businesses of a certain size, such as those that require larger companies to have "Committees of Hygiene and Security." Future research should explore systematically the connection between laws that only apply to large corporations and popular conceptions of the public/private divide.

24. The legal concept of violence, in fact, was extended to accommodate sexual harassment among coworkers in January 2002. See the Epilogue.

25. See Aeberhard-Hodges, "Sexual Harassment in Employment."

26. Sometimes French and American expectations about workplace regulations collide. When Disney opened a theme park in a suburb of Paris, it imposed its dress code, banning facial hair and requiring short haircuts, on its French employees. The latter expressed dismay and resentment over what they perceived as intrusive rules.

CONCLUSION

1. Marie-France Hirigoyen, *Le harcèlement moral: La violence perverse au quotidien* (Paris: Syros, 1998).

2. For particularly good discussions of collective consciousness, see, for instance, the work of Emile Durkheim, especially *Les formes elémentaires de la vie religieuse*; Moscovici, "The Phenomenon of Social Representations"; Maurice Halbwachs, *The Collective Memory* (New York: Harper and Row, 1980); and Michael Schudson, *Watergate in American Memory: How We Remember, Forget, and Reconstruct the Past* (New York: Basic Books, 1992).

3. Title VII of the Civil Rights Act of 1964, 42 U.S.C. §§ 2000e to 2000e-17 (1994).

4. See Chapter 2.

5. Gitlin, *The Whole World Is Watching*, p. 146.

6. Dworkin, "Harassment in the 1990s"; "Thank You, Anita Hill, for the Civil Rights Act of 1991." For a discussion of the merits of these claims, see Clegg, "A Brief Legislative History of the Civil Rights Act of 1991."

7. Zalesne, "Sexual Harassment Law."

8. *Burlington v Ellerth*, 524 US 742 (1998); *Faragher v City of Boca Raton*, 524 US 775 (1998). This is what some neo-institutionalists have called the "endongeneity of law." Edelman, Uggen, and Erlanger, "The Endogeneity of Legal Regulation." See also Dobbin and Sutton, "The Strength of a Weak State."

9. Badinter, "La chasse aux sorcières."

10. See Chapter 1.

11. See the Epilogue for a discussion of this reform and its significance.

12. For a discussion of international policy borrowing, see Richard Rose, *Lesson-Drawing in Public Policy: A Guide to Learning in Time and Space* (Chatham, N. J.: Chatham House Publishers, Inc., 1993).

13. See Schulhofer, *Unwanted Sex*.

14. See Friedland and Alford, "Bringing the State Back In"; Nicholas Pedriana and Robin Stryker, "Culture Wars 1960s Style: Equal Employment Opportunity — Affirmative Action Law and the Philadelphia Plan." *American Journal of Sociology* 103, no. 3 (November 1997): 633–91; Stryker, "Rules, Resources, and Legitimacy Processes."

15. See Frank Dobbin, "The Social Construction of the Great Depression: Industrial Policy During the 1930s in the United States, Britain, and France," *Theory and Society* 22 (1993): 1–56; Lamont and Thévenot, eds., *Rethinking Comparative Cultural Sociology*.

16. Ezekiel, "Anti-féminisme et anti-américanisme," pp. 59–76 ; Louis, "Harcèlement sexuel et domination masculine"; Scott, "Vive la différence!"

17. Bleich, *Race Politics in Britain and France*.

18. Rodney Benson and Abigail C. Saguy, "The Globalization of Social

Problems: Sexual Harassment and Immigration in the French and American News," presented at the American Sociological Association Conference (Anaheim, Calif., 20 August 2001).

EPILOGUE

1. Hirigoyen, *Le harcèlement moral*, p. 12.
2. Hirigoyen, *Le harcèlement moral*, p. 56.
3. Hirigoyen, *Le harcèlement moral*, p. 55.
4. Hirigoyen, *Le harcèlement moral*, pp. 59–60, 63.
5. Hirigoyen, *Le harcèlement moral*, p. 69.
6. Louise Fitzgerald, "Sexual Harassment: The Definition and Measurement of a Construct," in *Ivory Power: Sexual Harassment on Campus*, ed. Michael A. Paludi (Albany: State University of New York Press, 1991).
7. Hirigoyen, *Le harcèlement moral*, p. 70.
8. The three other categories of sexual harassment noted are: "seductive behavior," "non-desired sexual attention," and "sexual imposition."
9. Law 2001–1066, passed on 16 November 2001, introduced the concept of indirect discrimination to French law ("Loi no 2001–1066 du 16 novembre 2001 relative à la lutte contre les discriminations," *Journal Officiel*, no. 267: 18311). It is too soon to tell what the concrete effect of this will be on French jurisprudence.
10. Code de travail [C. Trav.] art. L. 122–49 (Fr.).
11. *Burlington Industries v Ellerth*, 524 US 742 (1998); *Faragher v City of Boca Raton*, 524 US 775 (1998).
12. In 2002, the European Parliament and European Commission revised the 1976 *directive* on sex discrimination to address sexual harassment as a form of sex discrimination. Unlike the European Commission's 1991 *recommendation* on sexual harassment, the *directive* will be binding on nation states when it goes into effect in July 2005. As such, it may have an important impact on national laws. See the European Parliament legislative resolution on the proposal for a Directive of the European Parliament and of the Council amending Council Directive 76/207/EEC on the implementation of the principle of equal treatment for men and women as regards access to employment, vocational training and promotion, and working conditions (COM(2000) 334 – C5–0369/2000 – 2000/0142[COD]) in Official Journal of the European Communities [O.J.] C47 E, volume 45, 21 February 2002, 173).

13. Le Magueresse, "Harcèlement sexuel au travail."

14. See Michel Schneider, "Désir, vous avez dit désir?" *Le Monde*, 6 March 2002, sec. Analyses & Forum.

15. Code pénal [C. Pén.] art. 222–33 (Fr.).

16. CLASCHES, "Petition contre le harcèlement sexuel dans l'enseignement supérieur," unpublished document. See also CLASCHES, "La fin d'un tabou à l'université," *Le Monde*, 6 March 2002, sec. Analyses & Forum.

17. Interview with the author, 22 April 2002. In what follows I draw on the account of this respondent.

18. Blandine Grosjean, "Harcèlement sexuel, la fac se rebelle." *Libération*, 28 January 2002, sec. Rebonds.

19. See Eric Fassin, "Actualité du harcèlement sexuel," *Le Monde*, 22 February 2002. sec. Analyses & Forums.

20. Emmanuel Pierrat, "Le droit de cuissage, une histoire française," *Le Monde*, 6 March 2002, sec. Analyses & Forum.

21. Arrêt n° 810 du 20 février 2001, Cour de Cassation — Chambre criminelle.

22. Blandine Grosjean, "Promotion université," *Libération*, 19 February 2002.

23. Robert Solé, "Plainte et chuchotements," *Le Monde*, 17 February 2002.

24. Pascale Krémer, "Les initiateurs de la pétition contre le harcèlement sexuel à l'université sont reçus au ministère," *Le Monde*, 27 March 2002.

25. Krémer, "Les initiateurs de la petition."

26. Cited in Solé, "Plainte et chuchotements."

27. Francis Terquem, "Harcèlement sexuel: La nouvelle inquisition." *Le Monde*, 26 February 2002, sec. Analyses & Forum.

28. Terquem, "Harcèlement sexuel."

29. Hervé Le Bras, "Chasse à l'homme." *Le Monde*, 19 March 2002.

30. Solé, "Plainte et chuchotements."

31. Le Bras, "Chasse à l'homme."

32. Elisabeth Zucker-Rouvillois, "Les mandarins gourous," *Libération*, 4 February 2002, sec. Rebonds.

33. Pascal Degiovanni and Nicolas Legrand, "Université: Casser les liens de dépendance," *Libération*, 8 March 2002, sec. Rebonds.

34. Terquem, "Harcèlement sexuel."

35. Grosjean, "Promotion université."

36. See, e.g., Emilie Lanez, "Une ancienne étudiante du démographe renommé Hervé Le Bras porte plainte pour harcèlement sexuel: Une première

en France," *Le Point,* 22 February 2002, p. 66. For a critique, see Eric Fassin, "Manipulation?" *Le Point,* 5 April 2002, p. 71.

37. Pierrat, "Le droit de cuissage, une histoire française."

38. "Plainte contre X avec constitution de partie civile," 28 December 2001.

39. Grosjean, "Harcèlement sexuel."

40. Lanez, "Une ancienne étudiante."

41. See Eric Fassin, "Pouvoirs sexuels: Le juge Thomas, le cour suprême et la société américaine." *Esprit,* no. 177 (December 1991): 102–30; Eric Fassin, "Un an sans puritains," *Le Monde,* 5 June 1997, sec. Analyses & Forum.

42. Fassin, "Actualité du harcèlement sexuel."

43. Personal discussion with Eric Fassin, 31 March 2002.

44. Fassin, "Manipulation?"

45. Krémer, "Les initiateurs de la petition." A member of CLASCHES told me the same thing in a discussion on 14 March 2002.

46. Solé, "Plainte et chuchotements."

47. Pierrat, "Le droit de cuissage, une histoire française." His exact language was: "Le délit de harcèlement sexuel n'a pas surgi dans notre droit hexagonal à la faveur d'un clonage de l'imagination hollywoodienne."

48. Fassin, "Manipulation?"

49. Thanks to Judith Ezekiel for our stimulating discussion on this point.

APPENDIX

1. To better assist those who reside outside of the capital, the AVFT has tried to develop networks with lawyers, *inspection du travail* government agencies (workplace inspectors), and local unions. Their success has been uneven across different regions.

2. I have intentionally avoided using the label "feminist" (except in quotes or as "self-defined feminist") to describe the respondents, since this label is itself highly contested. For instance, Camille Paglia calls herself a feminist, but her work is labeled "anti-feminist" in many feminist circles (Muriel Dimen, "Review of *Sexual Personae: Art and Decadence from Nefertiti to Emily Dickinson,*" *Psychoanalytic Psychology* 10, no. 3 [1993]: 451–62; Naomi Wolf, "Feminist Fatale: A Reply to Camille Paglia," *New Republic* [March 1992]: 23–25). Catharine MacKinnon calls herself a "radical feminist" while others label her a "prohibitionist" feminist. Elisabeth Badinter considers herself a feminist but this status is disputed in some French "feminist" circles. Disputes over the label "feminist,"

"radical feminist," etc., and the way they are articulated differently in France and the United States, are themselves topics ripe for investigation. I thank Eric Fassin for bringing this to my attention.

3. See Camille Paglia, *Sexual Personae: Art and Decadence From Nefertiti to Emily Dickinson* (New York: Vintage Books, 1991); Camille Paglia, *Sex, Art, and American Culture* (New York: Vintage Books, 1992).

4. See Elisabeth Badinter, *L'un est l'autre* (Paris: Odile Jacob, 1986); Elisabeth Badinter, *XY: De l'identité masculine* (Paris: Odile Jacob, 1992).

5. See Françoise Giroud, *Les françaises: De la gauloise à la pilule* (Paris: Fayard, 1999).

6. See Ozouf, *Les mots des femmes*. For a critique, see Ezekiel, "Anti-féminisme et anti-américanisme"; Scott, "Vive la différence!"

7. Dimen, "Review of *Sexual Personae*"; Wolf, "Feminist Fatale."

8. In contrast, the personnel representative at the American branch of FrenchCo was a full-time human resource employee who reported directly to the HR manager.

9. See Table 3, Chapter 4.

10. Laurent Thévenot encouraged me to use ambiguous vignettes as a way of leading the respondents to articulate judgments and clarify their criteria of evaluation.

11. *Le Monde* is the most widely circulated newspaper in France and is associated with the political center, as compared to the leftist *Libération* or conservative *Le Figaro*. The *New York Times* leads in newspaper circulation after the *Wall Street Journal* and *USA Today* (Robert Fanignetti, *The World Almanac and Book of Facts* [Mahwah, N. J.: K-111 Reference Corporation, 1996]). However, the former is more comparable to *Le Monde* in content and readership than these other two publications. The *New York Times* and *Le Monde* focus on political and societal events, while the *Wall Street Journal* focuses more on financial issues. While the *Wall Street Journal* is widely read in the corporate world, the *New York Times* and *Le Monde* are points of reference respectively for American and French intellectuals and the educated public. *USA Today* is less intellectual, more comparable to *Le Parisien* or *France Soir*.

12. *L'Express* has historically been the most widely distributed newsmagazine but in recent years, *Le Nouvel Observateur* has caught up with its competitor in sales. A larger gap separates *Time*, the most widely distributed newsmagazine, from its most serious competitor, *Newsweek*. *L'Express* and *Time* make for a neat comparison, since the founders of *L'Express* took *Time* as their model. The *Nouvel Observateur* is associated with the French Left while *L'Express* is located at the

political center. Since the 1960s, *Time* and *Newsweek* have been located at the political center.

13. Louis, "Harcèlement sexuel et domination masculine."

14. Louis, "Harcèlement sexuel et domination masculine."

15. A narrative description of the other variables is available upon request.

16. According to Lull and Hinerman ("The Search for Scandal," pp.11–13), there are ten components of a scandal, including: (1) *"social norms reflecting the dominant morality must be transgressed"* (emphasis in the original); the transgressions must be performed by (2) specific persons who carry out (3) actions that reflect an exercise of their desires or interests; individual persons must be (4) identified as perpetrators of the act(s), and be shown to have acted (5) intentionally or recklessly and be (6) held responsible for their actions. (7) The actions and events must have differential consequences for those involved. (8) The revelations must be widely circulated via communications media, where they are (9) effectively narrativized into a story that (10) inspires widespread interest and discussion. All of these criteria are present in the four scandals discussed.

BIBLIOGRAPHY

Abrams, Kathryn. "Symposium: The State of the Union: Civil Rights: Gender Discrimination and the Transformation of Workplace Norms." *Vand. L. Rev.* 42 (May 1989): 1183–248.

Aeberhard-Hodges, Jane. "Sexual Harassment in Employment: Recent Judicial and Arbitral Trends." *International Labour Review*, no. 135 (1996): 499–533.

Albert, Pierre. *La presse française*. Paris: La Documentation Française, 1998.

Apple, R. W. Jr., "Harassment Case Against Clinton Now at Highest Level." *New York Times*, 12 January 1997, sec. National Desk, col. 1, p. 16.

Assemblée Nationale. "Projet de loi relatif à la prévention et à la répression des infractions sexuelles ainsi qu'à la protection des mineurs," 202, 27 (1998).

AVFT. "Proposition d'amendement de l'AVFT." *Cette violence dont nous ne voulons plus* 10 (June 1990): 59–63.

———, ed. *De l'abus de pouvoir sexuel: Le harcèlement sexuel au travail*. Paris and Montreal: La Découverte/Le Boréal, 1990.

Axam, Hilary S., and Deborah Zalesne. "Simulated Sodomy and Other Forms of Heterosexual 'Horseplay': Same Sex Sexual Harassment, Workplace Gender Hierarchies and the Myth of the Gender Monolith Before and After *Oncale*." *Yale Journal of Law and Feminism* 11 (1999): 155–243.

Badinter, Elisabeth. "La chasse aux sorcières," *Le Nouvel Observateur*, 17–23 October 1991, 82.

———. "Ici, en droit, nous avons tout obtenu." *Le Nouvel Observateur,* 19 May 1994, 102–5.

———. *L'un est l'autre.* Paris: Odile Jacob, 1986.

———. *XY: De l'identité masculine.* Paris: Odile Jacob, 1992.

Bennett, W. Lance. *News: The Politics of Illusion.* New York: Longman, 2001.

Benneytout, Mirielle, Sylvie Cromer, and Marie-Victoire Louis. "Harcèlement sexuel: Une réforme restrictive qui n'est pas sans danger." *Semaine Sociale Lamy* 599 (1992): 3–4.

Benson, Rodney. "La logique du profit dans les médias americains," *Actes de la Recherche en Sciences Sociales* 131–132 (2000): 107–15.

———. "The Mediated Public Sphere: A Model for Cross-National Research." Working Paper 2001 series, Center for the Study of Culture, Organizations and Politics, University of California, Berkeley.

———. "Shaping the Public Sphere: Journalistic Fields and Immigration Debates in the United States and France, 1973–1994." Ph.D. diss., Department of Sociology, University of California, Berkeley, 2000.

Benson, Rodney, and Abigail C. Saguy. "The Globalization of Social Problems: Sexual Harassment and Immigration in the French and American News." Presented at the American Sociological Association Conference, Anaheim, Calif.: 20 August 2001.

Berger, Peter L. *The Sacred Canopy: Elements of a Sociological Theory of Religion.* New York: Anchor Books, 1969.

Berger, Peter L., and Thomas Luckman. *The Social Construction of Reality.* Garden City, N. Y.: Doubleday Anchor, 1967.

Bernstein, Anita. "Law, Culture, and Harassment." *University of Pennsylvania Law Review* 142, no. 4 (1994): 1227–311.

Bird, Robert C. "More Than a Congressional Joke: A Fresh Look at the Legislative History of Sex Discrimination of the 1964 Civil Rights Act." *William and Mary Journal of Women and the Law* 3 (Spring 1997): 137–61.

Bleich, Erik. *Race Politics in Britain and France: Ideas and Policy-Making Since the 1960s.* New York: Cambridge University Press, in press.

Boli, John, and George M. Thomas. "World Culture in the World Polity: A Century of International Non-Governmental Organization." *American Sociological Review* 62, no. 2 (1997): 171–90.

Boltanski, Luc. *The Making of a Class: Cadres in French Society.* Cambridge/ Paris: Cambridge University Press and Maison de la Science de L'Homme, 1987.

Boltanski, Luc, and Laurent Thévenot. *De la justification: Les économies de la grandeur.* Paris: Gallimard, 1991.

Bourdieu, Pierre. *Acts of Resistance: Against the Tyranny of the Market.* Trans. Richard Nice. New York: The New Press, 1998.

Boureau, Alain. *Le droit de cuissage: La fabrication d'un mythe XIIe-XXe siècle.* Paris: Albin Michel, 1995.

Brauer, Carl M. "Women Activists, Southern Conservatives, and the Prohibition of Sex Discrimination in Title VII of the 1964 Civil Rights Act." *Journal of Southern History* 49, no. 1 (1983): 37–56.

Brill, Steven. "War Gets the Monica Treatment." *Brill's Content* (July/August 1999).

Browne, Kingsley. "Free Speech." *Directions in Sexual Harassment Law,* edited by Reva Siegel and Catharine MacKinnon. New Haven, Conn.: Yale University Press, in press.

Brubaker, Rogers. *Citizenship and Nationhood in France and Germany.* Cambridge, Mass.: Harvard University Press, 1992.

Cahill, Mia. *The Social Construction of Sexual Harassment Law.* Aldershot: Ashgate, 2001.

Castro, Janice. "Sexual Harassment: A Guide: An Instant 'How-Not-to' Book Prompted by the Thomas Hearings Spells It out with Classroom Clarity." *Time,* 20 January 1992, sec. Business, 37.

Chancer, Lynn. *Sadomasochism in Everyday Life: The Dynamics of Power and Powerlessness.* New Brunswick, N. J.: Rutgers University Press, 1992.

CLASCHES. "La fin d'un tabou à l'université." *Le Monde,* 6 March 2002, sec. Analyses & Forum.

———. "Pétition contre le harcèlement sexuel dans l'enseignement supérieur." Unpublished document.

Clegg, Roger. "A Brief Legislative History of the Civil Rights Act of 1991." *La. L. Rev.* 54 (1994): 1459–71.

Cockburn, Cynthia. *In the Way of Women: Men's Resistance to Sex Equality in Organizations.* Ithaca, N. Y.: ILR Press, 1991.

Cohen, Lloyd R. "Sexual Harassment and the Law," *Society* (May/June 1991): 8–13.

Coignard, Sophie. "Médiations." *Le Point,* 25 January 1992, sec. Société, 63–69.

"Comment." *New York University Law Review* 51 (1976): 148.

"Compte rendu intégral: Séance du mardi 31 mars 1998." *Sénat Débats Parlementaires Journal Officiel de la République Française,* no. 25 (1 April 1998): 1369–70.

Cousins, Christine. "Women and Employment." In *Society, Work and Welfare in Europe,* 72–96. London: Macmillan Press, 1999.

Coyne, Christine. "*Anjelino v. New York Times Co.*: Granting Men Standing to Fight Injuries Received as a Result of Sexual Discrimination Towards Female Co-Workers." *Villanova Law Review* 45 (2000): 651–88.

Craib, Ralph. "Sex and Women at UC Berkeley — 2 Surveys." *San Francisco Chronicle*, 22 July 1977.

Crane, Diana, ed. *The Sociology of Culture: Emerging Theoretical Perspectives.* Oxford: Basil Blackwell, 1994.

Cromer, Sylvie. "France: AVFT." In *De l'abus de pouvoir sexuel: Le harcèlement sexuel au travail*, edited by AVFT, 223–30. Paris and Montreal: La Découverte/Le Boréal, 1990.

——. *Le harcèlement sexuel en France: La levée d'un tabou 1985–1990.* Paris: La Documentation Française, 1995.

——. "Histoire d'une loi: La pénalisation du harcèlement sexuel dans le nouveau code pénal." *Projets Féministes* 1 (March 1992): 108–17.

Cromer, Sylvie, and Marie-Victoire Louis. "Existe-t-il un harcèlement sexuel 'à la française'?" *French Politics and Society* 10, no. 3 (1992): 37–43.

Crowley, Steven P., and Jon D. Hanson. "The Nonpecuniary Costs of Accidents: Pain-and-Suffering Damages in Tort Law." *Harvard Law Review*, no. 108 (June 1995): 1785–917.

Crozier, Michel. *The Bureaucratic Phenomenon.* Chicago: University of Chicago Press, 1964.

de Pisan, Annie, and Anne Tristan. *Histoires Du MLF.* Paris: Calmann-Lévy, 1977.

Degiovanni, Pascal, and Nicolas Legrand. "Université: Casser les liens de dépendance." *Libération*, 8 March 2002, sec. Rebonds.

Dekeuwer-Defossez, Françoise. "Le harcèlement sexuel en droit français: Discrimination ou atteinte à la liberté?" *La Semaine juridique* 3662, no. 13 (1993): 137–41.

Desrosières, Alain, and Laurent Thévenot. *Les catégories socio-professionelles.* Paris: La Découverte, 1988.

Dimen, Muriel. "Review of *Sexual Personae: Art and Decadence from Nefertiti to Emily Dickinson.*" Psychoanalytic Psychology 10, no. 3 (1993): 451–62.

Dobbin, Frank. "The Social Construction of the Great Depression: Industrial Policy During the 1930s in the United States, Britain, and France." *Theory and Society*, no. 22 (1993): 1–56.

Dobbin, Frank, and John R. Sutton. "The Strength of a Weak State: The Rights Revolution and the Rise of Human Resources Management Divisions." *American Journal of Sociology* 104, no. 2 (1998): 441–76.

Douglas, Mary. *How Institutions Think*. Ithaca, N. Y.: Cornell University Press, 1986.

Duchen, Claire. *Feminism in France: From May '68 to Mitterrand*. London: Routledge & Kegan Paul, 1986.

Durkheim, Emile. *Les formes élémentaires de la vie religieuse: Le système totémique en Australie*. Paris: Quadrige/Presses Universitaires de France, 1960.

Dworkin, Terry Morehead. "Harassment in the 1990s: Sexual Harassment in the Workplace: Women in Business." *Business Horizons* 36, no. 2 (1993): 52.

Edelman, Lauren, Steven E. Abraham, and Howard S. Erlanger, "Professional Construction of Law: The Inflated Threat of Wrongful Discharge." *Law and Society Review* 26, no. 1 (1992): 47–83.

Edelman, Lauren B., and Mark C. Suchman. "When the 'Haves' Hold Court: Speculations on the Organizational Internalization of Law." *Law & Society Review* 33, no. 4 (1999): 941–91.

Edelman, Lauren B., Christopher Uggen, and Howard S. Erlanger. "The Endogeneity of Legal Regulation: Grievance Procedures as Rational Myth." *American Journal of Sociology* 105, no. 2 (1999): 406–54.

Elman, R. Amy. *Sexual Subordination and State Intervention: Comparing Sweden and the United States*. Providence, R. I.: Berghahn Books, 1996.

Entman, Robert. *Democracy Without Citizens: Media and the Decay of American Politics*. Oxford: Oxford University Press, 1989.

Epstein, Cynthia Fuchs. "Tinkerbells and Pinups." In *Cultivating Differences: Symbolic Boundaries and the Making of Inequality*. Edited by Michèle Lamont and Marcel Fournier, 232–56. Chicago: University of Chicago Press, 1992.

Esping-Andersen, Gosta. *The Three Worlds of Welfare Capitalism*. Princeton, N. J.: Princeton University Press, 1990.

Estrich, Susan. "Sex at Work." *Stanford Law Review* 43 (1991): 813–61.

Evans, Sara. *Born for Liberty*. New York: Free Press, 1989.

Ewick, Patricia, and Susan S. Silbey. *The Common Place of Law: Stories from Everyday Life*. Chicago: University of Chicago Press, 1998.

Ezekiel, Judith. "Anti-féminisme et anti-américanisme: Un mariage politiquement réussi." *Nouvelles questions féministes* 17, no. 1 (1995): 59–76.

"Fair Housing Law Is Applied in a Sexual Harassment Case." *New York Times*, 11 December 1983, sec. 1, p. 44.

Faison, Seth. "Sexual Harassment New as Legal Issue." *New York Times*, 7 October 1991, sec. A: National Desk, col. 1, p. 14.

Fanignetti, Robert. *The World Almanac and Book of Facts*. Mahwah, N. J.: K-111 Reference Corporation, 1996.

Farley, Lin. *Sexual Shakedown: The Sexual Harassment of Women on the Job.* New York: McGraw-Hill, 1978.

Fassin, Eric. "Actualité du harcèlement sexuel." *Le Monde,* 22 February 2002, sec. Analyses & Forums.

———. "Un an sans puritains." *Le Monde,* 5 June 1997, sec. Analyses & Forum.

———. "Manipulation?" *Le Point,* 5 April 2002, 71.

———. "PaCS socialista: La gauche et le 'juste milieu,' " *Le Banquet,* nos. 12–13 (1998): 147–59.

———. "Pouvoirs sexuels: Le juge Thomas, le cour suprême et la société américaine." *Esprit,* no. 177 (December 1991): 102–30.

Felgentrager, Margot. "Droit et harcèlement sexuel." *Pratiques psychologiques,* no. 3 (1996): 45–48.

Fiske, Susan T., and Patricia W. Linville. "What Does the Schema Concept Buy Us?" *Personality and Social Psychology Bulletin* 6 (1980): 543–57.

Fitzgerald, Louise. "Sexual Harassment: The Definition and Measurement of a Construct." In *Ivory Power: Sexual Harassment on Campus,* edited by Michael A. Paludi. Albany: State University of New York Press, 1991.

Franke, Katherine. "What's Wrong with Sexual Harassment?" *Stanford Law Review* 49, no. 4 (1997): 691–772.

Friedland, Roger and Robert Alford. "Bringing the State Back In: Symbols, Practices, and Institutional Contradictions." In *The New Institutionalism in Organizational Analysis,* edited by Walter W. Powell and Paul J. DiMaggio, 232–63. Chicago: University of Chicago Press, 1991.

Gamson, Joshua. *Freaks Talk Back: Tabloid Talk Shows and Sexual Nonconformity.* Chicago: University of Chicago Press, 1998.

Gamson, William. *Talking Politics.* Cambridge: Cambridge University Press, 1992.

Gans, Herbert. *Deciding What's News.* New York: Pantheon, 1979.

Gauthier, Ursula. "Suède: La fin des filles publiques." *Le Nouvel Observateur,* 14 January 1999, sec. Notre époque, p. 86.

Gibbs, Nancy. "Office Crimes: In a Matter of Hours, a New Vocabulary of Laws and Risks and Expectations Entered the Language of the Factory Floor and the Tower Suite." *Time,* 21 October 1991, sec. Nation, p. 52.

Giddens, Anthony. *The Constitution of Society: Outline of the Theory of Structuration.* Cambridge: Polity Press, 1984.

Ginsburg, Gilbert J., and Jean Galloway Koreski. "Sexual Advances by an Employee's Supervisor: A Sex-Discrimination Violation of Title VII?" *Employee Relations Law Journal* 3 (1977): 83.

Giroud, Françoise. *Les françaises: De la gauloise à la pilule.* Paris: Fayard, 1999.

Gitlin, Todd. *The Whole World Is Watching: Mass Media in the Making and Unmaking of the New Left.* Berkeley: University of California Press, 1980.

Goffman, Erving. *Frame Analysis: An Essay on the Organization of Experience.* New York: Harper Colophon, 1974.

Gold, Michael Evan. "A Tale of Two Amendments: The Reasons Congress Added Sex to Title VII and Their Implication for the Issue of Comparable Worth." *Duquesne Law Review* 19 (Spring 1981): 453.

Grattet, Ryken, and Scott Phillips. "Judicial Rhetoric, Meaning-Making, and the Institutionalization of Hate Crime Law." *Law & Society Review* 34, no. 3 (2000): 567–606.

Greenhouse, Steven. "Companies Set to Get Tougher on Harassment: Policies under Review after Court Decision." *New York Times,* 28 June 1998, sec. National, pp. A1, A14.

Griswold, Wendy. *Cultures and Societies in a Changing World.* Thousand Oaks, Calif.: Pine Forge Press, 1994.

Grosjean, Blandine. "Harcèlement sexuel, la fac se rebelle." *Libération,* 28 January 2002, sec. Rebonds.

———. "Promotion université." *Libération,* 19 February 2002.

Gusfield, Joseph R. *The Culture of Public Problems: Drinking-Driving and the Symbolic Order.* Chicago: University of Chicago Press, 1981.

Hager, Mark McLaughlin. "Harassment as a Tort: Why Title VII Hostile Environment Liability Should Be Curtailed." *Connecticut Law Review* 30 (1998): 375–437.

Halbwachs, Maurice. *The Collective Memory.* New York: Harper and Row, 1980.

Harris, Louis. "Le harcèlement sexuel: Enquête des français: Perceptions, opinions et évaluation du phénomène" (1991).

Heinich, Nathalie. "Pour introduire la cadre-analyse." *Critique* 535 (1991): 936–53.

Hirigoyen, Marie-France. *Le harcèlement moral: La violence perverse au quotidien.* Paris: Syros, 1998.

Hoffmann, Stanley. "Deux universalismes en conflit." *Tocqueville Review* 21, no. 1 (2000): 65–71.

"How Do You Handle Sex on the Job?: A Redbook Questionnaire." *Redbook,* January 1976, 74–75.

Hunter, Mark. *Le journalisme d'investigation.* Paris: Presses Universitaires de France, 1997.

Huret, Marie. "Au tribunal, parole contre parole." *L'Express,* 13 March 1999.

Inglehart, Ronald. *Culture Shift in Advanced Industrial Society.* Princeton, N. J.: Princeton University Press, 1990.

Jenson, Jane, and Mariette Sineau. *Mitterand et les françaises: Un rendez-vous manqué.* Paris: Presses de la Fondation Nationale des Sciences Politiques, 1995.

Jolibois, Charles. "Rapport." *Sénat: Session Ordinaire de 1997–1998,* 265 (1998).

Kanter, Rosabeth M. *Men and Women of the Corporation.* New York: Basic Books, 1977.

Kelly, Erin, and Frank Dobbin. "Civil Rights Law at Work: Sex Discrimination and the Rise of Maternity Leave Policies." *American Journal of Sociology* 105, no. 2 (1999): 455–92.

Krémer, Pascale. "Les initiateurs de la pétition contre le harcèlement sexuel à l'université sont reçus au ministère." *Le Monde,* 27 March 2002.

Kroeber, Alfred L., and Clyde Kluckhohn. *Culture: A Critical Review of Concepts and Definitions.* Cambridge, Mass.: Harvard University Peabody Museum of American Archaeology and Ethnology, 1952.

Kuhn, Raymond. *The Media in France.* London: Routledge, 1995.

Lacorne, Denis, and Jacques Rupnik. "Introduction: La France saisie par l'Amérique." In *L'Amérique dans les têtes: Un siècle de fascinations et d'aversions,"* edited by Denis Lacorne, Jacques Rupnik, and Marie-France Toinet, 11–44. Paris: Hachette, 1986.

Lamont, Michèle. *Money, Morals and Manners: The Culture of the French and American Upper-Middle Class.* Chicago: University of Chicago Press, 1992.

Lamont, Michèle, and Laurent Thévenot, eds. *Rethinking Comparative Cultural Sociology: Polities and Repertoires of Evaluation in France and the U.S.* Cambridge/ Paris: Cambridge University Press and Presses de la Maison des Sciences de l'Homme, 2000.

Lamont, Michele, and Robert Wuthnow. "Betwixt and Between: Recent Cultural Sociology in Europe and the United States." In *Frontiers of Social Theory: The New Synthesis,* edited by George Ritzer, 287–315. New York: Columbia University Press, 1990.

Lanez, Emilie. "Une ancienne étudiante du démographe renommé Hervé Le Bras porte plainte pour harcèlement sexuel: Une première en France." *Le Point,* 22 February 2002, 66.

Langelan, Martha J. *Back Off! How to Confront Sexual Harassment and Harassers.* New York: Fireside, 1993.

Lawton, Anne. "The Emperor's New Clothes: How the Academy Deals With Sexual Harassment." *Yale Journal of Law & Feminism* 11 (1999): 75–145.

Le Bras, Hervé. "Chasse à l'homme." *Le Monde,* 19 March 2002.

Le Magueresse, Catherine. "Harcèlement sexuel au travail." In *Dictionnaire des sciences criminelles* (Paris: Éditions Dalloz, 2003).

———. "Sur la nullité des mesures prises à l'encontre d'une salariée victime de harcèlement sexuel." *Droit Social* 5 (May 1998): 437–41.

"Loi no. 2001–1066 du 16 novembre 2001 relative à la lutte contre les discriminations." *Journal Officiel,* no. 267 (2001): 18311.

Louis, Marie-Victoire. *Le droit de cuissage.* Paris: Les Editions de l'Atelier, 1994.

———. "Harcèlement sexuel et domination masculine." In *Un siècle d'antiféminisme,* edited by Christine Bard. Paris: Fayard, 1999.

Lull, James, and Stephen Hinerman. "The Search for Scandal." In *Media Scandals,* edited by James Lull and Stephen Hinerman, 1–33. Oxford: Polity Press, 1997.

MacKinnon, Catharine. "Feminism, Marxism, Method and the State: An Agenda for Theory." *Signs* 7 (1982): 533–44.

———. *Sexual Harassment of Working Women.* New Haven, Conn.: Yale University Press, 1979.

Mannheim, Karl. *Essays on the Sociology of Culture.* London: Routledge and Kegan Paul, 1956.

Marshall, Anna-Marie. "Closing the Gaps: Plaintiffs in Pivotal Sexual Harassment Cases." *Law & Social Inquiry* 23, no. 4 (1998): 761–93.

Mathy, Jean-Philippe. *Extrême-Occident: French Intellectuals and America.* Chicago: University of Chicago Press, 1993.

McCann, Michael. *Rights at Work: Pay Equity Reform and the Politics of Legal Mobilization.* Chicago: University of Chicago Press, 1994.

McGee, Jack J. Jr. "Note, Sexual Advances by Male Supervisory Personnel as Actionable under Title VII of the Civil Rights Act of 1964: *Corne v. Bausch & Lomb, Inc., Williams v. Saxbe.*" *S. Texas Law Journal* 17 (1976): 409.

Meyer, John W., David Kamens, Aaron Benavot, Yun Kyoung Cha, and Suk-Ying Wong. "Knowledge for the Masses: World Models and National Curricula, 1920–1986." *American Sociological Review* 56, no. 1 (1991): 85–100.

Meyer, John W., John Boli, and George M. Thomas. "Ontology and Rationalization in the Western Cultural Account." In *Institutional Environments and Organizations: Structural Complexity and Individualism,* edited by Richard Scott and John Meyer, 9–27. Thousand Oaks, Calif.: Sage, 1994.

Minet, Michel, and Francis Saramito. "Le harcèlement sexuel." *Droit Ouvrier* (February 1997): 48–91.

Minow, Martha. *Making All the Difference*. Ithaca, N. Y.: Cornell University Press, 1990.

Moscovici, Serge. "The Phenomenon of Social Representations." In *Social Representations*, edited by R. M. Farr and Serge Moscovici. New York: Cambridge University Press, 1984.

Mossuz-Lavau, Janine. *Les lois de l'amour: Les politiques de la sexualité en France (1950–1990)*. Paris: Editions Payot, 1991.

Noiriel, Gérard. *Population, immigration et identité nationale en France XIXe-XXe siècle*. Paris: Hachette, 1992.

"Note, Legal Remedies for Employment Related Sexual Harassment." *Minnesota Law Review* 64 (1979): 151.

"Note, Sexual Harassment and Title VII: The Foundation for the Elimination of Sexual Cooperation as an Employment Condition." *Michigan Law Review* 76 (1978): 1007.

Nussbaum, Martha. "The Modesty of Mrs. Bajaj: India's Problematic Route to Sexual Harassment Law." In *New Directions in Sexual Harassment Law*, edited by Reva Siegel and Catharine MacKinnon. New Haven, Conn.: Yale University Press, in press.

Oppenheimer, David Benjamin. "Exacerbating the Exasperating: Title VII Liability of Employers for Sexual Harassment Committed by Their Supervisors." *Cornell Law Review* 81, no. 1 (1995): 66–153.

Ozouf, Mona. *Les mots des femmes: Essai sur la singularité française*. Paris: Fayard, 1995.

Paglia, Camille. *Sex, Art, and American Culture*. New York: Vintage Books, 1992.

———. *Sexual Personae: Art and Decadence From Nefertiti to Emily Dickinson*. New York: Vintage Books, 1991.

———. *Vamps and Tramps*. New York: Vintage, 1994.

Pedriana, Nicholas, and Robin Stryker. "Culture Wars 1960s Style: Equal Employment Opportunity—Affirmative Action Law and the Philadelphia Plan." *American Journal of Sociology* 103, no. 3 (November 1997): 633–91.

Picq, Françoise. *Libération des femmes: Les années-mouvement*. Paris: Seuil, 1993.

Pierrat, Emmanuel. "Le droit de cuissage, une histoire française." *Le Monde*, 6 March 2002, sec. Analyses & Forum.

Prentice, Deborah A., and Dale T. Miller. "Pluralistic Ignorance and the Perpetuation of Social Norms by Unwitting Actors." *Advances in Experimental Social Psychology* 28 (1996): 161–209.

Press, Aric. "Abusing Sex at the Office." *Newsweek*, 10 March 1980, sec. Justice, p. 81.

Remy, Jacqueline. "Les françaises accusent." *L'Express*, 13 March 1999.

Rivais, Rafaele. "La commission européenne s'attaque au harcèlement sexuel au travail." *Le Monde*, 9 June 2000, sec. Dernière page.

Rose, Richard. *Lesson-Drawing in Public Policy: A Guide to Learning in Time and Space*. Chatham, N. J.: Chatham House Publishers, 1993.

Rousso, Henry. *The Vichy Syndrome: History and Memory in France Since 1944*. Translated by Arthur Goldhammer. Cambridge, Mass.: Harvard University Press, 1994.

Roy-Loustaunau, Claude. "Le droit du harcèlement sexuel: Un puzzle législatif et des choix novateurs." *Droit social* 6 (June 1995): 545–50.

Rubinstein, Michael. "La dignité des femmes dans le monde du travail: Rapport sur le problème du harcèlement sexuel dans les états membres des communautés européennes." Brussels, 1987.

Rupp, Leila, and Verta Taylor. *Survival in the Doldrums*. New York: Oxford University Press, 1987.

Saguy, Abigail C. "Employment Discrimination or Sexual Violence? Defining Sexual Harassment in American and French Law." *Law and Society Review* 34, no. 4 (2000): 1091–1128.

———. "Puritanism and Promiscuity? Sexual Attitudes in France and the United States." *Comparative Social Research* 18 (1999): 227–47.

———. "Sexual Harassment in the News: The United States and France." *Communication Review* 5, no. 2 (2002): 109–41.

Schmitt, Eric. "Aftermath of Tailhook: The Pentagon's Accountant Takes over a Troubled Navy." *New York Times*, 12 July 1992, sec. 4, Week in Review Desk, col. 4, p. 2.

Schneider, Elizabeth. *Battered Women and Feminist Lawmaking*. New Haven, Conn.: Yale University Press, 2000.

Schneider, Michel. "Désir, vous avez dit désir?" *Le Monde*, 6 March 2002, sec. Analyses & Forum.

Schudson, Michael. *Watergate in American Memory: How We Remember, Forget, and Reconstruct the Past*. New York: Basic Books, 1992.

Schulhofer, Stephen J. *Unwanted Sex: The Culture of Intimidation and the Failure of Law*. Cambridge, Mass.: Harvard University Press, 1998.

Schultz, Vicki. "Reconceptualizing Sexual Harassment." *Yale Law Journal* 107, no. 1683 (1998): 1732–805.

Scott, Joan W. *Only Paradoxes to Offer*. Cambridge, Mass.: Harvard University Press, 1996.

———. "'La Querelle des Femmes' in the Late Twentieth Century." *New Left Review*, no. 226 (1997): 3–19.

———. "Vive la différence!" *Le Débat* 87 (November–December 1995): 134–39.

Serusclat, Frank M. "Rapport du sénat." *Seconde session ordinaire de 1991–1992*, 350 (1992), pp. 16–17.

Seymour, William C. "Sexual Harassment: Finding a Cause for Action under Title VII." *Labor Law Journal* 30 (1979): 139.

Skrentny, John David. *The Ironies of Affirmative Action: Politics, Culture and Justice in America*. Chicago: University of Chicago Press, 1996.

Smolowe, Jill. "The Feminist Machine: Women Candidates Hope to Make 1992 a Banner Year, but Will Enough Voters Share Their Rage About Abortion Rights and Anita Hill to Make a Difference at the Polls?" *Time*, 4 May 1992, sec. Cover Stories, 34.

Snow, David, and Robert D. Benford. "Ideology, Frame Resonance and Participant Mobilization." *International Social Movement Research* 1 (1988): 197–217.

Snow, David A., E. Burke Rochford, Jr., Steven K. Worden, and Robert D. Benford. "Frame Alignment Processes, Micromobilization, and Movement Participation." *American Sociological Review* 51, no. 4 (1986): 464–81.

Solé, Robert. "Plainte et chuchotements." *Le Monde*, 17 February 2002.

Strang, David, and John Meyer. "Institutional Conditions for Diffusion." *Theory and Society* 22 (1993): 487–511.

Stryker, Robin. "Rules, Resources, and Legitimacy Processes: Some Implications for Social Conflict, Order and Change." *American Journal of Sociology* 99, no. 4 (January 1994): 847–911.

Sunstein, Cass. "Damages in Sexual Harassment Cases." In *Directions in Sexual Harassment Law*, edited by Reva Siegel and Catharine MacKinnon. New Haven, Conn.: Yale University Press, in press.

Swidler, Ann. "Culture in Action: Symbols and Strategies." *American Sociological Review* 51, no. 2 (1986): 273–86.

Tarrow, Sidney. "Mentalities, Political Cultures, and Collective Action Frames: Constructing Meanings Through Action." In *Frontiers in Social Movement Theory*, edited by Aldon D. Morris and Carol McClurg Mueller, 174–202. New Haven, Conn.: Yale University Press, 1992.

Taub, Nadine. "Keeping Women in Their Place: Stereotyping Per Se as a Form of Employment Discrimination." *Boston College Law Rev.* 21 (1980): 345–418.

Terquem, Francis. "Harcèlement sexuel: La nouvelle inquisition." *Le Monde*, 26 February 2002, sec. Analyses & Forum.

"Thank You, Anita Hill, for the Civil Rights Act of 1991," *Christian Science Monitor*, 29 October 1991, sec. Editorial.

Toinet, Marie-France, Hubert Kempf, and Denis Lacorne. *Le libéralisme à l'américaine: L'état et le marché*. Paris: Economica, 1989.

Tomlinson, John. "And Besides, the Wench Is Dead: Media Scandals and the Globalization of Communication." In *Media Scandals*, edited by James Lull and Stephen Hinerman, 65–84. Oxford: Polity Press, 1997.

Tong, Rosemarie. *Women, Sex and the Law*. Totowa, N. J.: Rowman & Allanheld, 1984.

Toobin, Jeffrey. "The Trouble with Sex: Why the Law of Sexual Harassment Has Never Worked." *New Yorker*, 9 February 1998, sec. Annals of Law, 48–55.

U.S. Merit Systems Protection Board. *Sexual Harassment in the Federal Workforce: Is It a Problem?* Washington, D. C.: U.S. Government Printing Office, 1981.

UFF, "Propositions de loi pénale de l'UFF," *Clara* 19 (Summer 1991): 23–27.

Valiente, Celia. "Sexual Harassment in the Workplace: Equality Policies in Post-Authoritarian Spain." *Politics of Sexuality: Identity, Gender, Citizenship*, edited by Terrell Carver and Veronique Mottier, 169–79. London: Routledge, 1998.

Vhay, Michael D. "The Harms of Asking: Towards a Comprehensive Treatment of Sexual Harassment." *University of Chicago Law Review* 55, no. 1 (1988): 328–62.

Walt, Vivienne. "Regarding Sexism on the Job: Plus Ça Change . . ." *New York Times*, 24 May 2000, sec. G, col. 1–3, p. 1.

Whitehead, John. "Eleventh Hour Amendment or Serious Business: Sexual Harassment and the United States Supreme Court's 1997–1998 Term." *Temple Law Review* 71 (1998): 773–837.

Williams, Christine. *Still a Man's World: Men Who Do Women's Work*. Berkeley: University of California Press, 1995.

Wolf, Naomi. "Feminist Fatale: A Reply to Camille Paglia." *New Republic* (March 1992): 23–25.

Working Women United Institute, *Sexual Harassment on the Job: Results of a Preliminary Survey*. New York, N. Y.: Working Women United Institute, 1975.

Wright, Erik Olin, Janeen Baxter, and Gunn Elizabeth Birkelund. "The Gender

Gap in Workplace Authority: A Cross-National Study." *American Sociological Review* 60, no. 3 (1995): 407–35.

Wuthnow, Robert. *Meaning and the Moral Order: Explorations in Cultural Analysis.* Berkeley: University of California Press, 1987.

Zalesne, Deborah. "The Intersection of Socioeconomic Class and Gender in Hostile Housing Environment Claims Under Title VIII: Who Is the Reasonable Person?" *Boston College Law Review* 38, no. 4 [1997]: 861–902.

———. "Sexual Harassment Law: Has It Gone Too Far, or Has the Media?" *Temple Political & Civil Rights Law Review* 8, no. 2 (1999): 351–76.

———. "Sexual Harassment Law in the United States and South Africa: Facilitating the Transition from Legal Standards to Social Norms." *Harvard Women's Law Review* 25 (2002): 143–220.

Zecchini, Laurent. "Accusé de harcèlement sexuel, un tenor du sénat américain démissionne." *Le Monde,* 9 September 1995, sec. International.

Zelizer, Viviana. "The Purchase of Intimacy." *Law & Social Inquiry* 25, no. 3 (2000): 817–48.

Zippel, Kathrina. "Comparative Perspectives of Sex Equality Policies in Germany, the European Union, and the United States: The Example of Sexual Harassment." Ph.D. diss., Department of Sociology, University of Wisconsin, Madison, 2000.

Zucker-Rouvillois, Elisabeth. "Les mandarins gourous." *Libération,* February 4 2002, sec. Rebonds.

INDEX

Compositor:	BookMatters
Text:	10/15 Janson
Display:	Janson
Printer and Binder:	Malloy Lithographing, Inc.